W9-CZM-755

Dialectic of Salvation

DIALECTIC

OF

SALVATION

Issues in Theology of Liberation

Anselm Kyongsuk Min

State University of New York Press

BT
83.57
.M55
1989

Published by
State University of New York Press, Albany

© 1989   State University of New York

All rights reserved

Printed in the United States of America

No part of this book may be used or reproduced
in any manner whatsoever without written permission
except in the case of brief quotations embodied in
critical articles and reviews.

For information, address State University of New York
Press, State University Plaza, Albany, NY 12246

Library of Congress Cataloging-in Publication Data

Min, Anselm Kyongsuk, 1940-
    Dialectic of salvation: issues in theology of liberation/Anselm
Kyongsuk Min.
        p.   cm.
    Bibliography: p.
    Includes index.
    ISBN 0-88706-908-8. — ISBN 0-88706-909-6 (pbk.)
    1. Liberation theology. I. Title.
BT83.57.M55   1989   88-39150
261.8—dcl9   CIP

10 9 8 7 6 5 4 3 2 1

CONTENTS

PREFACE

Most of the research for this book was done during my sabbatical year (1984-1985) at Vanderbilt University. I thank its graduate department of religion for the financial assistance that made my stay at Vanderbilt possible, and its theology faculty, especially Peter Hodgson, Eugene TeSelle, Sally McFague, and Edward Farley for their valuable conversations on the subject of this book in general and on the first drafts of some of its chapters. They are not, of course, responsible for any inadequacies of this book.

I also thank Artin Arslanian, my dean at Belmont Abbey College, for his constant encouragement and support, and my colleagues on the Faculty Development Committee for finding my project worth supporting by partially subsidizing my sabbatical leave and funding my research and writing during three successive years (1985, 1986, 1987).

I acknowledge my debt to Professor Paul Lakeland of Fairfield University and the anonymous reviewer for their critical comments on the first version of this book. They should know that their suggestions were extremely helpful, although I have not been able to accommodate all of them.

Mr. William D. Eastman, director of the State University of New York Press, also deserves my gratitude for his friendliness, patience and promptness during the long process of publication. Also to be thanked is Bernadine Dawes, production editor at the Press, whose meticulous care in the editing process added greatly to the intelligibility and readability of my otherwise very awkward and convoluted philosophical prose.

Part of chapter 2 originally appeared, under the title "The Vatican, Marxism and Liberation Theology," in *Cross Currents,* 34:4 (Winter 1984-85), 439-55. Part of chapter 3 was published under the title "Praxis and Theology in Recent Debates" in the *Scottish Journal of Theology,* 39:4 (November 1986), 529-49. They have been revised for inclusion in this book. I thank the publishers of the two journals for their permission to reprint the articles. I also thank the Orbis Books for permission to quote from Gustavo Gutierrez, *A Theology of Liberation* and *The Power of the Poor in History,* and Clodovis Boff, *Theology and Praxis.*

Finally, for sharing the burdens of relocation during the sabbatical year and cheerfully enduring the countless hours of my silence since, I thank my wife, Soonja, and my two children, Jeehey and Kihong.

To all the anonymous sisters and brothers struggling on the liberation front throughout the world, often languishing and dying in jails, I dedicate this book.

Anselm Kyongsuk Min
Belmont Abbey College
Belmont, North Carolina
February 18, 1988

CHAPTER I

Theology of Liberation: Issues and Challenges

HISTORY AND THEOLOGY

Theologies, even dominant theologies, come and go. During the present century alone we have seen a rapid succession of theologies, each associated with the name of its founder (Barth, Bultmann, Tillich, Rahner) or its underlying philosophical movement or method (existentialist, dialectical, transcendental, critical, political, process, or praxis). The pace of change is so rapid that one often despairs of ever being able to read, digest, and evaluate even a single movement before another appears on the scene, each with its own demand for serious, immediate attention. The all-too-natural temptation under the circumstances is to dismiss all new movements in theology as so many superficial "fads" and to decide to stick with either one of the classical theologies (Augustine, Aquinas, Eastern Fathers, Luther, or Calvin) or one of the modern ones (Barth, Tillich, Rahner, and others), with the conviction that the theology of one's choice is truly enduring and "classical" in its insights.

This temptation, however, is myopic in two ways. It often assumes that theological pluralism is something unique to our day. It forgets that even in the past—although perhaps at slower pace—competition has always existed among dominant and emerging theologies, and that the emergence of new theologies, competition between old and new, and coexistence of different theologies have always been a fact of theological history.[1] It also assumes that there is a "classical" theology, be it Thomistic, Augustinian, Schleiermacherian or Barthian, which, despite its "minor" imperfections, still remains adequate and relevent for all ages. This assumption is usually buttressed by the further assumption that changes in theology—or, for that matter, in intellectual history as a whole—are solely the products of the genius and caprice of the individual thinker, and that the

1

demands of changing history, as such, make no essential difference either to the emergence of new theologies or to the relevance and validity of classical theologies. If the first myopia is the forgetting of plurality of theologies as a historical fact, the second myopia is the reduction of historicity as such to an incidental factor in the genesis and validity of intellectual movements.

Since the awakening of the so-called historical consciousness at the beginning of the last century, there has been a significant shift in the attitude of theologians towards the historical dimension of human existence as a whole and of theoretical activity in particular. Until the recent emergence of political and liberation theologies, however, most theologians—with the notable exception of Troeltsch—have generally understood "history" in the sense of factuality, as opposed to mere fiction or myth. This is understandable. The theological sense of history originally emerged in the context of the historical criticism of the Bible and a resultant preoccupation with the factual authenticity of events, statements, and personages against the Enlightenment critique of the biblical foundation of Christian faith as mythological and superstitious. Even now, much energy of biblical studies is devoted to establishing the historical authenticity of the Bible in this sense.

There is, however, another, and in many respects more profound, sense of history originating from the tradition of Hegel, Marx, and critically oriented historians and sociologists. There are two aspects to this sense of history or historicity. One is that the individual's relation to history—meaning, the ever-changing totality of economic, political, and cultural conditions—is intrinsic and essential to the very constitution and development of human subjectivity, and not an incidental episode in the life of a subject already constituted as a subject even apart from history. The subject is born and develops in all its thoughts, desires, and hopes only under the situational pressures, challenges, and opportunities provided by history. The subjectivity and freedom of an individual is thus conditioned—though not determined except in limit cases—by the sociohistorical conditions under which that person lives. It is in history that ideas emerge, and it is in history in all its particularity that they are also tested and proven to be relevant or irrelevant, adequate or inadequate, true or false. It is in history that humanity also develops a consciousness of its own identity and essence. The essence of humanity does not exist apart from history. Just as it is of the very essence of humans that they can exist and develop only in history, so it is in history alone that such essence can be discovered and developed. Any system of ideas, including theology, that seeks to serve humanity must prove its power to serve and transform humanity precisely under the changing and challenging conditions of history that constitute an essential and intrinsic dimension of human existence.

The other aspect of historicity is that history is something made by humans, not something purely natural or given. The totality of sociohistorical conditions constituting history not only conditions the development of individuals and groups but is also conditioned by what humans do as individuals and groups. History does not just happen; it is a product of human actions, if not always of conscious human designs. If history does not always correspond to the intentions of either individual or collective actions, it is, nonetheless, a result of human actions and human purposes—a result for which humans are responsible and which they can do something to transform. Just as humans are subject to the historical conditions under which they exist, so these conditions themselves do change through the contributions of individuals and groups—in the way and to the degree that their actions and intentions are coordinated and mobilized for a common purpose.

History, then, is not a neutral and external environment of theology. History enters into the constitution and development of theology as an intrinsic and essential condition. It provides the basic intellectual horizon that governs the particular concepts and categories of theology as well as the challenges and tasks theology sets for itself in each age. Insofar as history means change, the guiding horizon and agenda for theology also change with each new epoch. Thus, every theology is historically conditioned and necessarily bears the marks of the age, while each age provides positive opportunities and challenges for the creativity and energy of the theologian in the endless task of making the Gospel concretely relevant to the present. The truths of Christian faith must prove their universality not outside of history but precisely in the concrete changing context of each new historical epoch and thus prove themselves concretely universal and relevant to all ages.[2]

The question to raise in the face of new theologies, then, is not whether we need them or whether they are passing fads like new fashions in dress and automobiles; rather, we need to ask, given the necessity of new theological tasks in each age, whether they indeed address the central problems of the age, and which of them does so in a way that is most faithful to the demand of the Gospel and the insights of the Christian tradition and is most adequate to the urgency and magnitude of the problems posed by the age.[3] This requires a constant dialectic of listening to the Word of God in Scripture and tradition and discerning the signs of the times. This is a question of a real dialectic between the past and the present, of illuminating the ambiguities and hopes of the present in light of the Word of God, and of re-reading the Word of God in the fresh light of such present challenges and tasks, not of a unilateral application of the wisdom of the past to the present or of the present perspective to the past.

One of the theologies to approach the theological task with precisely this dialectical sense of historicity is the Latin American theology of liberation (TL). More than perhaps any other theology past or present, TL is self-consciously historical. It considers the liberation of the poor and oppressed in the Third World as the central problem of our age and seeks to elaborate a theology that is most effective in assisting such liberation while remaining faithful to the message and demand of the Gospel. Unlike many theologies which claim, implicitly or explicitly, to be *the* universal truth, TL consciously limits its claim to that of accomplishing its particular task for the present moment of history, and disclaims all intention to do theology for all time.

ISSUES IN THEOLOGY OF LIBERATION

Since its official emergence in 1968, in the documents of Medellin, TL has proven its impact beyond the borders of Latin America. It has challenged much academic theology in Europe and North America, stirred an outburst of theological effort to create a theology of liberation in a way relevant to the indigenous situation of each country and region in Africa and Asia, and certainly unsettled the peace of the Vatican enough to have received its notice in the form of numerous papal speeches, two major documents of the Congregation for the Doctrine of the Faith, and frequent censures and threats of censure for some of its representative theologians. It has also been an object of special concern, investigation, and even harassment on the part of a category of people who could not normally care less about anything so academic and speculative as theology—generals, police chiefs, prime ministers, and presidents. This, I think, is something unique about TL. One strains the imagination to visualize Hitler becoming upset over the theology of Barth and Bultmann or President Johnson losing sleep over the theologies of the Secular City and the Death of God. In TL we have a theology which does disturb secular powers—which, in fact, most disturbs them in particular.

Apart from the distinctly political threats TL has also been challenging contemporary academic theology on a number of fronts. It has questioned even the modern conceptions of God prevalent in theologies of correlation and in "revisionary" theologies (Tracy), disputed the dehistoricized Christologies of both traditional and contemporary Christianity, and criticized the harmonistic and authoritarian models of prevailing ecclesiologies. It has also called into question the still generally prevailing dualism of transcendent salvation and historical liberation. It has challenged, above all, the academic and theoretical orientation of theology and its methods, which has prevailed in Christianity for over a millennium. For TL, theology is a practical, not a theoretical, science. There is no major area of theology that it has left undisturbed. Although not a "theology of revolution" in the sense of the 1960s, TL has perhaps shown itself to be the most revolutionary theology yet in its impact, challenge, and implication.

The revolutionary character of TL has been perceived by no one better than by its official critic, Joseph Cardinal Ratzinger, the Prefect of the Congregation for the Doctrine of the Faith in the Vatican. In a private document preceding the publication of the famous Instruction of August 1984, Ratzinger states the radical challenge posed by TL as follows:

> It does not intend to add a new theological treatise to those already existing, i.e., it does not wish to develop new aspects of the Church's social ethics. Rather it sees itself as a new hermeneutics of the Christian faith, a new

way of understanding Christianity as a whole and implementing it. Thus it affects theology in its basic constitution, not merely in aspects of its content. So too it alters all forms of Church life: the Church's constitution, liturgy, catechesis, moral options.[4]

He goes on to explain the revolutionary departure of TL from the classical tradition, despite the seeming continuity in theological language:

> A theologian who has learned his theology in the classical tradition and has accepted its spiritual challenge will find it hard to realize that an attempt is being made, in all seriousness, to recast the whole Christian reality in the categories of politico-social liberation praxis. This is all the more difficult because many liberation theologians continue to use a great deal of the Church's classical ascetical and dogmatic language while changing its signification. As a result, the reader or listener who is operating from a different background can gain the impression that everything is the same as before, apart from the addition of a few somewhat unpalatable statements, which, given so much spirituality, can scarcely be all that dangerous.
>
> The very radicality of liberation theology means that its seriousness is often underestimated, since it does not fit into any of the accepted categories of heresy; its fundamental concern cannot be detected by the existing range of standard questions.[5]

Just as TL has presented myriad challenges, so it has itself been challenged on various fronts. It has been accused of an arbitrarily selective use of Scripture and of ignoring those traditions not directly relevant to the problem of liberation; of reducing salvation to politics; of advocating violent class struggle and partisanship with the poor; of sacrificing the objectivity and critical spirit of theology in a blind commitment to the oppressed; and of being Marxist in the guise of Christian theology. For all its emphasis on the concrete and on praxis, it has been said, TL lacks an adequate social theory, neglects substantive social analysis, and ignores the practical ways of producing wealth that would benefit the poor. It has been pointed out that TL in principle rules out theological anthropology and ethics, reducing both to a theology of history which is itself based on an uncritical, fundamentalist acceptance of the Exodus paradigm as a historical fact. Its claim to be a product of the Latin American historical situation has been contradicted: the ruling intellectual categories of TL are products of Europe, not of Latin America. It has also been criticized for laying exclusive emphasis on the economic source of oppression and forgetting its sexist, psychological, and racist origins, and accused of being Pelagian and utopian and of leaving no room for divine grace and Christian realism. The criticisms of TL have come from all sources—from liberals and conservatives, Marxists and capitalists, the Vatican and the Heritage Foundation; such criticisms have also been variously theological, political, and sociological in content.[6]

Along with these criticisms there have also been those who, while accepting the fundamental idea of liberation, have tried to develop a theology of liberation on different foundations. These attempts share the urgency of liberating the poor and oppressed with those of the Latin American theorists, but dispute the latter's theological method. In a world increasingly oppressive for the vast majority of humankind, the Vatican and Schubert Ogden, for example, seem to share the need for some sort of a theology of liberation, yet both disagree with the dialectical approach of TL and seek to provide their own alternatives as more authentic or more adequate. The Vatican's alternative—spelled out in John Paul II's Puebla address of 1979 and the two Instructions of 1984 and 1986 on liberation theology—is based on personalism. Ogden's alternative is based on an existentialist approach to theology.[7]

In this regard the significance of the 1984 Vatican Instruction[8] on TL cannot be exaggerated. In both theoretical and practical sense, TL has been the most provocative of all post-conciliar theologies, a veritable sign of contradiction responsible for the rise and fall of many and revealing where a Christian stands with regard to the gravest issues facing Christianity in the present decades of world history. No wonder that the opposition to TL—religious and secular, theological and political—has, after a sporadic beginning in the early 1970s, coalesced and crystallized around the Vatican position, even as the defenders and sympathizers of TL have strained their theological and political resources to minimize the document's impact on the survival of their theology. The document is a clear demonstration of how far the Vatican is willing to go in meeting the challenge of historical liberation, as well as of the theological outlook underlying such a stance.

Despite the attempt of many liberals to put the best possible interpretation on the document, it should be clear that it was in reality a condemnation, not the mere "warning" it professed to be. (Whether there was a significant shift of attitude or "about-face," as one journal put it, in the Easter 1986 letter of John Paul II to the Brazilian hierarchy and the 1986 Instruction on Christian Freedom and Liberation, will be discussed in chapter 5.) It claims to address itself only to "certain aspects" (title) and "certain forms of liberation theology" (Introduction; vi, 9), but these aspects and forms, however misinterpreted, turn out to be the very heart and substance of TL, that which makes it distinct, original, and challenging. Like the early chapters of Genesis, the document states first the original sin of TL; i.e., its alleged political and historical reductionism, leading to the denial of the transcendent character of salvation, faith, and sin. Second, it points to the cause of the fall, namely, the seduction by Karl Marx, his method of sociohistorical analysis, and his ideology of atheism and totalitarianism. Third, in a relentless crescendo of criticism item by item, it enumerates all the dogmatic errors resulting from that seduction, in Christology, theology of redemption, ecclesiology, and anthropology.

The charges include the exclusively political "re-reading" of Scripture; the reduction of Jesus to a revolutionary symbol; the introduction of class struggle into ecclesiology; the denial of the objectivity of truth; the advocacy of blind and systematic violence; and the identification of the poor of the Bible with the proletariat of Marx. Judging by the criteria for "authentic" theology of liberation laid down by John Paul II in Puebla in 1979, the document finds the liberation theologians guilty of error on all three counts: the truth about Jesus Christ, the truth about the Church, and the truth about humankind (v, 8). In the eyes of the Vatican, TL is "a perversion of the Christian message" (ix, 1), full of "serious ideological deviations" (Introduction), and "actually constitutes a practical negation" (vi, 9) of Christian faith. The indictment of TL is radical and sweeping; the only thing it finds acceptable is the commitment to "the preferential option for the poor," which by itself, of course, is not sufficient to turn a theology into a theology of liberation. The errors of TL are so numerous and fundamental that one only wonders why the Vatican issued only a "warning" rather than an outright "condemnation" as, for example, in the case of Modernism.

The responses of the defenders and sympathizers of TL have varied. Some tried to dismiss it as not speaking to them, often by minimizing the Marxian element in their theology. Others even tried to welcome it as an approval of TL by calling attention to its affirmation of the preferential option for the poor and dismissing its negative criticisms as either peripheral or irrelevant. A third response has been that of Juan Luis Segundo, for whom such responses betray "false confidence." For Segundo, "the document consciously goes beyond the mere denunciation of particular, rare, or peripheral excesses."[9] What is at stake in the conflict is a conflict between two irreconcilably opposed theologies. As Segundo puts it, "my theology (that is, my interpretation of Christian faith) is false if the theology of the document is true—or if it is the only true one."[10] Again, "in all sincerity, if my theology (which I have formulated in my books for almost twenty-five years, and have practiced pastorally) is correct and complete, the document's theology is certainly mistaken."[11] Furthermore, such a theology amounts to a reversal of the logic and dynamism of Vatican II.[12]

TL is a theology still in process. It has yet to produce its *Summa Theologiae* or *Church Dogmatics*. As a new theology it has many loose ends to tie up and many gaps to fill, a fact partially responsible for much misunderstanding and criticism. The phenomenal, continuing productivity of many of its representative theologians—Juan Luis Segundo, Jon Sobrino, Clodovis and Leonardo Boff, Gustavo Gutierrez, and others—has already gone far towards filling such gaps and developing a comprehensive theological synthesis. As a new way of doing theology with new assumptions and from a different perspective, TL has provoked and will continue to provoke criticisms from widely different perspectives, as it continues to vigorously assert itself against intensifying political and religious pressures to suppress it. As TL insists, the problem of thelogy of liberation is not, in the final analysis, about theology but about the actual liberation of the poor and oppressed, who are an absolute majority in Latin America and the world and whose cry for liberation cannot be silenced or suppressed too long, as witness the events of the past decade in Chile, Nicaragua, Haiti, the Philippines, South Africa, and South Korea. As long as the problem of liberation remains a problem, so long will theology of liberation remain to articulate it. As long as the scandal of the poor continues to provoke, so long will theology of liberation continue to scandalize.

PURPOSE AND SCOPE OF THIS BOOK

The purpose of the following chapters is both constructive and polemical. I want to present in a systematic way the philosophical sources of TL (Marx and Hegel) and its chief doctrines on theological method (i.e., the dialectic of the hermeneutic and socio-analytic mediations on the basis of praxis) and the relation between salvation and liberation, between personal and social sin. I do so in the context of the polemical issues raised by and against TL. In each case I begin with the criticisms of TL, go on to present its position on the issues at stake at some length, and end with responses to the critics. The most important critic of TL has been the Vatican, whose criticisms will be examined and responded to and whose alternative theology of liberation, especially its anthropological assumptions will in turn be subjected to an extensive critique. This also defines the scope of this book. It is limited to the issue of Marxism, theological method, and the relation between transcendent salvation and sociohistorical liberation. It does not propose a comprehensive survey of all the themes, topics, and issues bearing on liberation.

This book is limited in another way. 'Theology of liberation' is a generic term of which there are many variants, ranging from the feminist and black theologies of North America to the liberationist theologies of the Third World. These theologies do share certain common concerns and perspectives, but there are also significant differences. This book is limited to the Latin American theology of liberation and the issues it has provoked. The theology of liberation (TL) discussed in this book refers solely to its Latin American version.

In addition to this introductory chapter, there are five chapters in this book. Chapter 2 deals with the philosophical sources of TL, Marx and Hegel, and presents the basic philosophical categories operative in TL. It is an essential preparation for the discussion of substantive issues in the chapters that follow. In Chapter 3, I discuss the theological method of TL, focusing on the relationship between theory and praxis, the historicity and historical task of theology, the theoretical necessity for practical solidarity with the poor, and the hermeneutic circle. Chapter 4 presents the relationships between God and history, salvation in the transcendent sense and liberation in the political–historical sense, and personal and social sin. In Chapter 5, I examine in some detail the Vatican's own version of theology of liberation, especially the personalist anthropology underlying its conceptions of the relationships between God and history, personal and social sin, and freedom and liberation. Finally, in chapter 6, I reflect on the larger significance of the confrontation between TL and the Vatican. At the level of theory the confrontation is one of two opposed anthropologies, the dialectical anthropology of TL and the personalist anthropology of the Vatican. At the deeper level of praxis the confrontation is political and poses a profound challenge to the institutional church—the most urgent challenge of all, that of the poor and the oppressed of the world. The real issue is not whether TL or Marxism is compatible with orthodoxy but whether—and how—the highest leadership in the church is prepared to respond to the cry for liberation around the world.

Let me now present the background of each chapter in some detail. Chapter 2 deals with the philosophical sources of TL. Like any theology, TL draws from many sources, both classical and contemporary, both philosophical and theological: official teachings, biblical studies, and sociohistorical and economic studies. In the area of theology proper, it is indebted to the entire range of contemporary theology, from Barth and Bonhoeffer to Karl Rahner, Dorothee Sölle, Johannes Metz, Jürgen Moltmann, and Wolfhart Pannenberg.[13] Philosophically, it has drawn from the entire range of philosophical developments from Kant, Hegel, Feuerbach, Kierkegaard, and Marx to Maurice Blondel, existentialism, critical Marxism, and hermeneutics. TL is thoroughly conversant with the categories and problematics of modern and contemporary philosophy and has shown a capacity—as great as that of any contemporary Christian theology—to incorporate and synthesize a wide range of philosophical options. This contact of TL with philosophy, while often direct, is just as often mediated through its source theologies. Among the diverse philosophical sources it draws from, however, the Hegelian-Marxian tradition stands out as the dominant influence on the *Denkform* of TL, a tradition often mediated by such twentieth-century figures as Antonio Gramsci, Louis Althusser, Georg Lukacs, Herbert Marcuse, Karl Mannheim, and members of the Frankfurt School.

It is noteworthy that it is precisely around the theological appropriation of the "dialectical" approach and perspective of Hegel and Marx that so much furor and debate have arisen, especially between the Vatican and TL. Despite its traditional openness to philosophy and 'natural theology,' Roman Catholicism in the modern world has had its difficulties with new philosophical developments ever since Kant, the modernist controversy being one of the critical examples. It has positively accepted modernity only in the form of neo-Thomism and personalism (Buber, Scheler, Marcel, Mouroux) and only tolerated the fragments of Kant, Hegel, and Heidegger in the transcendental Thomism of Joseph Marechal, Karl Rahner, Emerich Coreth, and others. Attention has always been focused on the negative aspects of these philosophies—Kant's subjectivism and agnosticism, Hegel's pantheism and immanentism, Heidegger's atheism and pessimism—and no attempt has been made to come to grips with the fundamental questions being raised or the new philosophical horizons and methods opened up by these thinkers.

It is no wonder that this fundamental suspicion of modernity on the part of official Catholicism should become outright hostility and rejection when that modernity takes the form of Marxism and finds its way into the philosophical presuppositions of TL. As is well known, Marxism is not just another philosophy, which would be relatively harmless, but a philosophy which seeks to change the existing power structures by means of organized political praxis. As a philosophy it has been atheist, and as a political movement it has had a history of deviations and corruptions—just as has Christianity—often culminating in totalitarianism. At the same time, however, it would be difficult to deny that Marxism has been the only major intellectual movement to try to understand, analyze, and transform existing societies from the perspective of the poor and exploited majority. It is also undeniable that the cry of the poor—the vast majority of humankind today—constitutes the most fundamental crisis and challenge confronting all those with power, religious or secular. It is quite understandable, therefore, that the Vatican responds to the challenge of Marxism, modernity at its most cutting edge, with outright rejection. All other issues raised by TL, one might say, are footnotes to this fundamental issue, how and to what extent Christian theology may appropriate Marxism for its own purposes and still remain Christian theology.

In Chapter 2, I try to confront this issue. Instead of trying to reduce TL to Marxism, in the fashion of the ideological right, or to deny the existence of Marxian elements in TL, as some liberation theologians do, I try to discuss to what extent and how Christian theology can and must use philosophical sources for its own theological purpose; to what extent Marxism, at least in its generalized form, has already become part of the social doctrine of the Catholic church as it has become part of the general intellectual culture of the contemporary world; the nature and scope of the Marxism TL has been appropriating and the attitude towards Marxism inherent in such appropriation; and, finally, the Hegelian element in TL. The Marxian connection of TL has generally been well publicized (although not always properly understood and often greatly exaggerated), but the Hegelian connection, I am afraid, has scarcely been noticed. In my view, it is the Hegelian dialectic which mediates TL and Marxism. This is not a book on Marx, Hegel, or the larger question of the general relationship between Marxism and Christian faith as such, and my discussion here is limited to the above issues. Once the Marxian and Hegelian elements in TL have been isolated, we can see, in the following chapters, how such elements are integrated into TL proper. Since the main purpose of this book is not to show how TL integrates such elements—which would only divert attention from the real issue raised by

TL, namely, the historical urgency of liberation—but to discuss the substantive claims of TL in its own right, my references to Marx and Hegel in the following chapters will be only occasional and limited. One has only to remember the Marxian and Hegelian concepts and categories discussed in this chapter to see how they are integrated into TL.

In Chapter 3, I deal with the question of the nature and method of theology, an issue increasingly important in recent theological debates. Until very recent times, theology had been considered to be wisdom—i.e., knowledge of the ultimate and transcendent finality of human existence, a theoretical science whose goal is knowledge of truth for its own sake. As the activity of the contemplative intellect in its transcendent finality, it prided itself on its separation and autonomy from— often verging on contemptuous indifference to—the exigencies of human action or praxis in the relative, ambiguous world of history and society. It claimed its own methods—ranging from contemplation and meditation through appeal to Scripture and tradition to deduction and analysis—but all such methods remained firmly within the realm of theory.[14] Generally, it did not consider its own basis in the concrete historical praxis of human existence; theologians did not consider the "disclosive," epistemological function of such praxis essential to their own methods, nor did they regard contribution to such praxis as an essential goal of their own activity. TL challenges this theoretical conception of theology with its claim of the priority and primacy of praxis over theory and insists that theology is a practical, not a theoretical science, whose knowledge derives its origin, content, and purpose from historical praxis. This practical conception of theology has in turn been challenged by many, who may accept the cognitive contribution of praxis as one among other sources of theology, especially in the area of practical theology, but who do not wish to accord to praxis a foundational and unifying role for all theology, including systematic theology, as does TL.

As is well known, a revolution in the conception of the relation between theory and praxis began with Hegel, Kierkegaard, and Marx in the nineteenth century, and was continued through existentialism, phenomenology, pragmatism, and neo-Marxism in the twentieth. A vast literature has grown up on the subject. It is only in recent decades, however, that Christian theology began to take serious notice of these developments, and it is natural that the very recent attempts of political and liberation theologies to appropriate such developments have been received with mixed reactions. My concern in this chapter is not to review the entire history of the concept, which indeed goes back to Plato and Aristotle, but only to examine and evaluate the recent theological controversies occasioned by TL. To be discussed are the objections posed by the Vatican, Schubert Ogden, and Dennis McCann and Charles Strain, and the possible responses of TL to such objections; my argument is based on a lengthy presentation of the position of TL on such issues as the relationship between faith and praxis, the historical conditioning of the origin, content, and task of theology, the preferential option for the poor, and the hermeneutic circle.

In chapter 4, I go into the theological center of the controversy between TL and the Vatican: the relation between salvation and liberation (or transcendence and history) and between personal and social sin. Ever since the Enlightenment critique of the traditional dualism endemic to Christian faith, the issue of the theological or salvific significance of our earthly existence, especially our political efforts to humanize and transform society and history, has been the primary challenge to Christian theology. This challenge has been not only theoretical, as in the case of Feuerbach, Nietzsche, Freud, Dewey, and Sartre, but also practical, as in the case of the various socialist political movements of which Marxism has been the chief intellectual inspiration and reflection. From the *Rerum Novarum* of 1891 to the *Gaudium et Spes* of Vatican II to the *Sollicitudo Rei Socialis* of 1987, the Catholic Church has tried to respond to the practical challenge by means of social doctrine.[15] Although in the process the traditional dualism of natural and supernatural, secular and sacred, has softened significantly, it seems clear that the official theological position has always remained ambivalent, as witness the Vatican reactions to Henri de Lubac's *The Mystery of the Supernatural,* Karl Rahner's "supernatural existential," and Teilhard de Chardin's *The Phenomenon of Man* and *The Divine Milieu.*

The controversy between the Vatican and TL is the latest and perhaps the most explosive in this series of conflicts between the highest magisterium of the church and a theological movement on the most challenging issue of the day. Since Vatican II it has been generally recognized that there is indeed a relation between salvation and liberation; they are neither opposed nor indifferent to each other. They are distinct, but not separable. What, then, is this distinct but inseparable relation between salvation and liberation? Is it one of primary and secondary importance (Vatican), or one of formal distinction and material identity (TL)? Is liberation intrinsic to and constitutive of salvation (TL), or are they inseparable yet extrinsic to each other (Vatican)? Does the positing of an intrinsic and constitutive relation between salvation and liberation necessarily lead to reduction of the former to the latter, to "temporal messianism" and "historicist immanentism," as the Vatican charges? Furthermore, is our relation to transcendent salvation primarily mediated through personal, i.e., individual, conversion or through cooperative social praxis of structural change? Is personal sin the only sin in the proper sense, whereas social sin is sin only in the analogical sense? Is social sin merely the sum of personal sins, or is it a sin in its own right with a structure of its own and in need of something more than the conversion of individual hearts? These questions, of course, are derived from and are variations on the more fundamental theological question—i.e., What is the relationship between God and history? In chapter 4, I discuss these questions first by presenting the Vatican's critique of TL and then by elaborating the latter's position.

In chapter 5, I discuss the Vatican's own version of a theology of liberation, which it calls more "authentic," with its emphasis on "integral" liberation. Based on its two Instructions of 1984 and 1986 as well as on other works of John Paul II and Joseph Ratzinger, I examine in some detail the Vatican's own conception of the relationship between salvation and liberation, personal and social sin, and freedom and liberation, and its theological justification of the Christian's participation in historical liberation. In the process I try to disclose the anthropological presuppositions—a personalist anthropology, with an emphasis on interiority, transcendence, and individuality—underlying its theology of liberation. I conclude that the Vatican's personalist anthropology is incompatible with its own theology of liberation; either it needs a different anthropology for its theology of liberation or the latter is at best inconsistent and half-hearted, for the basic reason that its anthropology suffers from an as yet unresolved dualism despite its claims to the contrary. I also show that there is not much substance to the rumors spread in the media that the 1986 Instruction meant a rapprochement between the Vatican and TL, for the fundamental difference dividing them, clear enough in the 1984 Instruction, became even clearer in the 1986 document.

In chapter 6, I offer concluding reflections on the preceding discussions in the book, especially on the historical significance of the confrontation between TL and the Vatican. There are two aspects to the confrontation, theoretical and practical. Theoretically, they represent two irreconcilably opposed theologies, as Segundo and Ratzinger both admit, largely because of the differences in their mode of thinking and anthropological presuppositions. The Vatican's theology is dominated by Thomist and, at best, personalist approaches, with their classical, dualist emphasis on the primacy of transcendence, interiority, and individuality. TL operates with a dialectical anthropology of *concrete totality* (Hegel and Marx), which tries to see the intrinsic, constitutive mediation between transcendence and history, between the individual and social existence, without denying their real distinction. The difference, therefore, is ultimately not so much theological as philosophical. If the magisterium has no divinely guaranteed expertise, still less infallibility, in matters of philosophy—unless, of course, philosophy directly contradicts basic dogmas and doctrines on faith and morals—any more than it does in matters of economics and social analysis, this leaves plenty of justification for a continuing discussion between TL and the Vatican.

At the practical level, and this is the more significant and decisive of the two, the confrontation between TL and the Vatican is a political confrontation between the global challenge of liberation of the poor and oppressed and the response of the institutional leadership of the Catholic Church. The ultimate issue is not TL as theology, but the political challenge of the huge masses of poor, exploited, and oppressed humanity in a divided world and the adequacy of the response of the ecclesiastical leadership. The Catholic Church has somehow weathered the many theoretical challenges of modernity since the Enlightenment—not always successfully, to be sure, nor without losing its intellectual credibility. The challenge of TL is whether it can also survive the political challenge of the existence of degraded but increasingly self-conscious masses of humanity around the globe, without losing its evangelical credibility as a Christian church. Can the politics of the Vatican be as radical as the challenge of global liberation that it must address?

CHAPTER II

Philosophical Sources of Liberation Theology

Ever since the emergence of Marxism as a theory and as a social and political movement in the nineteenth century, the relation between Christianity and Marxism has been one of unbending hostility. True, there was some enthusiasm for dialogue in the nineteen-sixties in the limited circle of Eastern European Marxist theoreticians and Christian theologians, notably the members of the German *Paulusgesellschaft.* There was also some very cautious opening towards Marxism in the encyclicals of John XXIII and Paul VI. Nevertheless, the social doctrine of the Catholic Church, from the *Rerum Novarum* of 1891 to the *Laborem Exercens* of 1981, has been predominantly hostile and invariably critical towards Marxism, just as Marxism has been towards Christianty. In this regard the attitude of the Church has been no different from that of the capitalist world as a whole. It is no surprise that the Vatican has recently focused its critique of TL on the Marxian elements in the latter.[1]

Marxism is not simply a social theory or merely a philosophy of history. In its own self-understanding it is more a socio-historical movement for the practical realization of certain ideals, a movement self-consciously rooted in history and seeking to transform that history. As such it not only has its own history or a "development of dogma," from Marx and Engels through Lenin and Kautsky to the critical and humanistic Marxists of today. It also has a history of institutional and organizational developments, from the first Communist International to countless labor movements and political regimes in different countries of the world, each with its own variation. In this regard Marxism has been precisely what Christianity has been, not a pure theory but a *social movement,* whose theory is itself subject to the dialectic of concrete history in all its ambiguities; one must keep this fact in mind in any discussion of Marxist theory and Christian theology.

At the theoretical level there are many issues at stake. Theologians and Marxist philosophers have argued about whether atheism and totalitarianism are inseparable from the essence of Marxism, a debate which has not been and, in my view, *cannot* be conclusive, given the fundamental differences in intellectual horizon among the participants in the debate.[2] Economists and social theorists argue whether Marxist analysis of capitalism is valid and relevant. Again, for precisely the same reason, the debate has been far from conclusive. The Marxist critique of capitalism seems no more dead or passé, as the ideologues of capitalism have been announcing, than is Christian faith, as might be claimed by atheists. We can also evaluate the history of the attitudes of the Christian churches towards Marxism and discuss whether such attitudes have been based more on paranoia than on reality.[3]

In this chapter I cannot go into these complex issues. My purpose here is limited to the discussion of the relation between Marxism and TL in the context of the issues raised by the Vatican. I discuss three issues in particular. The first issue is whether and to what extent one system of thought (i.e., TL) can borrow concepts and categories from another (i.e., Marxism) for its own purposes. The second issue is the nature and scope of the Marxism that TL does accept, whose role in TL I neither want to minimize or exaggerate. The third is the role of the Hegelian dialectic, which in my view mediates the synthesis of Christian faith and Marsixm in TL but whose importance, although not as great as that of Marxism, has generally been ignored or only insufficiently appreciated in the current debates. Both Marxism and Hegel's thought constitute the chief philosophical sources of TL.

THEOLOGICAL APPROPRIATION OF MARXISM

The Vatican's basic charge against TL is that it uses Marxist concepts and categories as a "determining" principle of its own theology (viii, 1)[4] and that as a result it is no longer *Christian* theology. The response of TL has been that it is possible to convert and baptize Karl Marx on condition that he repent and be purged of his sins, atheism and totalitarianism, to which the Vatican replies by saying that Marx will not repent and therefore remains irredeemable.

Is it possible, then, to borrow certain categories from Marx and still to transform their meaning by placing them into the new context of Christian faith? According to the Vatican, it is not; Christian faith only ends up by being corrupted and perverted by the categories. For the Vatican, the context in which a category originates also determines its meaning. For example, the concept of class struggle in the original Marxian context means something more than "severe social conflict" in an empirical sense (vii, 8). The document goes further: "Certain formulas are not neutral, but *keep* the meaning they had in the original Marxist doctrine" (ibid.; emphasis added). That is, not only does the context determine the meaning of a category, but the category is also so indissolubly wedded to its original context that no divorce is possible. No matter what the new context, a category retains its old, original meaning. A critical and transformative appropriation of concepts from another system, then, seems impossible.

The first response to this stricture has been an appeal to the history of theology itself. Is there any great philosopher whose concepts have not been appropriated by one theologian or another in the last two thousand years? Plato, Aristotle, neo-Platonists, Kant, Hegel, Heidegger, Whitehead, and the existentialists seem to be ready examples of such critical appropriation. If Aristotle, then, why not Marx as well, as Dom Helder Camara once asked at the University of Chicago?[5] This response, however, raises two issues. The first is that such appropriation has not always been a happy one. What if such appropriation has in fact been a corruption of the Christian faith, as many have been saying since Harnack? What if the new context, instead of transforming the concepts it borrows, is itself corrupted by them? On the other hand, and this is the second issue, can Christian faith avoid borrowing concepts from other sources without falling into an impossible biblical fundamentalism? These issues, however, are too complex to go into here, and I will simply leave them aside. Besides, the argument from history is too general and formalistic. It may indicate the general necessity for borrowing philosophical categories, but it does not settle the issue of whether it is valid and prudent to borrow from any particular philosopher. What if there should be something unique about a philosopher, say, Marx, which makes such appropriation invalid, imprudent, or both?

This, I think, is precisely the point that the Vatican is making about Marxism. In arguing for the inseparability of method, which TL does admit that it is borrowing from Marx, from his ideology, which it claims ro reject, the document says:

> the thought of Marx is such a global vision of reality that all data received from observation and analysis are brought together in a philosophical and ideological structure, which predetermines the significance and importance to be attached to them. The ideological principles come prior to the study of the social reality and are presupposed in it. Thus no separation of the parts of this epistemologically unique complex is possible. If one tries to take only one part, say, the analysis, one ends up having to accept the entire ideology. That is why it is not uncommon for the ideological aspect to be predominant among the things which the "theologians of liberation" borrow from Marxist authors. (vii, 6)

Quoting from Paul VI's earlier warning, it goes on to say that

> it would be "illusory and dangerous to ignore the intimate bond which radically unites them, and to accept elements of the Marxist analysis

without recognizing its connections with the ideology, or to enter into the practice of class struggle and of its Marxist interpretation while failing to see the kind of totalitarian society to which this process slowly leads." (vii, 7)

The search for a systematic unity, of course, is not unique to Marxism. The very dynamism of human reason seems to be to seek to comprehend the relationships among things and organize such relationships according to a unifying principle. The goal of every philosophy has been a vision of reality as a unity, a totality of necessarily interrelated parts. It is also precisely in elaborating these interrelationships, and in the degree of necessity with which one part is related to another in a totality, that a philosophical system rises or falls.

It is one thing, however, to say that something is necessarily related to other parts *within* a particular system, and quite another to say that it is so inseparable from that system that its meaning is exhausted by its place within that system. The meaning a concept actually possesses within a system need not be the only meaning it may have, unless that system is so comprehensive and so penetrating as to exhaust all reality without remainder. Even Hegel's system did not claim such perfection. The meaning of a concept may transcend its particular embodiment within a given system, just as a different system or a new context may disclose a new meaning of the concept not evident or present in the old. A concept and a context can enrich and transform each other in a positive dialectic, just as they can impoverish and corrupt each other in a negative. In neither case is a concept inseparable from its old context and its meaning simply exhausted by it. In a real sense, the whole history of philosophy is a history in which parts of a system get separated from their old matrix and emigrate to a new home, a new system with which they enter into a dialectical relationship. This phenomenon is also evident in the history of the relationship between philosophy and theology, from the New Testament to Paul Tillich and Karl Rahner.

John Paul II himself is, I think, a good example of this dialectic. He takes the concept of 'person' in Boethius, Thomas, Kant, Scheler, and others, criticizes it, and transforms its meaning with his own interpretation in his *The Acting Person.*[6] He also takes terms and ideas, undoubtedly Marxian in origin, such as 'labor,' 'social labor,' 'alienation,' 'proletarianization,' 'social subject,' 'the priority of labor over capital,' 'praxis,' 'exploitation,' and others, and personalizes their meaning. It is not merely these concepts but also the viewpoint and social analysis associated with such concepts that he incorporates into his own analysis of contemporary society. The U. S. bishops point out in their pastoral letter of 1980 on "Marxist Communism" that "even our Holy Father, Pope John Paul II in his first encyclical, *Redemptor Hominis,* partly appropriates Marx's critique when he writes," and go on to quote from #15 of the encyclical, which says:

The man of today seems ever to be under threat from what he produces, that is to say from the result of the work of his hands and even more so, of the work of his intellect and the tendencies of his will. All too soon, and often in an unforeseeable way, what this manifold activity of man yields is not only subjected to "alienation," in the sense that it is simply taken away from the person who produces it, but rather it turns against man himself, at least in part, through the indirect consequences of its effects returning on himself. It is or can be directed against him. This seems to make up the main chapter of the drama of present-day human existence in its broadest and universal dimension.[7]

How this passage echoes the young Marx's analysis of alienation in his *Economic and Philosophic Manuscripts of 1844,* of course, is all too evident.

In fact, it should not be too difficult to trace the Marxian origin of the analysis of capitalist society common to the encyclicals from *Quadragesimo Anno* through *Populorum Progressio* to *Laborem Exercens.*[8] The popes have routinely analyzed capitalism in terms of the profit motive, the inversion of subject and object in the economic process, the concentration of wealth, exploitation of the worker, increasing power of 'things' over 'persons,' the growing division and conflict between rich and poor, the political and cultural consequences of such conflict, international colonialism and imperialism, and the need for collective action and structural change, all of which are, without question, Marxian in their origin. And there is nothing unusual about this. So much of Marxism has become part of the very intellectual culture of today that we use its categories without even noticing their origin. As pointed out by Oswald von Nell-Breuning, the former advisor to Pius XI, an authority on Catholic social doctrine and a man whose orthodoxy has never been questioned, "we are all riding on Marx's shoulders."[9]

The real question, therefore, is not whether particular concepts and even the mode of analysis are separable from the overall ideology or world view of the system in which they originate; they are, as the actual history of philosophy clearly shows. It is not relevent to recognize that the method of social analysis and the overall ideology (anthropology, ontology) are indeed found mutually inseparable *within* the system of Marx, a fact Enrique Dussel, a liberation theologian himself, insists on and which leads him to argue for a non-Marxian, Christian socialism.[10] In any system and certainly in a dialectical system (Hegel, Marx), and to the degree to which it is systematic, there is a dialectic among the parts, where they illumine the meaning of one another, as well as between the parts and the whole with their mutual coloring. As I argued earlier, this does not mean that the meaning the parts have within the system is the only possible meaning they can have. The dialectic recognizes not only the necessary interaction or relation among the parts, but also the irreducible mutual otherness, or difference among them. This is , after all, why there can be such a thing as the collapse of a system due to its *internal* contradictions, as various parts refuse to give up their identity and obey the demands of other parts or of the whole. What the thesis of inseparability requires, then, is not to abandon the attempt to learn and borrow from other systems, but to do so with caution and criticism.

Nor is the real question whether theology may use philosophy for its own purposes. Theology must do this, and has always done so.[11] It is not relevant whether the ideology of a system one borrows from is atheistic and totalitarian. Aquinas did not mind borrowing from Aristotle, although Aristotle's God is a far cry from the God of Abraham, Isaac, and Jacob, and he denied the immortality of the soul. As Pedro Arrupe, the former General of the Jesuits, put it,

> Marxist analysis is not the only analysis mixed with such elements.
> . . . Especially the social analyses commonly used in the "free world"
> imply a materialistic and individualistic view of the world, which are
> likewise opposed to Christian values and attitudes.[12]

The real question, as the Vatican itself put it, is whether such non-theological categories and analyses operate as the determining principle (viii, 1) of a theology which uses them, and whether they control the elaboration of the theological content in such a way that the content of faith, the *principia* of theology, and the horizon of transcendence proper to theology as theology are themselves subordinated to the requirements of such categories and analyses. Here much depends on how critical and undogmatic one is in the actual theological integration of such categories, as well as on the nature and intrinsic merit of such categories. In the final analysis, however, the dispute will always remain as to whether such categories are controlling or being controlled by the theological system they inform, for such judgments depend, as I shall argue in chapter 3, on the horizon of the judge's presuppositions.

THE MARXIAN MOMENT OF LIBERATION THEOLOGY

Regarding TL's appropriation of Marxism there are three questions to ask, especially in view of the fact that the Vatican document makes it appear as though liberation theologians have been buying Marxism lock, stock, and barrel. It repeatedly accuses them of borrowing Marxian concepts "uncritically," concepts which are in its judgment "perhaps impossible to purify" in any event (Introduction). The three questions are: (1) Why does TL feel the need to resort to Marxism in the first place? (2) What sort of Marxism is it that TL has been appropriating? and (3) What is the spirit or attitude with which such appropriation is made? Whether TL has actually managed to keep Marxism subordinate to the demands of faith can be answered only after its whole theology has been examined. I shall attempt an answer in chapter 4.

Why Marxism?

Regarding the first question we can begin with the starting point of TL, which is always the shocking awareness of the contradiction between the demand of Christian love, with its preferential option for the poor, and the sense of human powerlessness—often concealed as the virtue of resignation—regarding the situation of poverty and marginality. This consciousness, along with its sense of responsibility, compels the intellectual and practical search for ways of making brotherly love—the center of the message of Jesus—historically effective. This involves getting to know the actual situation of poverty and oppression, not merely its appearance but also its structural causes, in order to develop effective strategies to respond to it.

Where, then, should one turn for this knowledge? Sciences are not neutral. The picture and analysis of society produced by the intellectuals of the ruling class tend to cover up the most decisive characteristics of social reality, especially its conflictual, discriminatory and exclusivistic aspects, even when they are most sincerely Christian and well meaning, a fact of which the Boff brothers reminded us in their critical analysis of the U.S. bishops' pastoral letter on the economy.[13] The dominant analyses tend to attribute the poverty of the masses to a sad but inevitable fate. In this situation it becomes clear to committed Christians that love for the poor involves taking sides in the historical conflict. This taking of sides is certainly a matter of praxis and ethical choice, but there is also an intellectual or theoretical aspect to it, the decision to look at society and history from the standpoint of the oppressed, from the underside of history. At this point it is not surprising that Christian activists turn to Marxist theory, which has historically been the only major theory to do precisely that. It is not that the poor of the Gospel are simply identified with the proletariat of Marx, as the Vatican claims. Rather, it is a question of, in Girardi's words, "perceiving the connection between them, in the dynamics of a Christian consciousness which seeks to live according to the Gospel of Jesus in the midst of history."[14] In short, the discovery of Marxism is a result of the search for efficiency and coherence of praxis in meeting the demands of Christian faith and love, a love which goes beyond the sentimental moralism that may be subjectively gratifying but is incapable of changing the objective situation of the poor it means to love.[15]

The Marxism of Liberation Theology

What, then, is the scope and content of the Marxism appropriated by TL? Here, I think, the answer is not easy. First of all, Marxism is not as monolithic as the Vatican document makes it appear to be.[16] The sheer variety of Marxist doctrine existing today makes it as difficult to define its essence as it is to define the essence of Christianity. Secondly, the Marxian content varies from one liberation theologian to another. My presentation is based on certain concepts, generally considered Marxian, that are accepted as such by the majority of the liberation theologians.

TL's appropriation of Marxism has, I think, been generally critical and selective (although, understandably, not critical and selective enough in the eyes of the Vatican and the right-wing critics).[17] The ultimate criterion for such appropriation is the dynamics of faith in its search for historical ways of "actualizing" Christian love. Marxism is accepted "precisely to the measure to which it corresponds to the demands of such search."[18] In this sense there has never been a question of accepting Marxism as a "systematic totality," not even implicitly.[19] Theologians of liberation reject its atheism, metaphysical materialism, and historical determinism. They also reject, quite contrary to the Vatican's accusation (iv, 15), the tendency of dogmatic Marxism to reduce all forms of alienation to the economic as the source of all alienation. They agree with the Vatican that "sin" is the "most radical form of slavery" (iv, 2) and "the source of all evils" (x, 7) and that all other forms of slavery and alienation "derive ultimately from sin" (Introduction). For TL, sin is the "basic" alienation, "the ultimate root of all injustice and oppression,"[20] and "the cause of all evil."[21] Against Marxism's purely immanentist horizon, TL accepts the "eschatological reservation": salvation is not simply reducible to historical liberation, and no achievement of liberation is immune from the eschatological critique.[22] It does not share Marx's confidence that history by itself contains an immanent and necessary dynamism which will negate its negativities and transform them into a "kingdom of freedom." As Gutierrez put it, "the process of liberation will not have conquered the very roots of oppression and the exploitation of man by man without the coming of the Kingdom, which is above all a gift."[23] TL also points out that historical materialism is not itself empirically verifiable and thus requires transhistorical faith for its justification.[24] It does not like Soviet totalitarianism any more than does John Paul or Michael Novak, and looks for different models of socialism more appropriate to the indigenous conditions of Latin America and its different regions.

What, then, are the aspects of Marxism TL finds worth appropriating for its own historical task? According to the combined list of Clodovis Boff and José Miguez Bonino, there are six such interrelated basic concepts. They are: (1) the concept of society as a totality; (2) the economic interpretation of history; (3) the sociohistorical understanding of human existence; (4) the concepts of class struggle and of the revolutionary role of the proletariat; (5) the primacy of praxis within the unity of theory and praxis; and (6) the utopian vision of the dialectic of history.[25] Let me elaborate on each of these in order, adding my own reflections where helpful.

Society as Totality. The conventional approach to society is to divide it into separate spheres or areas of activity, such as politics, economics, and culture; to consider each sphere as autonomous and independent of one another, related to one another at best accidentally or extrinsically; and thus to regard society as the resulting sum of such extrinsically related spheres. This is based on a social division of labor, where each sphere is left up to the interpretation and decision of professionals with their specialized training in that particular sphere. Sickness is left to the doctors of medicine, politics to the professional politicians, business to the men and women in business, morality to the clergy and ethicists, and so forth. A sense of the whole is lacking, and the result has been the fragmentation and alienation of human existence and a prevailing sense of powerlessness to change this. In contrast, following Hegel's dialectical approach, Marxism sees society as a 'concrete totality.'[26] Society is concrete in the sense that it is internally differentiated into relatively autonomous spheres of activity as well as groups and classes of people, each of which is intrinsically (or 'constitutively') related to or conditioned by one another and shapes itself in a dialectic of appropriation and contradiction in relation both to other parts and to the whole. Society is a totality in the sense that it is both the a priori condition for the process, or 'becoming,' of the parts and the a posteriori result shaped in its turn by such becoming, often collapsing as a totality as when it can no longer sustain the conflicts and contradictions among its parts. This view insists on the need to study each sphere in itself, according to its own relatively autonomous logic of operation, but it also stresses the prime necessity of informing and guiding such study at the same time (not after its completion) with a vision of the whole and other spheres. This view makes it possible to understand a society *as* society in its structure, function, and movement. Thus, it corresponds not only to the inherent dynamism of human reason—often called "architectonic" or "speculative" (Hegel)—but also to the needs of sociopolitical action geared towards the structural change of society.

The Economic Interpretation of History. History is constituted by the dialectic of society as a concrete totality. In this dialectic, not all spheres have equal influence on the shaping of the whole or in relation to other spheres. Like Hegel, for whom the (absolute) spirit is identical with itself yet "overreaches" or conditions its Other and thus serves as the unifying or totalizing principle (cf. Sartre) in this dialectic of identity and difference, but unlike Hegel, who locates the unifying and shaping principle of history ultimately in the Absolute Spirit and then in the cultural objectifications of that Spirit in the sphere of philosophy, religion, and art, Marxism sees one particular sphere as exercising such a totalizing role, but locates it in the *economic* sphere with an internal dialectic between the means and relations of production, not in God or in the "higher" regions of culture and politics.

The economic sphere, of course, is first of all the sphere in which humans produce and reproduce the material conditions on which they depend for their very existence. It is the sphere in which our materiality as humans and our dependence on nature become most manifest, a sphere without which there could be no human existence, still less the "higher" things of life, a fact expressed in the powerlessness of the poor and the greed of the wealthy as well as suppressed by those who pretend to be indifferent to such "material" things in their pursuit of the higher things of life. The economic sphere, however, is also something more. It is not only the sphere of the production of material things but also the sphere of social interdependence, in which we can produce such things only in mutual dependence on our fellows. It is the juncture of our dependence on nature and our dependence on other humans, at once the materialization of our social relations and the socialization of our material relations. We depend on our fellows not only for the things on which we depend for our very existence, but also for the very possibility of our political independence and our cultural self-expression. The economic sphere, therefore, is not just one sphere among others; it is also a unifying, totalizing sphere, in its own way, with a shaping power over other spheres and the whole. It conditions not only the production and distribution of material things but also, through such production and distribution, the relations of power among and over human beings (politics) and the quality and availability of certain types of culture (ideology). This economic conditioning of politics and culture, of course, means precisely that, conditioning, not mechanistic determinism.[27]

This economic interpretation—known as 'historical materialism'—is a deliberate rejection of idealism in the broad sense, including rationalism, intellectualism, voluntarism, and spiritualism; these perspectives look at human life from 'above,' whereas the economic interpretation looks at it from 'below.' As Miguez Bonino puts it, "history is not primarily the unfolding of man's consciousness or of his ideas but the dynamics of his concrete activity, the main form of which is the work through which he transforms nature in order to respond to the totality of his needs."[28] This is in clear contrast to the traditional model of human nature that has ruled both theology and philosophy, for which the human person is basically a consciousness—a thinker, a 'feeler,' or at most a 'willer,' to use neologisms, still more or less confined within the circle of inwardness. This model, of course, did not deny that the person is also an actor in the concrete world or that he or she has to make a living, but this dimension of human activity in relation to the transformation of the material world, along with its political and ideological implications, remained at best peripheral, an afterthought, to its understanding of the person. The economic interpretation makes this transformative activity the essential, unifying principle of our humanity without denying the reality or importance of our spiritual and intellectual life. In doing so, it denies that reason or thought is totally autonomous or separable from the concrete totality of human existence. Human life is not an aspect of thought; rather, thought is an aspect of human life. It also recognizes our basic, internal dependence on nature and our finitude as material beings. Angelism belongs to the angels, not to humans.

The Sociality of Existence. Human existence is essentially social in the most concrete, historical sense. Humans are born into a determinate society with its determinate economic structure, political institutions, and cultural horizons. It is in a dialectic with the pressures and challenges of that society that humans develop their individuality. Capitalist individualism ignores this social a priori of individual existence. It considers society as only an aggregate of isolated individuals—isolated in the sense of having no antecedent relations and ties— and claims both the power and the right of such individuals to be self-sufficient, while in reality individuals can be individuals only in manifold forms of inter- dependence on others, individualism itself being a social product of a particular culture. Christian spirituality likewise regarded our social relationships as either harmful to our salvation or at best an occasion of good works, and advocated withdrawal into the inwardness of our souls where we could presumably establish a direct relationship with God. In contrast, TL, along with Marxism, insists that "man is not the single individual but a communal unity in the form of a concrete social formation with its structures, relationships and self-understanding (ideology)."[29] This need not deny that humans have a transcendent dignity or that they are subjects of their own thought. It does mean that such dignity is necessarily bound up with the concrete social structures for the possibilities of both its promotion and oppression, and that the thoughts which are indeed our own are also conditioned, positively or negatively, by our social environments.

This insight also provides all the more reason why a critique of ideology and a transformation of social structure are necessary, although not sufficient, for the attainment of truth and the promotion of our transcendent dignity. Ad- vocates of individualism and privatism affirm the transcendence of human dignity and truth, but too often fail to recognize those conditions that nurture them. This failure can lead them to accept the grossest violations of this dignity and to become unconscious, uncritical dupes of ideologies. It is obvious that the possibility of this critical transcendence of ideological conditioning and the at- tainment of objective truth are subject to the basic historicity of human existence and available only within its limits; the objectivity of human knowledge can never be that of a suprahistorical being, any more than the transcendent dignity of humans can be based on an actual capacity to transcend all history.

Class Struggle and the Proletariat. The concepts of class struggle and the revolutionary role of the proletariat have perhaps been the most scandalous and offensive of all the elements of Marxism to the traditional Christian con- sciousness. Due to its peculiarly individualistic conception of sin and spiritualistic understanding of conversion as a purely interior act, coupled with a basically ahistorical vision of social reality as something immutable, the theological and philosophical tradition confined its ethics to that of the individual, regarding social ethics as at best an extension of individual ethics. It failed to perceive the theological meaning of basic social divisions and conflicts or to recognize the social evil of oppressive institutions and structures which generate and conceal such conflicts. Instead, it generally tended to accept the reality of the status quo as a divine, immutable order of things. It could not perceive the ethical demand of structural evil, still less believe in the possibility of a structural change for the better. That the Church has been basically reactionary in the face of the many modern revolutions, therefore, is no surprise.

In this regard the role of TL is both similar to and different from that of Kierkegaard and existentialist theology. Both stress the reality of rupture in human life, but the nature of the rupture remains different. In an age dominated by bourgeois smugness and easy rationalism, Kierkegaard accentuated the character of Christian faith as epistemological rupture, an "offense" and "absolute paradox" demanding the "crucifixion of the understanding." In the contemporary world, fraught with explosive class conflicts and their globalization between North and South yet complacent enough to conceal them in a harmonistic vision, TL accepts without apology the sociological rupture of class struggle and the necessity of revolutionary—i.e., structural—change in all their sting and scandal. Neither Marx nor TL invented class struggle or advocates it for its own sake. It is simply a question of recognizing a historical reality which has always been there and reflecting, from the viewpoint of effective faith and love, on what is to be done about that reality. Class struggle is no more than a sociohistorical expression of that basic conflict which is in some sense built into the situation of concrete human existence as we know it. Given the scarcity of material resources upon which humans so deperately depend, the social relations that always govern the production and distribution of such resources, and the reality of the varying degrees of human greed recognized by both Christianity and capitalism, those who possess those resources also necessarily acquire and exercise a social power over those who do not possess but need them. This relationship of struggle and domination eventually becomes objectified into social institutions and structures and develops appropriate ideologies to justify and legitimate them.

Those with power and privilege will not voluntarily share their power with those who are without, not necessarily because they lack good will as individuals but because the weight of reified structures based on a division of classes will overrule such a good will. Appeal to the conversion of their individual hearts is not unimportant, but such conversion, unless made concrete and effective in organized political solidarity with the oppressed majority, would prove only an ineffectual gesture, perhaps consoling to their individual conscience but leaving the situation of oppression just as it was. Likewise, history has shown no significant example of a ruling class abolishing itself *as* a class in a mass conversion.

What, then, does this situation of class conflict, often as explosive as in Latin America and much of the Third World, require of Christian faith and love? To say that we must wait for the mass conversion and voluntary self-abolition of the ruling class as a class would be to accept the oppression of the majority till the *eschaton*. To say that we must remain neutral and impartial in the face of such conflicts would be both to accept the moral claims of the respective classes as equally valid and to legitimate the status quo of oppression in fact if not in intention. The only option, therefore, is the preferential option of solidarity with the poor and oppressed, who together suffer basic social conflict in its most degrading form and therefore also have, objectively, both the strongest motivation for and a shared interest in organizing for their own emancipation.

TL thus accepts the reality and dynamics of class struggle and the necessity of a revolutionary class in a broad, general way, without the dogmatism often associated with them in the Marxist tradition. It is fully aware of the ongoing dynamics of capitalism and the subtle changes in the relations between classes. It does not accept Marx's nineteenth-century explanation as it was, and does not simply identify the agent of revolution with the industrial proletariat. It insists on the necessity of continuing empirical analyses and broadens the meaning of the proletariat to refer to the "poor" as such, the poor "not as an isolated and haphazard phenomenon, but in their organic and structural existence as oppressed classes."[30]

Primacy of Praxis. For Marxism the essence of human existence does not lie primarily in thought, rationality, or any form of inwardness, as in much of traditional philosophy stemming from Plato and Aristotle, or in 'existence' in the Kierkegaardian or Heideggerian sense. It lies in action, activity, or praxis, whereby humans objectify, activate, and actualize their subjectivity, potentialities, and inwardness so as to become concretely free. To act, at the same time, is always to act in a determinate sociohistorical situation. Action is the locus of the dialectic of thought and being, subjectivity and objectivity, individuality and sociality, the weight of the past which necessitates the action and the promise of the future it hopes to actualize. It is above all through action that the human essence becomes concrete and effective. The dialectic of action thus captures in itself all the dimensions of human existence both in their concrete density and in their mutual relatedness, such as the subjectivity of thought and self-determination, the historicity of social relations in which such subjectivity must become actual, and the necessity of social cooperation and social transformation. The actual human subject, then, is not the thinking, willing, or feeling subject but the acting subject, of which thinking, willing, and feeling are aspects or dimensions. In this sense praxis or action is the unifying, totalizing principle of all the dimensions of concrete existence.

It is this acting subject, shaped by the challenges and pressures of the concrete objective situation, which thinks, wills, and feels. The distinction between thinking and acting, theory and praxis, is a distinction made and posited within the unity of the subject, which is essentially the acting subject or subject of praxis. As an intrinsic dimension of this acting subject, theory takes its origin, impetus, condition, and goal from the exigencies of concrete, determinate sociohistorical praxis. There is, of course, a dialectic between the self-transcending and self-critical dynamism of theory and the confining pressures and challenges of historical praxis, but this unity in difference is a unity within praxis as the unifying and totalizing principle and in this sense within the primacy of praxis. In this anthropological view, theory is essentially oriented towards praxis in history and society; the task of theory is not merely to interpret the world but to change it, as Marx said in his famous eleventh thesis on Feuerbach. At the same time the praxis of changing the world under constant exposure to its contradictions and ambiguities also has the epistemological function of disclosing or revealing to theory those aspects of the social reality that are inaccessible to ahistorical, abstract, merely contemplative theory.

It is no surprise that TL should find in this Marxian view, which takes human existence at its most concrete, a sorely needed corrective against traditional anthropology, which regarded the person as basically a thinker, and traditional epistemology, which regarded truth as a static correspondence between the contemplative mind and objective reality. When these are introduced into Christian theology, the result has been to confer primacy on the intellectual or 'knowing' aspect of faith over the 'doing' of faith, and to relegate such doing or praxis to a secondary position as merely an application of a faith antecedently constituted in its own right apart from praxis. The emphasis, therefore, has naturally been on orthodoxy, often leaving orthopraxis, as Schillebeeckx well pointed out, to non-Christians.[31] The relation between knowing and doing in faith, as well as the relation between the theory of theology and the praxis of faith, must be radically reconceived and brought closer to the concrete reality of the believing and theologizing subject.

The Utopian Vision of History. Whether Marx really thought of the total abolition of classes as a real historical possibility is still a much debated issue. He certainly has been accused by his critics of harboring such a utopian dream. Nevertheless, it would be difficult to deny that Marx's historical vision of a reconciled society achievable by human effort, a society of sisters and brothers liberated from the artificial barriers of class domination, has provided a powerful inspiration and impetus to the many modern movements of liberation on the part of the exploited and oppressed masses around the world. It has brought hope to the despairing masses and awakened confidence in historical action where apathy and resignation, long preached as virtues, have suppressed the human powers of active self-liberation into oblivion. It has served as a powerful corrective against the fatalism and ideology of grace, which has so long thrown a damper on the collective human will to liberation in the name of human depravity and dependence on God, as though such dependence ever dispensed with the necessity of human initiative. It is not surprising that TL, faced with the tragic reality of Latin America, should find in such a utopian vision a source of hopeful action and historical confidence, a welcome antidote against the despairing passivity so often characteristic of exploited peoples.

This thematic classification of the Marxian contribution to TL, I think, can be usefully complemented by another approach, that of Ignacio Ellacuria, who classifies the contribution in terms of ethics, epistemology, and philosophy.[32] This brings out the dialectic among the themes as well as between the themes and Christian theological concerns. First, the ethical contribution of Maxism lies in awakening the consciousness of social injustice as the most important moral challenge of today. Marxism gives ethical meaning to the historical praxis of justice and historical content to our ethical commitments. In doing so, it seeks to overcome the dualism of personal ethics and political praxis: one must find personal fulfillment in political praxis and fill such praxis with ethical meaning. By giving a concrete, materialistic, and political meaning to the poor, who are often considered victims of unavoidable fate and mere accidents, it calls attention to the structural causes of poverty and overcomes the long history of the 'spiritualization' of the poor. Its utopian vision gives historical content to hope and lends itself to the reconceptualization of God as a power in history, as the power of effective utopia.

In the area of epistemology, the Marxian critique of ideology sensitizes us to the hidden interests lurking in prevailing theories, including theology. In interpreting history from below, from the standpoint of the exploited proletariat, it invites theology to also look at history from the standpoint of the poor. There is a convergence—a relation, not a direct transference—between the proletariat as the locus of the knowledge of history and the poor as the locus of theological interpretation. The doctrine of the unity of theory and praxis compels a reconceptualization of the theoretical status of theology itself, and confers on orthopraxis the status of a necessary, if not sufficient, condition for the authenticity of theological theory. The fundamental importance attributed by Marxism to the struggle in the economic sphere assists TL in overcoming the purely spiritualistic conception of salvation and giving it concrete historical content. In contrast to the traditional deductive–metaphysical, transcendental, and phenomenological methods, the dialectical method enables theologians to understand reality in its totality, dynamism, and conflicts, and thus to be more relevant and effective in their historical task.

The basic philosophical contribution of Marxism lies in its interpretation of reality as history. In looking at history as a process in which reality is manifested, it opens up new perspectives which enable theology to see history as a history of salvation, as the locus in which God manifests herself/himself and humans must work for their salvation, in a way similar to the perspective of the Old Testament. Marx's historical materialism can lead to a new appreciation of the materiality of human existence and guard us against the traditional temptations to false spiritualism and transcendentalism which have long contributed to the legitimation of injustice and domination. It can also lead to a healthy realism in looking at reality, avoiding irrelevant moralism and impotent idealism. Marx's vision of a new humanity created by transformed 'history' after the long dark night of the 'prehistory' of mutual domination can help us rediscover the Christian vision of utopia, the 'New Heaven' and the 'New Earth,' opening up new perspectives for the praxis and theory of theology and saving us from the excessive pessimism and passive understanding of the doctrine of original sin. Above all, the rediscovery through Marxism of the conflictual character of sociohistorical existence gives a new, historical dimension to the struggle against sin—so often reified and removed from concrete history—as well as to the concepts of the cross, suffering, persecution, and love, which henceforth can no longer be spiritualized and idealized as in the past. It also sensitizes us to institutional and structural violence so that we may unmask it for what it really is.

These, then, are the basic concepts and categories of Marxism that TL admits it has taken over and in fact insists that it must. I have tried to present them in the context of intellectual history and theological concerns. The list is by no means exhaustive, and much depends on one's classification. It does give us, however, a sufficient indication of the extent to which TL is indebted to the Marxist tradition. As should have been noticed, these ideas are taken over not in the precise technical formulation that they have received in the Marxian tradition but rather in their generality as basic ideas or perspectives which allow us to look at human existence and human history in a new way. This leads us to the third question, namely: What is the spirit or attitude with which TL appropriates these concepts and categories?

Attitude of TL Towards Marxism

I stated earlier that the appropriation of Marxism by TL is critical and selective. It rejects those elements of Marxism that are clearly incompatible with the basic affirmations of Christian faith, such as its atheism, totalitarianism, historical determinism, and immanentism. Let me now add that TL retains its critical approach even with regard to those elements which it admits it has taken over from Marxism. This critical approach, which I think is shared by theologians of liberation as a whole, is summed up in their insistence on the primacy of faith over all human theories and of the faith imperative to liberate the poor over all interpretations of the sociohistorical reality, as well as in their consequent deabsolutizing of the status of Marxism from an absolute, closed system to a scientific method or perspective subject to all the limitations of human sciences.

Clodovis Boff has recently formulated, on the basis of the actual practice of TL, certain "rules for the theological use of Marxism," which I find extremely helpful in understanding the spirit or attitude with which TL takes Marxism.[33] The first rule is to treat it as science, not as religion, prophecy, gnosis, or holy scripture. We must guard against the temptation to elevate it to an absolute, closed system of comprehensive, immutable truths. The second rule is to take this science in the sense of the scientific method. A method, by nature, is something flexible and open to further testing, verification, and reformulation. It certainly does not dispense with the need for ongoing empirical analysis of the dynamics of particular situations. What it does is to provide certain ways of approaching, interpreting, or dealing with social reality.

The Marxian elements discussed above constitute the content of this method, which means that it is not merely a method of social analysis in the usual sense in which it is distinguished from ideology. It does include certain philosophical interpretations of human existence and history as a whole, or, if one prefers, a metaphysics in the broad sense. At the same time, these metaphysical interpretations are to be taken not as an absolute, immutable system but precisely as perspectives, horizons, or as *medium quo*—that in light of which reality is looked at. It is as a perspective of this sort that Marxism helped TL in its rediscovery of certain basic themes of Scripture, such as the theological meaning of oppression, the historically enduring conflict between rich and poor, the identification of God and Jesus with the oppressed in society, the Christian vision of a redeemed society based on justice, equality, and love, the meaning of Jesus' conflict with the status quo for Christology, and many others. These elements have always been there in Scripture, but it has taken the shock of the experience of massive oppression and human degradation *and* the Marxian dialectical perspective on history to rediscover and appreciate them as something central to Christian faith.

The third rule is to use Marxism as a theory of historical reality, not to exaggerate its competence as some sort of *mathesis universalis* or universal theory. As every science has its own formal object, so does Marxism, whose object is the social and historical dimension of reality and whose competence is therefore limited to that dimension. To claim universal competence in all areas and dimensions of reality would be a sign of arrogance. Even within the areas of its own competence there are, we must recognize, many domains of social life Marxism has yet to investigate. As Gutierrez adds, we should also recognize that Marxism is not the only social science there is.[34]

The fourth rule is to treat Marxism as a *tool*, and therefore only for its instrumental value. What is important is not Marxism for its own sake but the understanding of reality that it opens up, more precisely of the reality of oppression and the possibilities of liberation. It is only an instrument at the service of higher ends. As an instrument it is always open to correction and improvement. As knowledge it is subject to the 'epistemological breach,' the irreducible gap between knowledge and reality; contrary to the view of ideocracy, the knowledge of something is never identical with its reality. It is this instrumental use of Marxism which gives theology a certain flexibility in dealing with the claims and issues of Marxist theory as well as in using it for its own theological purpose.

The fifth and last rule is to use Marxism as a mediation of faith, not as faith itself. It is a mediation which begins from faith and is controlled by faith. The faith in the absolute sovereignty of God and the Gospel must always remain as a critical and relativizing principle for all finite mediations of faith. As God is the absolute measure of all that is finite (science, Marxism, revolution, history, and so on), so does faith have the power to 'detheologize' totemistic Marxism, 'detotalize' totalitarian Marxism, and 'deabsolutize' absolutized Marxism.

In its own self-understanding, then, the relationship of TL to Marxism is a critical, selective, and instrumental one. Some critics may, of course, question whether TL has always observed such a relationship in its actual theological practice of appropriating Marxism for its own synthesis. It is the burden of the following chapters (3 and 4) to show how TL actually integrates the Marxian sources into its theological construction.

THE HEGELIAN MOMENT OF LIBERATION THEOLOGY

To speak of Marx, of course, is to speak of Hegel. Despite the undeniable differences between the absolute idealism of Hegel and the historical materialism of Marx, there is also an intimate connection between them, an intrinsic relation of appropriation which links Marx to Hegel and without which there would have been no Marx as we know him. Many of the major ideas of Marxism discussed here—history as a dialectical movement, the role of contradiction in that history, society as a concrete totality, the primacy of the actual over the merely ideal, the sociohistorical understanding of human existence, history as the history of the actualization of freedom, the idea of a historical subject—are undoubtedly Hegelian in their origin and form although different in their content.

It is not, however, solely through this Marxian content that Hegel enters into the constitution of TL as one of its essential moments. Hegel also enters into it in his own right. As I shall try to show in the following chapters, the Marxian contribution to TL lies chiefly in the area of its articulation of the tasks of Christian faith and theology in relation to the urgencies of liberation *within* history. These tasks, however, presuppose two things if they are to remain theological, not sociological. It presupposes that secular and profane history is already pregnant with salvific significance; that is, it presupposes the overcoming of the traditional dualisms of sacred and profane, transcendent salvation and historical liberation. It also presupposes that the concern for the liberating tasks in history has a protection against the temptations of 'immanentism,' that object of the Vatican's special concern and criticism. In this properly theological area Marxism as such has no important contribution to make, whereas Hegel's specific contribution to TL, I think, lies precisely here. Hegel articulates the relationship between God and history as something posited by God as God's self-mediation. Due to this mediation, human history is not something extrinsic to God but an intrinsic moment in God's own life. God is at work in human history as God's own Other, which preserves duality (Other) but overcomes dualism (God's own) because the duality is itself posited by God and subject to the unifying and totalizing power of God, which also protects against the immanentist claims to self-sufficiency. In other words, Hegel provides the necessary mediation between the Marxian emphasis on historical liberation and the Christian theological emphasis on God and God's transcendent salvation, and enters into TL as the organizing principle for its final synthesis of Christian faith and Marxism.

This properly Hegelian moment in TL, unlike its Marxian moment, is more assumed and hidden than explicit and elaborated. As I shall try to show, however, its presence is real and of substantial theological significance to the Christian integrity of a TL that seeks to be Christian theology, not sociology. This is no place to go into all the problems of Hegel interpretation, as controversial as in

the case of Marx. I shall confine myself to those aspects of Hegel relevant to
TL according to my own interpretations elaborated elsewhere.[35] In any event,
it seems essential to call attention to this Hegelian presence in TL, first because
its importance has generally been neglected and unacknowledged in the raging
debates on TL, and secondly because it provides a significant theological corrective against the conservative exaggerations of the Marxian presence in TL,
which are intent on accusing it of historicist reductionism and condemning it
as Christian theology.

Let me begin with a summary of the relevant aspects of Hegel's dialectic.
As a method of dialectical reason it begins with a recognition of the *otherness*
or division among things, parts, or dimensions of reality, but goes on, as analytic
reason—"understanding"—does not, to show the *inner* relatedness of things that
are other within the *unity* of the whole, which both renders the totality concrete
and provides an immanent *teleological* thrust towards reconciliation as the self-
sublation *(Aufhebung)* of its inner contradictions. The totality as such, then, is
a *movement* resulting from the inner mediation both among the parts themselves
and between the parts and the whole, in which the movement of the parts concretizes and makes actual *(wirklich)* that of the whole but does so precisely within
the unity of the whole and thus as inner moments of the *self-mediation* of the
whole whose efficacy and teleology as a totality transcend those of the parts as
parts. Otherness or negativity, internality of relations, unity of and within the
whole, contradiction and its teleological sublation in reconciliation, the concretizing self-mediation of the whole through the parts; these are the basic categories
of dialectical reason. For Hegel, these are not merely the subjective tendencies
of human reason, but also the aspects of the very structure, come to consciousness
in humans, of the objective reality which is the Absolute Spirit.[36]

According to Hegel, the essence of God or the Absolute Spirit lies in action,
which means both actualization and manifestation of divine subjectivity by means
of an Other. To act is to actualize what otherwise would remain merely potential
and abstract, and it is also to reveal what otherwise would remain hidden and
opaque. This self-actualizing and self-expressive activity constitutes the eternal
life of the immanent Trinity. Because God is the pure act in this dynamic sense,
God also can and does create a world and a history as his Other in relation to
which he actualizes and reveals himself. God is really related to and involved
in human history, and reveals who he is through his historical action.
Transcendence and history are not two independent, mutually external realities.
They are indeed distinct; the infinite is *not* finite. But they are also dialectically
united through God's own activity which overreaches the finite as *his* Other, that
is, through God's unifying and totalizing power. God creates and appropriates
the finite as his own Other from within. It is God's own praxis of creating,
redeeming, and reconciling which constitutes history *as* history.

It is important to note here the way in which Hegel tries to reconcile the
traditional dichotomy of God and creature, transcendence and history, infinite

and finite. For him, an infinite which is only opposed and external to the finite is not truly infinite. It still has something outside itself and thus remains limited by the latter. By the same token, the finite ceases to be truly finite when it is opposed to the infinite as something external to itself. For Hegel, to be finite means to be dependent on the infinite and this as a matter of an intrinsic ontological characteristic of finitude as such: by itself the finite cannot even be finite. The opposition, originally motivated by the desire to preserve the transcendence of the infinite over the finite, ironically ends up by finitizing the infinite and infinitizing the finite. The "true" infinite requires that the finite itself be construed not as something outside the infinite but as something internal to it, that is, as something posited by the infinite itself as an Other and therefore as in some sense really distinct from the infinite, but also as *its* Other which it posits and through which it manifests and incarnates itself, and which therefore is ultimately subject to its own transcendent efficacy and finality. In this view, then, the intrinsic striving of the finite towards the infinite is both the act of the finite and the self-mediation of the infinite to itself. In this sense, the true infinite must be construed as Absolute Spirit— absolute because it is not conditioned by anything external to itself but is instead inclusive of the finite as *its* Other without losing its own transcendence over the finite as finite. In short, the true infinite is possible only as a *concrete universal* or *concrete totality.*

Hegel's philosophy of history interprets history as a process in which the Absolute Spirit becomes a concrete totality through the inner mediation of finite spirits in the realm of contingency and externality. The essence and immanent *telos* of spirit is freedom; that is, it seeks to actualize its transcendent dynamism and become itself concretely, not abstractly; objectively, not merely subjectively. As a historically conditioned, situated freedom, however, it can do so only by sublating the contradiction between its own ever-transcendent ideals and the limitations of existing institutions, and thus by objectifying and concretizing such ideals in ever-new institutions and structures at once historically concrete and socially effective. In the immanent order the agency of historical transformation belongs to certain 'world-historical' individuals and states, who have both the passion and receptivity to actualize the newly emerging 'spirit of the times' but whose historical destiny is always temporary and relative to the needs of a particular time. Their agency is subject to the transcendent agency and *telos* or 'providence' of the Absolute, who inspires and effects the self-liberation of finite spirits and, through such liberation, its own concretion in history, while also transcending any of its particular historical embodiments. For Hegel, then, history is a history of liberation, with a twofold meaning: in its historical content, it is political, but in its absolute finality it is also religious and transcendent, and the one cannot exist without the other. The political content is meaningful only as the historically particular concretization of the absolute finality, as the absolute is absolute, not another particular finite, only by virtue of its power to concretize itself through such historical particularity without losing the power to transcend such particularity in its historical limitation.[37]

These, then, are some of the salient points of Hegel's theology which I think are important for an understanding of TL, especially its attempt to connect transcendent salvation and historical liberation without falling into reductionism. The notion of God as an absolute, true infinite inclusive of the finite, the dialectic of the concrete univesal actualizng itself through the particular and of the particular as the incarnation of the universal, the emphasis on action as both actualization and manifestation, history as the locus of the dialectic of the divine universal and the historical particular, concrete liberation as the effective, immanent *telos* of that history: these are useful to keep in mind in the following chapters, especially in chapter 4 as we discuss the relationship between salvation and liberation or transcendence and history. As always, the appropriation of these Hegelian categories by TL is not a case of direct transference but one of transformation for its own purpose and in its own context.

CHAPTER III

Theology and Praxis

One of the many challenges of TL has been the need to rethink the relation between theory (theology) and praxis. Are theory and praxis two coequal dimensions of human existence, or is the one derivative from the other? What exactly is the relation between the two? Are they parallel activities—each with its own object, end, and sphere—or is there a dialectic of mutual constitution and interaction between them, even as they remain mutually distinct and irreducible?

In the religious sphere proper, TL has challenged us to ask whether Christian faith is primarily a matter of theory, belief, and truth or primarily a matter of praxis, action, and justice—is it only a reflection *on* faith or a reflection *in* faith as well? What is the relation between theology and contemporary historical praxis? Does theology have to remain external to that praxis because such *historical* praxis is simply irrelevant to the transcendence of theology in its goal (God) and foundation (revelation) and/or because theology must preserve its critical objectivity and ensure its ideological neutrality vis-a-vis all ideologies of historical praxis? Or should we say that participation of theology in that praxis is the very condition of its transcendence and objectivity? In the latter case, what is the proper role of theological theory in and for the praxis of faith, and how can it preserve its transcendence and objectivity against the ideological pressures of that praxis? How does the a priori "preferential option for the poor"—so insisted on by TL—not vitiate but confirm the integrity of theology? I believe that these questions, with their assumptions about the relation between theory and praxis, are central to theology as such; they have to do not so much with the truth or validity of particular affirmations of theology as with the very foundation—

37

at least the anthropological—for the possibility of theology as such. The challenge of TL in this regard is not, as I stated at the beginning, 'one of the many challenges' but *the* challenge to contemporary Christian theology.

The problem of theory and praxis is as old as philosophy and implicitly as old as human life itself. As such it contains all the basic problems of philosophy, such as subject and object, consciousness and reality, transcendence and history, ideality and actuality, philosophy and politics. This comprehensive character of the implications of the problem is quite understandable, given the structure of human existence as a unity of transcendence and history, from which arise all the relations and contradictions between the polarities of existence. Humans are not simply merged in and with the given but are burdened with the task of transcending the given in view of their ends, of both rendering it intelligible in thought and humanizing it in action.

For the classical tradition of Aristotle, which has ruled the relation between theory and praxis ever since, this task generally takes three forms in accordance with their respective object and end. The first consists in 'making' or *poiesis*. Its object is material things in nature; its end, to transform them into instruments of human needs. *Poiesis* thus covers the entire sphere of material production. The second consists in action or *praxis*, whose object is not material things but human actions in society and history and whose end is to transform and order human actions ethically so as to make possible a community (*polis*) of free citizens. The human need for transcendence, however, is not confined to the transformation of material and political existence in history, with all its contingency and variability. It also manifests itself in the need to know and attain what is necessary, immutable, and unconditioned, and this for its own sake, not as a means to material and political ends within history. From this need follows the third form of human existence, *theoria*. Its object is the unchanging and necessary, and its end the enjoyment of truth for its own sake. This is the sphere of theology (knowledge of God as the ultimate, unchanging source and end of all changing things), metaphysics (knowledge of the universal, necessary structures of all beings *as* being), and, by extension, the 'theoretical' aspects of the empirical sciences, insofar as they are 'disinterested' inquiries into the (relatively) stable regularities and uniformities in nature and society.

This classical conception of three forms of life, of course, was not free of ideology. It arose from the existing social divisions in the ancient and medieval world among three classes of people—the manual laborers, holders of political power, and the intellectuals (philosophers and theologians)—and, in turn, served to legitimate the hierarchical organization of society. Based on the dualistic anthropology of the material and the spiritual, it ignored the essential social and historical context of human existence taken as a concrete totality which necessarily introduces a disturbing dialectic into the relation among the economic, political, and intellectual spheres of human activity, undermining the all-too-neat distinctions according to formal object and specific end by which such distinctions were made and justified.

As briefly indicated in the preceeding chapter, it is this social and ideological division of labor that was radically challenged by the historical materialism of the Marxist tradition. As far as Christian theology is concerned, however, it has been as though the Marxian critique had never existed. Until very recently, the prevailing conception of theology as primarily a theoretical, contemplative science, and separate from the critical problems of economic exploitation and political oppression, went largely unchallenged. It has been left to TL to challenge this dominant conception and save theology from its lofty isolation from historical praxis and integrate it into the concrete totality which is human life. Why theology, otherwise so sensitive to the contributions of existentialism, phenomenology, personalism, analytic philosophy, and process thought, had for so long remained oblivious of the contributions of ideology critique remains a fertile territory for a sociology of knowledge to explore.

The purpose of this chapter is neither to review the entire history of the concepts of theory and praxis nor to discuss their contemporary developments and their ramifications in theology, philosophy, and the empirical sciences.[1] My purpose is limited to the presentation and discussion of the specific issues raised by and against TL. Ever since Gutierrez challenged contemporary academic theology with his new definition of theology as "a critical reflection on Christian praxis in the light of the Word"[2] and his claim that "the theology of liberation offers us not so much a new theme for reflection as a *new way* to do theology,"[3] the challenge has been met with critical counter-challenges from different quarters, each with its own conception of theology and its own theological agenda. In what follows, I shall first present three important criticisms of TL, those of the Vatican, Schubert Ogden, and Dennis P. McCann and Charles R. Strain; then will go on to discuss, at some length, the position of TL, covering such topics as the historicity of theology, solidarity with the poor, and its theological method, i.e., the "hermeneutic circle"; and finally will respond to the critics.

CRITICISMS OF THEOLOGY OF LIBERATION

The Vatican

In its virtual condemnation of TL[4], the Vatican points out that TL subordinates every affirmation of faith and theology to a political criterion, evaluating it from an a priori "classist" (x, 2) point of view and claims that "the viewpoint of the oppressed and revolutionary class" "is the single true point of view" (x, 3). In this perspective "orthodoxy, or the right rule of faith, is substituted for by the notion of orthopraxy as the criterion of the truth," relativizing "theological criteria for truth" and subordinating them to the imperatives of the class struggle (ibid.). The truths of faith are not respected "beforehand for their transcendent value" (ix, 6). It also seems clear that such a "partisan" conception of truth would discredit in advance all views which do not share the same commitment to the class struggle and make impossible real dialogue with other points of view "with objectivity and attention (x, 1 & 3). Other positions, considered "only reflections of class interests," would not have to be examined "in themselves" (x, 1).[5]

What, then, is the Vatican's understanding of the theological significance of praxis, especially the political praxis of solidarity with the oppressed? The Vatican does recognize that there is a kind of "practical orientation, which is proper to traditional theology in the same way that speculative orientation is" and which should not be confused with the "privileged priority" given to the revolutionary praxis "as the supreme criterion for theological truth" (x, 3). As the Vatican puts it:

> A healthy theological method no doubt will always take the praxis of the church into account and will find there one of its foundations, but that is because that praxis comes from the faith and is a lived expression of it. (ibid.)

In addition to the Gospel, the social teachings of the church, and contributions of theologians and other thinkers to the reflection of the church, the Vatican states that

> likewise the experience of those who work directly for the evangelization and for the advancement of the poor and the oppressed is necessary for the doctrinal and pastoral reflection of the church. In this sense it is necessary to affirm that one becomes more aware of certain aspects of truth by starting with praxis, if by that one means pastoral praxis and social work which keep its evangelical inspiration. (xi, 13)

Praxis, then, is authentic only insofar as it "comes from the faith and is a lived expression of it" or "keeps it evangelical inspiration," and becomes relevant as a theological method or as "one" of its foundations by making us "more aware of certain aspects of truth" in "simply drawing attention to the consequences and political implications of the truths of faith, which are respected beforehand for their transcendent value" (ix, 6). For the Vatican, faith is primarily a matter of truth or orthodoxy, and praxis is only a subsequent "expression" of faith. Praxis must respect the truth of faith "beforehand," and its only contribution to faith as truth lies in drawing the "consequences" and "implications" of the latter and making us "more" aware of them. In short, praxis is neither an intrinsic moment of faith itself, which is primarily a matter of truth, nor an essential moment in the very disclosure of the content of faith, which is basically already known apart from praxis.

Schubert Ogden

One of Ogden's many criticisms of TL[6] is that it confuses the witness of faith, which is indeed binding on the theologian *as* believer, with critical reflection on that witness, which distinguishes the theologian *as* theologian. Existing theologies of liberation "are not so much theology as witness," and "they tend rather to be the rationalization of positions already taken than the process or product of critical reflection on those positions."[7] They are guilty of "uncritically assuming that the claims of the Christian witness are true" and "that the liberation it promises is one and the same with that for which men and women today are asking."[8] As a result, they are, along with the vast majority of theologies in the past, "Christian ideologies, in the precise sense of rationalizing the prior claims of the Christian witness instead of critically inquiring as to their meaning and truth."[9] The only critical function of traditional theology "has been restricted to criticizing particular witnesses of faith by reference to whatever has been understood to constitute normative Christian witness, whether Scripture and tradition, or, rather Scripture alone."[10] It did not try to ask, and answer, "the radical question" about the truth of that normative witness itself.[11]

For Ogden, liberal theology, of course, took one step further and tried to criticize traditional Christian faith on the basis of human experience and reason as understood in the context of modernity. Nonetheless, it too remained more a rationalization of positions already taken than a critical reflection on the truth of those positions insofar as it originated in "a prior option and commitment to secular self-understanding" which it simply took for granted and in terms of which it tried to rationalize the Christian witness.[12] Theologies of liberation typically charge that all pre-liberationist theologies are ideological; they claim that the liberation of theology from ideology is possible only on the basis of a prior option and commitment to an effective solidarity with the oppressed, and that theology is truly liberated only as a reflection in and on the praxis of political emancipation. This claim of theologies of liberation, however, is "simply one more proposal for the bondage of theology."[13] Even though the term of bondage has shifted from the oppressor to the oppressed, the bondage to the latter still remains bondage. What is necessary is a reconceiving of the very task of theology from the rationalization of positions already taken to the critical reflection on such positions.[14] A "radically free" theology is free "from" all positions so that it may be free "for" all positions. Theological reflection is free to *result* in positions reflecting solidarity with the oppressed, as does Ogden's own reflection, but it is not in such solidarity that theology should *originate.*[15]

Is Ogden, then, advocating the possibility of a wholly presuppositionless theology, a theology without any prior option and commitment? He is aware that such a theology is not possible. He does distinguish, however, between a first-order commitment to a particular position as *given* in tradition or praxis, which he rejects as uncritical, and a second-order commitment to the critical search for truth as such and to human beings who seek the truth, which he accepts as the indispensable and only valid commitment for the theologian. The only prior option of theology is "simply the prior option and commitment of any and all critical reflection—namely, human existence as such in its profound exigency for the truth that alone can make us free."[16] In fact, "theology as such exists, above all, to respond to this deep human need for truth."[17] To put it differently, theology as a *process* of reflection

> is committed simply to understanding the meaning of the Christian witness and to assessing its truth, and, therefore, to any and all human beings insofar as, being human, they are somehow moved by the question of the ultimate meaning of their existence to which this witness presents itself as the answer.[18]

As a *product* or result of such a critical process, theology is committed not only to the truth of the Christian witness but also to

> giving reasons for the claim that this witness is true. As such, it is, once again, a commitment to any and all human beings insofar as, being human, they not only ask about the ultimate meaning of their existence but are also bound to seek only the truth in doing so.[19]

Ogden distinguishes between theology as critical reflection and theology undertaken as a Christian vocation. Insofar as a theologian assumes theological responsibilities as his or her vocation as a Christian, a theologian too must make the same prior first-order commitment that must be made by any other Christian. Even in this case, however, it is not the commitment of faith one shares with other Christians but the element of critical reflection on the truth of that faith that makes one a theologian. An involvement in the process of liberation is necessary if the work of a theologian is to remain a Christian vocation, but what makes it concrete and scientific is the critical testing of the truth of the claims implied in such involvment. Without the latter, theology remains a reflection *in* faith, but not a reflection *on* faith, which theology should be. The connection between theology as a Christian vocation and theology as critical reflection, for Ogden, is "contingent," and the error of TL is to confuse a contingent with a necessary connection. In short, praxis of faith is necessary for the Christian believer but contingent for the theologian *as* theologian.[20]

The service of theology to praxis, then, "can be only the *indirect* service of critically reflecting on the positions that such praxis implies," which is "the only service that a truly free theology is in a position to perform."[21] A direct service to the Christian witness and political praxis would turn theology into a rationalizing ideology.[22] Theology is itself a way of bearing witness to faith, but the way it does is neither the "explicit" one of proclaiming the Gospel nor the "implicit" one of liberating praxis[23] but that of subjecting to critical reflection all of one's beliefs, including the very belief that we are saved not by our own good works but solely by God's grace accepted in faith, and thereby acknowledging that our beliefs are at best our own intellectual good works. Only a theology that is itself genuinely free can bear witness to "a God whose gift and demand are radical freedom."[24]

McCann and Strain

A third criticism of TL comes from Dennis P. McCann and Charles R. Strain, who in a way combine the criticisms of the Vatican and Ogden. For McCann and Strain, as for Ogden, TL lacks a formal, theoretical reflection on the truth and validity of its own substantive claims, and, as for the Vatican, it is guilty of absolutistic dogmatism. But whereas Ogden proposes as a remedy critical reflection on the meaning and truth of the substantive Christian beliefs from a position committed only to human existence in its need for truth and the Vatican insists on obedience to the magisterium of the church, McCann and Strain's remedy lies in founding practical theology on a public discourse free from domination and constraint as well as from commitment to all substantive positions, the only justifiable commitment being the "readiness to reason together."[25]

The central problem of practical theology, for McCann and Strain is how to decide on the appropriate political programs (e.g., socialism vs. capitalism) and political strategies and actions to achieve such programs. The trouble with TL, that of Segundo and Gutierrez in particular, is that it dogmatically opts for socialist praxis as the only form of orthopraxis without providing a procedural mechanism whereby such an option could be arrived at without violating the values of pluralism and tolerance. TL brands all other forms of praxis as heteropraxis and makes absolutistic and exclusivistic claims for its own position. It does not allow theory, i.e., intersubjective rationality, to inform praxis, thus recognizing no genuine dialectic of theory and praxis. Religious praxis is held hostage to the political strategies of whatever group happens to have the power to define it. Ironically, according to McCann and Strain, the so-called primacy of praxis in TL perpetuates the primacy of theory in a new form, merely transferring sacral authority from doctrines to political strategies and tactics. The sacralism, which used to attach to orthodoxy with its pretense of exclusive moral validity and religious absolutism, now clings to orthopraxis and threatens totalitarianism as an ever-present possibility.[26]

How, then, does one avoid this theological totalitarianism? For McCann and Strain, practical theology is a "discourse about the religious foundations of the *res publica*,"[27] and the only way for practical theology to avoid totalitarianism is "by adhering to an ideal of public discourse that transcends all the particular communities within a pluralistic culture."[28] Drawing on the thought of Jürgen Habermas,[29] who had to grapple with the similar problem of orthodoxy and orthopraxis in Marxism, McCann and Strain propose to shift the discussion from substantive issues and positions to the formal conditions and criteria for the possibility of authentic discourse about such issues. Such authentic discourse is a discourse "among *all* qualified participants,"[30] free from all distorting external constraints—including that of the immediate pressures of action—and committed to no substantive prejudgments and class interests, the only commitment being "the formal commitment to providing publicly scrutable reasons"[31] in a free community of rational inquirers. The norms and criteria derived from the transcendental analysis of such discourse would then guide all critical reflection on praxis, on political programs, strategies, and actions. The foundation of practical theology must be sought in a theory of public discourse. Only in this way is it also possible to preserve the integrity of theory and a genuine dialectic of theory and praxis. For "praxis is not blind activism. It is action generated by communities self-consciously constituted through public discourse."[32] It should be noted here that for McCann and Strain, theory is not conceived as an intrinsic moment of praxis itself; it is external to and coequal with praxis, and only as such could it guide orthopraxis. The dialectic of theory and praxis involves the interaction of two elements, each constituted independently of the other.[33]

HISTORICITY OF THEOLOGY

Faith and Praxis

Referring to the basic challenge facing theology today, Gutierrez quotes from Johann Metz:

> Properly speaking, the so-called hermeneutic problem of theology is not the problem of how systematic theology stands in relation to historical theology, how dogma stands in relation to history, but what is the relation between theory and practice, between understanding the faith and social praxis.[34]

The challenge today, in other words, is not one of integrating the history of theology into contemporary systematics or one of understanding the development of dogma or even of founding theology on a critical basis in Ogden's or McCann's sense, but one of understanding faith in relation to social praxis and its demand. Systematics, historical theology, dogma, critical theology, and their mutual relationship: these are problems within theology, within the realm of theory. The essential challenge today, however, is not intratheoretical; it has to do with the very relationship between theory and praxis.

In response to this challenge Gutierrez defines theology as "a critical reflection both from *within*, and *upon*, historical praxis, in confrontation with the Word of the Lord as lived and accepted in faith," "a reflection *in*, and *on*, faith as liberation praxis," "an understanding of the faith from an option and a commitment," "from a point of departure in real, effective solidarity with the exploited classes," "from a commitment to create a just society," "a theological reflection that

becomes true, verified, in real and fruitful involvement in the liberation process."[35] How are we to understand this radically different definition of theology
and its uncomfortably close marriage with praxis?

TL begins with a full recognition, as does any theology, of the irreducibly
transcendent dimension of faith, the primary object of its reflection. In its origin
faith is a product of divine grace, not human work. In its *fides quae* it is directed
to transcendent realities as to its object, the Trinity, the Kingdom, creation and
redemption, grace, and so forth. As Clodovis Boff puts it:

> Faith, as a theological virtue, a "gift of God," signifies an absolute open-
> ness to an absolute meaning: the Meaning of meanings. Faith is not and
> cannot be adequately identified with any of its possible or real human
> expressions, be they in the theoretical order or in the practical. Exuberant
> dynamism that it is, faith is not exhausted in any of its manifestations.[36]

This transcendence defines the "essence" of faith. This essence, however, is never
found in its pure transcendence. In its concrete, historical "existence" as *human*
faith, Boff claims that

> faith is nothing without the particular realizations of its aim and intent. It
> exists in *concreto* only in altogether determinate structures. Apart from its
> historical concretizations, faith, for a human being, is but an abstraction,
> or, better, only the transcendental possiblity of particular realizations.[37]

It is not only the inevitable historicity of human existence in which faith
must be incarnated if it is to be *human* faith which necessarily renders the
manifestations of faith historically particular and determinate. It is also the very
source of faith, God's grace inviting us to accept God, and the very nature of
the object of faith, the Trinity, the Kingdom, creation and redemption of history,
which demands the concrete realization of our faith, which can only be historically particular. The very element of truth in faith, as Kierkegaard pointed out,
is something salvific and existential, with an intrinsic demand for appropriation and realization in historical praxis—not some existentially neutral, purely
objective piece of information or a set of propositions meant only for the
understanding, as the classical intellectualist tradition would have it.[38] The truth
of faith precisely in its objective reference to the transcendent reality of God
is meant to be a "basic life option" or orientation and a transformation of the
totality of our existence. It is "the intrinsic dynamism of faith that necessarily
impels it to assume concrete 'incarnations',"[39] and it is only in and through such
incarnations that faith is historically real.

The transcendence of faith this side of the *eschaton,* then, does not lie in
the transcendence of all history but "in the form of realizations ever to be renewed,
radicalized, and deepened"[40] in history. Inherent in faith is a dialectic of

transcendence and immanence, and the locus of such a dialectic is not somewhere between heaven and earth but history itself called to transcendent transformation. This dialectic of transcendence and history *in* history, of course, is itself theologically meaningful only because it is posited and legitimated by the dialectic of divine existence, the absolute sovereignty of God, and thus only "on the horizon of transcendence."[41] (I shall deal with this self-incarnating dialectic of divine existence in the following chapter.)

It is in this dialectical sense that the relation between faith and praxis is to be understood. Faith and praxis are not, as the Vatican would have it, two independent, mutually external realities that must be brought together following their constitution as independent realities, where the one is conceived of as the "consequence," "implication," or "expression" of the other. Their relation is mutually internal and "constitutive."[42] Faith by its own nature demands actualization in praxis, as (Christian) praxis by its own nature is constituted by the informing and transforming demand of faith. Praxis is not an application of faith, an application extrinsic to faith but the realization of faith's own intrinsic demand. For praxis is precisely "faith *qua operata—qua* lived, realized."[43] This demand for the unifying realization of faith by praxis also contains the moment of opposition between the two: the transcendence of faith challenges the self-complacency and reifying tendency of praxis and calls it to constant self-transcendence, just as praxis challenges the apolitical escapism of faith into pure privatism and interiorism and calls it to historical realization and relevance.

Abstractly, "essentially" or undialectically considered, faith corresponds to the theoretical dimension of subjective inwardness and divine transcendence, while praxis refers to objective concreteness and historical realization; however, "existentially" and dialectically, they are two moments of an intrinsic totality, which may be called faith from the teleological horizon of transcendence or praxis from the perspective of the historical realization inherent in faith itself. The special danger today, according to liberation theologians, is apolitical escapism in the name of faith. Hence their emphasis on faith as praxis, as deed. The point of TL is to preserve the existential integrity of faith that "works through charity" (Paul), not to glorify the deed divorced from faith or to advocate justification by works. In this sense, "true orthodoxy is orthopraxis,"[44] where the "is" must be taken dialectically. "In the final analysis what basically counts is the deed."[45] "After all, apart from works, faith is only words! Faith without practice is sermonizing."[46] Worse, "a 'pure' faith, faith devoid of all concrete mediation, is hypocrisy pure and simple."[47]

Theology and Praxis

As a critical reflection on the content of faith, theology also shares in the dialectical structure of faith. It has, first of all, a theoretical and a transcendent dimension. As theory, it has its own autonomy and consistency, a logic and purpose of its own not reducible to the immediate pressures and demands of praxis. The immediate end of theology is the discursive, systematic, and critical cognition of the transcendent content of faith. It is not itself faith, praxis, revelation, or salvation, just as its immediate function is not to preach. This critical distance between theology and its object must be preserved, precisely for the sake of the integrity of its object—i.e., to understand the object in its true identity and not to reduce it either to theology (theory) or to ideology, mindless activism, idolatry, and narcissism, the many practical perversions to which faith in its immediacy is always prone. The best theology is the most rigorously theoretical or scientific theology.[48] TL does not confuse the critical function of theology with the immediacy of witness any more than Ogden does.

The transcendent dimension of theology is constitued by its reference to the content of faith, the absolute sovereignty of God and the primacy of the Kingdom, which is not reducible to any particular historical reality. The theological dimension of theology lies in this "horizon of transcendence," in which the Kingdom remains "ever the *proton* in intention and the *eschaton* in hope."[49] In both the epistemological locus or horizon from which it speaks—i.e., revelation—and the meaning it seeks to disclose of temporal realities *sub specie Dei*, theology is transcendent.

This theoretical and transcendent dimension, however, is not all there is to theology. Like faith and everything else human, theology too shares in the historicity of human existence, and it is within the conditions of history that theology must perform its function as a critical instrument of faith. Theology as a *human* science is inevitably a dialectic of theory and praxis, of transcendence and history. Let me now look at this dialectic a little more closely, largely on the basis of the sophisticated analysis found in Clodovis Boff's *Theology and Praxis*, perhaps the best treatment of the subject in TL.[50] Boff discusses this dialectic under three headings, the *topos, kairos,* and *telos* of theology; these are the three mediating categories of the relation between theory (theology) and praxis.

First to be considered is the *topos* or locus of theology. Theology is done by concrete human beings and thus within history, not outside, not within history taken abstractly and generally but "within a determinate socio-historical situation."[51] When they do theology, they do so "in and from some determinate social locus, make use of the means society offers them, and formulate cognition and meaning endowed with a determinate social existence and finality."[52] Even before a theologian may consciously and subjectively take a political *position* and *option,* this is the objective sociological *situation* and *datum:* all theology, like all theory, is sociohistorically situated. By virtue of its insertion into the historical situation and the role it plays objectively in that situation, every theology, whether conservative or liberal, consciously historical or ahistorical, politically committed or indifferent, has its political and ideological consequences, and in this sense the most traditional theology is no less politically "committed," at least indirectly, than the most radical theologian of liberation. This is simply the limitation imposed by the concrete sociality and historicity of human existence on all theology and theory. The only question is whether and to what extent a particular theologian is subjectively conscious of it and what kind of a position or option he or she consciously takes—for whom? for what cause? for whose interest and power? and on what basis?[53]

This general relation between theology and its sociopolitical locus, however, has to be understood dialectically—i.e., as a unity in difference. Theology is the work of the human mind, whose basic capacity is that of critical self-transcendence. It has its own autonomous logic and dynamism not mechanistically determined by the needs and pressures of an order different from itself. The theologian as an epistemological subject and the theologian as a social subject, cognition and power, epistemology and sociology of knowledge—all belong to two different orders or levels, and "there is no direct, immediate, continuous relationship"[54] between the two. There is an "epistemological breach" posed by the human mind with its own dynamism and generative originality. In this sense, labels such as 'theology of the center,' 'theology of the periphery,' and 'Third World theology' point to the *topos* and even the ideological and political functions of such theologies, but they do not by themselves settle the analytic and evaluative questions concerning the truth of such theologies.[55]

There is, however, an essential, although mediate, relationship of unity between the two different orders. This is due to the concrete historical unity or totality of the two orders, cognition and action, knowledge and politics, the theological subject and object, and the political subject and object. After all, the subject of theological cognition is also the subject of political commitment. The mind of the thinking theologian is always an incarnate, situated mind, "not an absolutely free, creative mind or spirit like the divine mind."[56] It is from its own situation that the theological mind receives its impulses and pressures for theologizing, just as we can comprehend God "only within the purview of our historical possibilities."[57] The transcendence of all history is possible only as an eschatological hope, not as a present achievement. It is thus that each age leaves its mark on the theologian and one theology is differentiated from another, as one's political options leave their marks on one's choice of theological style, vocabulary, subject matter, and basic emphasis. The same is true of the *object* of theological reflection and political commitment. Our practical position furnishes us with materials for our theoretical reflection, as we tend to choose our theoretical object in view of our political commitments. The political object becomes the theological object.

This mediate relation between one's theological reflection and one's political option is of course not a mechanistic or causal, but a reflective relation in which the political option pressures the reflection in a certain direction and thus 'permits' the theologian to see the relevance and urgency of certain issues and themes and 'prohibits' him or her from entertaining the possibility of others. Thus, the political option is an antecedent epistemological condition for developing a certain kind of theology. As such, it is only a necessary, not a sufficient, condition; the work of reflection, once oriented in a certain direction, must still be performed according to its own logic.[58]

Second, Boff examines the *kairos*, or historical relevance, of theology. Theology (theory) and history are not coequal, mutually independent realities, as we are often led to believe under the linquistic spell of the word "and," any more than history can be reduced to concepts or be substituted for by ideas, as theoreticism, "that aristocratic form of idealism,"[59] would have it. Theory is itself rooted in our primordial experience of 'being,' 'life,' 'world,' or 'history' as the totality of our existence and praxis, and emerges from this totality only as a result of a self-conscious breach and abstraction, without, however, ever leaving that totality or being able to reduce the totality to its own conceptualities. As in classical critical realism, reality, being, and world are prior to cognition, logic, and awareness. Although there is no reality simply given apart from interpretation, such interpretation is itself a function of the prior challenge of reality as perceived in the pre-theoretical or pre-reflective sensibility of the *Lebenswelt*.[60]

It is as a response to the challenge of this lived, historical world that theology arises. It tries to respond to the *kairos*, the propitious moment, the 'signs of the times' of each historical epoch, and thus to acquire its relevance. Do theological questions address the historical moment and its real crises, difficulties, and contradictions, or do they deal with only trivial, peripheral, irrelevant issues? What are the problems demanding the theologian's attention today? What is the contemporary task of theology? What are the theologians to theologize about? The answer varies from age to age. What is relevant in one age becomes irrelevant in another. Theological interest changes as a function of the historical context of each theology, as witness the different concerns of the fathers of the church, the medieval scholastics, and contemporary theologians. Even within the same age, not everyone is interested in the same theology. What one group considers relevant is dismissed as irrelevant by another. Implicit in the debate on the relevance or irrelevance of a theology is a sociological interpretation of the needs and urgencies of a society. In this sense, even the most conservative theologies are relevant (at least indirectly) vis-à-vis the prevailing social order that they try to justify, although such relevance often remains tacit until and unless they are challenged, by the rise of competing social forces, to declare their political position. Strictly speaking, no theology is totally irrelevant. Relevance is always a function of a given situation, set of interests, or political causes. The real question to ask, then, is, Relevant to what social situation, for which political cause, to the interest of which class?[61]

How, then, does one go about answering these questions? For Boff, the answer would depend on the dialectic of two things, ethical or prophetic sensibility and social analysis. Prophetic sensibility refers to the pre-theoretical, global experience of a situation, born of the concrete praxis of life in a determinate social position. As the lived 'feel' of the situation in all its painful contradictions, it permits the perception of what is relevant in the situation. It is expressed in the language of indignation, criticism, denunciation, and demands for change. This prophetic sensibility, with its capacity for discerning real historical crises and problems, is possible only through the lived experience of such crises as confronted in praxis. For a genuine insertion into this 'flow of history,' however, one also needs the capacity for social analysis and criticism. The demand for social change must be based on an objective analysis of the realities of the situation to be changed—its contradictions, their causes, the real possibilities of transformation, the historical dynamics of the situation, and so forth. Without such analysis, sensibility remains blind and ends up in empty illusion and ineffective protest, just as analysis without sensibility can degenerate into pure technique and cynicism. What is necessary is a ceaseless dialectic of the two moments, theory and praxis, reason and experience.[62]

The third aspect is the *telos* or finality of theology, or the practical interests and causes in view of which theology is done. Here again, it is not to be denied that theology as theory has its own theoretical *telos*, knowledge. It has its own conceptual finality and mode of operation, an epistemological interest immanent in and constitutive of the theoretical inquiry. In this sense theology (theory) is an end in itself, disinterested or neutral with regard to non-theological, practical ends and objectives. On the other hand, at a different level, as sociology of knowledge has shown, every theory is also a social reality with its own social function—even if not subjectively intended by the scholar—within a determinate social totality. There is no body of knowledge that is not socially situated and politically oriented, in one manner or another. "All knowledge is, in fact, power, in virtue of its factual insertion into the fabric of social interests,"[63] a fact well confirmed in the massive attempts of governments and organized groups to control the production and distribution of knowledge and information. As a form of social power, then, no theory is politically and ideologically neutral and impartial. This does not mean that this practical social finality exhausts the theoretical, immanent finality of theory. Depending on the merit of a theory, its "truth," it may transcend the merit of its historically conditioned sociopolitical function. Still, theory does have such a practical function, which it cannot ignore in the name of pure neutrality. Thus, while we may still learn from the theology of Aquinas with its theoretical finality, we cannot remain indifferent to its objective ideological function in defense of feudalism.

The relationship of theory and praxis, however, is far more intimate and dialectical than mere coexistence at two different levels. Theory is itself a dimension and activity within the concrete historical totality of human existence and cannot be divorced from praxis and its end, the solution of the problems of that existence. Ultimately, it is praxis and its finality that "get theory going," that "fire the logical mechanism of the cognitive process."[64] It is the challenge and pressure of praxis that motivate and orientate the process of theoretical reflection.

It is within the pervasive finality of praxis that theory pursues its relatively autonomous course, asking new questions and arousing new interests. The dialectic of theory and praxis is itself a dialectic *within* praxis. Within the dialectic of historical praxis, "the *immediate* end of theory is cognition, but its *mediate* and terminal end is praxis itself."[65]

Given this ultimate primacy of praxis over theory, the question for theology is not *whether* it is interested or disinterested, but *where* its objective interest lies, for *what* cause it is being done, and, further, how to narrow "the gulf separating—on the social plane—subjective interests and objective interests, goals and outcomes, conscience and consequences,"[66] truth and justice. The answer, as discussed earlier, can only lie in a living synthesis of a religious, moral sensibility and critical social analysis of the historical realities of a situation.

The Historical Particularity of Theology

It is on the basis of this analysis of the dialectic of theory and praxis and of the historicity of that dialectic that we have to understand the insistence of TL on self-conscious acceptance of the historical particularity and provisional character of all theologies, including TL, and the necessity of pluralism in theology. TL is systematically conscious of its own historicity. As Gutierrez puts it, it "springs up out of the material foundations of society,"[67] and "addresses us from a precise location, speaks the Word of the Lord to us in the vernacular."[68] Likewise, to recognize this historicity is also to recognize that every theology is "transitional" in its task, as Hegel clearly saw that no philosophy transcends its own time.[69] If the intellectual challenge of the nonbeliever was the historical basis of modern liberal theology, the historical basis of TL is the practical challenge of the 'nonperson,' the oppressed of the Third World.[70] TL is "only the new consciousness, in communion with the church, that one Christian generation has of its faith in a given moment in history,"[71] as, for Hegel, philosophy is "its own time comprehended in thought."[72] It is precisely under the challenge of contemporary history that theology renders its critical service to faith, making the praxis of faith more self-critical, more prophetic, and thus more radical, profound, and efficacious.[73]

This does not negate the transcendence and universality of the Word of God intended by theology. Rather, the historical particularity of theology is an intrinsic demand of that very transcendence and universality. If faith in its transcendence and universality is to be concretely meaningful for *all* ages, not outside of all ages, and if each age has its own intellectual horizon and historical tasks, it is imperative that faith enter into a dialectic with each age, making itself intellectually credible and proving its transcendence by liberating and transforming human praxis according to its own demand, and thus concretely show its transcendence and universality. Faith must demonstrate its truth by being tested in praxis, "the proving ground of all theory."[74] This is all the more urgent today when, for TL, the challenge is not only epistemological—i.e., how to make faith intelligible to modern consciousness on the basis of an existentialist or transcendental "critique" of traditional theology—but also and primarily social and praxical—i.e., how to make faith in the goodness of God and the Kingdom credible by transforming the sinful, oppressive structures of power.[75] The content of faith is essentially a "concrete universal"; it is universal, not as an abstraction from all history, but as a concrete transforming power operative in every age. To incarnate faith in and for a particular age is not to deny its transcendence—faith is not exhausted by a particular historical expression of it—but rather to fulfill the demand for historical concretion inherent in its content.

The relation between theology and history, then, is neither contingent (Ogden) nor external (the Vatican) but necessary and internal. History enters into the very interpretation of the very content of faith and its praxis which would incarnate faith in that history. Theology does not merely "apply" universal truth, somehow apprehended apart from historical context, to a particular situation, but rethinks that universal truth itself in light of the particular situation and tries to make it concrete, as it also reflects on the particular situation in light of the universal. Every generation must rethink the dogmas of faith, incorporate them, and make them true in their historically conditioned praxis.[76] Theology, then, is an essentially historical dialectic, a dialectic of transcendence and history, universal and particular. In this sense, the church's "historical and social coordinates, its here and now, have a bearing not only on the adequacy of its pastoral methods. They also should be at the very heart of theological reflection."[77] That is, the particularities of a historical situation are relevant not only for the evaluation of pastoral practices, social doctrines, or 'practical theology,' which are often considered practical applications of timeless truth to particular circumstances, but also for the rethinking of this timeless truth itself—i.e., including Scripture, creeds, and systematic or dogmatic theology.

This imperative of faith as a concrete universal means not only that every theology is and must be historically particular but also that no human theology can exhaust the universal and transcendent content of faith and claim to be *the* theology for all times and places; every theology is necessarily provisional and must remain open to other theologies in other historical circumstances. Theology must give up its pretensions to absolute, ahistorical, universal truth, as well as its attempt to remain above the conflicts of concrete history in the name of timeless truth. Such a claim is at best "phony," "ideological," and guilty of "theological ethnocentrism,"[78] as has long been the case with European theology. Thus, TL recognizes the validity of other theologies under different historical situations, such as black theology, feminist theology, Minjung theology (Korea), and other Third World theologies. Unlike traditional theologies, TL also recognizes that it is itself only provisional, transitional, and open to replacement by other theologies when the basic historical situation changes. A theology may be both necessary in its own time and provisional in relation to other times and places. To sum up:

every theology develops de facto as a particular—and in some way political—theology. The theology that recognizes this condition, and presents itself as what it is de facto, at the same time acknowledges the transcendence that belongs to the faith by right and permits it a potentially infinite manifestation of concrete possibilities, as well in the theoretical as in the practical order. By contrast, a theology that ignores its historicity and political nature, and presents itself as *theology itself*—the rigid, dogmatistic expression of the meaning and imperatives of faith—this theology, which claims that it coincides with the voice of revelation itself, can only be an ideology. It adopts an erroneous position, be it in the area of theory (illusion) or politics (lie).[79]

THEOLOGY AND SOLIDARITY

The Disclosive Function of Solidarity

How, then, does TL pursue its contemporary theological task? How does it relate to Scripture and the theological tradition on the one hand and to the challenge of contemporary Latin American history on the other? How does it relate these two relations into a theological synthesis? How does it settle the question of the social locus, historical relevance, and political objective of theology without reducing theology to ideology? In short, what is the method of TL?

The method of TL lies basically in the dialectical circle—guided by prophetic sensibility—of the hermeneutic mediation, the interpretation of Scripture and the theological tradition, and the socio-analytic mediation, the critical analysis of the dialectic of contemporary history, its contradictions and possibilities of transformation. Let me begin with the prophetic sensibility.

The basic challenge to the contemporary task of theology is how to find concrete access to the central crises and contradictions of our time so as to be able to reflect on faith—the hermeneutic mediation—and to produce relevant incarnations of that faith—the socio-analytic mediation—from the perspective or the horizon *internal* to that crisis. A purely external and abstract approach does not provide a real access to the concrete, lived situation of praxis with its crises, challenges, and ambiguities. A theology that reflects on a situation from outside without a real inner experience of that situation will impose abstractions on the concrete, abstractions which have not grown out of the concrete, which miss the real lived crisis of the concrete, and are ultimately ignored or resisted by the concrete as irrelevant or, worse, ideological. In the final analysis such a theology would be as guilty of extrinsicism as was the traditional dualistic theology now rejected by humanists and contemporary theology alike. The whole anthropological turn in modern theology has in fact been an attempt to reflect on faith precisely from the viewpoint of modern consciousness. However, today's primary challenge, as least as seen by TL, does not come so much from modern consciousness as from modern reality.

It is as a way of acquiring the inner standpoint or perspective of contemporary crises as a condition for theological reflection that TL insists on participation in the praxis of concrete solidarity with the oppressed in their struggles for liberation.[80] This participation or lived experience concretely discloses truths about the human situation under contemporary historical conditions, and poses questions to the traditional interpretations of faith and the prevailing justifications of the existing social structure—an epistemological function with theological and political cutting edges not accessible to purely theoretical theology, which merely observes the crises from outside. It "affords a perception of aspects of the Christian message that escapes other approaches."[81]

> Involvement in the liberation process introduces Christians to an altogether unfamiliar world. They must make a quantum leap. They must now subject the social order and its familar ideology to a new, radical questioning. In a word, they must break with the old ways of knowing.[82]

Such an experience makes one aware concretely, not abstractly, of the plight of the oppressed, the irrationality and inhumanity of the system of which they are victims, and the urgency of structural change. Confronted with the poor, "my world changes,"[83] and I acquire a new perspective, a perspective from the "underside of history." The problem with the theologies of development and revolution in the 1960s was that they merely tried to 'apply' theology to a situation from outside. They were "not theology done from within and upon faith as liberating praxis. But when theology is finally done in this locus, perspectives will change."[84] In this sense, then, just as, for Kierkegaard, the "subjective" thinker was "a thinker with a relation to existence,"[85] so the theologian becomes "a thinker with a relation to *social* existence," that is, "an organic intellectual" (Gramsci), "a thinker with organic links" with the popular struggle and the community of faith sharing in that struggle. Theology becomes a reflection with a concrete sociohistorical base.[86]

Three Models of Solidarity

How directly should the theologian participate in the struggles of the poor? What degree of solidarity with the oppressed is required of the theologian of liberation for the authenticity of his or her theology? The question, perhaps the most discomfiting aspect of TL to the academic theologians of the First World, does not admit of a single definite answer. The basic thrust of TL in this regard has clearly been some sort of 'real' participation—that is, a participation concrete and painful enough to effect a conversion of perspective. How this would apply to individual theologians in the concrete particularities of their situation has not always been clear. Here again I would like to rely on Clodovis Boff, the only theologian that I know of who has done systematic reflection on the subject. On the basis of the actual praxis of liberation theologians, Boff mentions three possible models: the specific contribution model, the alternating moments model, and the incarnation model.

In the *specific contribution* model, the theologian makes a contribution to the struggles of the poor not in a directly political way but in a way specific and proper to the theologian *as* theologian—that is, within the realm of theory. It is a theoretical synthesis of theology and politics, in which the theologian takes a political position and fights political battles—e. g., criticizing and unmasking the ideologies of dominant theologies—within theology itself, according to its own rules and from its own locus. The political identification of the theologian with the poor will be reflected in the choice of theological themes and styles. For some this would entail genuine intellectual conversion in terms of issues, themes, and language. The assumption here is that in the dialectic of the social totality the theoretical activity of the theologian would also have its effect on politics just as politics affects theory. In this model the theologian as an epistemological subject coincides with the theologian as a social subject. On behalf of a group or political movement, the theologian performs

> the specific task of reflecting upon its activity precisely in its theological meaning. Thus, in and by the intellectual or scholarly *profession* itself, the theologian performs social work and exercises a political option.[87]

Given the ultimate conditioning of theory by praxis, however, this model cannot be realized in a pure form. The theologian cannot remain solely within the realm of theory and still acquire the prophetic sensibility to the issues of political praxis. The theoretician must enter into relations with the extra-theoretical realm, through, for example, meetings, collaborative projects, or other contacts with a given political movement. "A more or less direct participation in concrete practices is necessary for the well-being of the theory itself."[88] This model would have to incorporate some of the elements of the following models.

According to the *alternating moments* model, the theologian alternates between being a scholar—e. g., a seminary professor for six months—and being a political militant—e. g., working directly with the poor for the other six. As a political subject, the theologian synthesizes theology and politics by taking a political position in the political arena itself, not within the realm of theory. It is the unity of an all-embracing project or basic option, undertaken by one and the same person, that provides unity to the theologian's alternating activities.

In the *incarnation* model, the most complex and most demanding of the three, the synthesis of theology and politics takes the form of social insertion in an organic, even physical way, sharing in the life conditions of the poor. This existential identification—solidarity at its strongest—involves dislocation of the theologian in terms of class and even space. The synthesis will result in a theory rooted in praxis in the most intimates sense, incarnating itself as the self-consciousness of praxis. This model is generally meant when TL speaks of the social commitment of the theologian as a condition of theology. The main problem here, of course, is whether the theologian, in working and living with the poorest and *as* the poorest, would have even the minimum material conditions necessary for doing theology at all, let alone doing good theology. It is quite possible that the theologian may give up theology as irrelevant and give himself or herself totally to a given pastoral or political activity in view of the urgency of a particular situation.[89]

These models, however, are not meant as prescriptions. The specific model appropriate for a theologian depends on the particularities of subjective and objective situations, for each model is "a *living* synthesis of a person and a locus," which "must remain open to modification, in accordance with the continuous, enigmatic circularity prevailing between its terms."[90] Furthermore, the actual choices made by liberation theologians have been made not as a matter of purely theoretical reflection but as a result of "the dynamics of events, operative within a given conjuncture, that has placed them in that situation, and led them, as a result of personal existential views and options, to take such and such a concrete political position."[91] The important thing is to remain sensitive and committed enough to the dialectic of situation and option, objective and subjective conditions, so as to acquire and maintain a prophetic sensibility with which to reflect on faith "from within concrete praxis itself."[92]

Dialectic of Magisterium, Avant-garde, People

Although TL characteristically stresses identification with the poor as the hermeneutic locus of theology and defines theology as reflection on the praxis of the poor, it is important, for a balanced picture of TL, to note that the praxis of the poor is not the only source of theological reflection, and that liberation theologians are fully aware of the danger of absolutizing and idealizing the poor as such. In this sense Juan Carlos Scannone speaks of theology as a critical reflection on a three-dimensional dialectic—wherein the poor maintain indeed a privileged but not the only position—among the pastoral praxis of the church as an institutional body, especially the episcopate; the political praxis of the activist Christian elite; and the praxis of the poor, the believing masses, or people in their totality.[93]

The pastoral praxis of the institutional church refers to the prophetic role of proclamation and denunciation as witnessed, e.g., in Medellin. This praxis is expressed theoretically in countless official documents issued by episcopal conferences and individual bishops. The theology inspired by this praxis emphasizes 'integral' liberation and its 'evangelical' content, and considers the political implications of pastoral activity but almost always from the viewpoint of the heirarchy. In the reciprocal interaction of the three dimensions of liberating praxis, the theological, anthropological, and political (more on this in the next chapter), it stresses the non-reductive identity of each dimension more than the interaction as such. This position tends to forget that the function of the bishops is not the only function in the church, and thus neglects to develop theologically the salvific substance of liberating praxis, which as such is proper to the laity who must heed the signs of the times in the midst of daily political struggle and experimentation with new social forms.

In contrast, members of the Christian avant-garde, politically the most conscious and active, opt for the praxis of radical social change and live their faith in terms of this praxis. Their tendency is to overemphasize the interaction among the three dimensions of praxis over and against their irreducible specificity. Some of them make use of Marxian categories for social analysis and social change, although they do so—not always successfully—critically and from the Christian perspective. The danger of this position has been its tendency to separate itself from the praxis of the mainstream of the people and to project an abstract utopia and an abstract negation of the social totality, abstract because not mediated by the concrete history of the people and their church and not based on real possibilities and concretely realizable strategies of liberation. A theology solely based on the political praxis of this group tends to lose in complexity of perspective. It fails to grasp the total scope of liberating praxis as *integral* praxis by identifying liberation as political in the narrow sense, which is indeed an important dimension but not the only one. It is, of course, the merit of this theology to remind us that there is a political dimension—the ordering of society to the common good—to all other aspects of our social existence, such as the religious, educational, socioeconomic, and cultural.

The third approach is based on the praxis of the believing people—where the poor are the majority—as an organic, historical community. These people possess a deep sense of their own dignity and justice. Faith plays a decisive role in their historical experience and their historical projects for justice and freedom. The folk wisdom resulting from their historical struggles, informed by faith, can be critically reflected on by theologians in light of the Word of God. This approach, however, has its own dangers, which the other two approaches may help to avoid. It may confuse the different dimensions of praxis—the theological, anthropological, and political—with one another by stressing the incarnation of the people of God in a particular people as understood in the civic and cultural sense. Fixed on the local situation, it may also lose sight of the universal. It may likewise run the danger of hypostatizing 'the people' romantically or populistically by idealizing them as though they were free from sin and alienation, placing them outside history and its ambiguities. Here the first approach can serve as a corrective by reestablishing a contact between the local and the universal church as well as between the present praxis of the people and the eschatological hope. The second approach, on the other hand, can help the theologian recognize the alienations of the people by means of the critical theory and praxis of the elite and in light of the liberating, properly mediated utopia.[94]

These three approaches are not mutually exclusive. Not only do they enrich one another; they also can lead to mutual critique through reciprocal mediation. Among them there can be a three-dimensional dialectic corresponding to the organic unity of the people of God, in which the poor have their privileged place. Today, the emphasis must be placed on the third approach, which is at the heart of TL, without denying the magisterial function of the authorities in the church or the critical function of the politicized elite, provided neither of them are separated from the people. After all, liberation must serve the people, the main subject and object of liberating praxis. Furthermore, the practical wisdom of the people, which grows out of their history and their praxis of liberation, must be reflectively and critically tapped for its theological substance and theoretically formulated in theology. In fact, that remains the primary hermeneutic locus today.

THE HERMENEUTIC CIRCLE

The Socio-Analytic Mediation

As stated earlier, the method of TL consists in the dialectic of the hermeneutic mediation and the socio-analytic mediation, under the historical horizon of the crisis of the times as embodied in the poor and oppressed majority and perceived by a prophetic sensibility. Let me now turn to the socio-analytic mediation. As a theology of the concrete praxis of liberation, TL, more than any other theology, finds itself under the necessity of defining the relationship between theology and social praxis—i.e., of answering the question of *how* theology is to guide praxis. There are, according to Clodovis Boff, five ways in which one is *not* to relate theology and praxis; these must first be discussed and dismissed before going on to suggest a correct relationship. They are: empiricism, purism, theologism, semantic mix, and bilingualism.

The *empiricist* approach takes historical reality as it is given in the intuitive immediacy of consciousness and proceeds to interpret it theologically without attempting a prior analysis of it. It is not aware that all human knowledge is mediated, consciously or unconsciously, by numerous assumptions and ideologies. As a result of this epistemological naivete, it mistakes appearances for reality and ultimately reduces theology to ideology. It is strong on denunciation, sincerity, and struggle, but weak on critique, logic, and rigor, which are essential to any truly "concrete" theology.[95] Methodological *purism* is the epistemological equivalent of the dogma of *sola fides*. It insists on the self-sufficiency of theology and feels no need to appropriate the results of other disciplines. It is not aware that the content of faith and revelation is itself mediated by human concepts and categories, our historical and cultural experiences.[96] *Theologism* considers theological interpretation as the only true version of reality and substitutes itself for social analysis—assuming its own interpretation is total and adequate, it sees other interpretations as partial and inadequate. As the theoretical correlative of the practical attitudes commonly known as 'supernaturalism' and 'spiritualism,' it is critical of materialism and is content with stating timeless truth as the theological response to all situations. This approach is implicit in the ideologies of 'Christendom,' 'apoliticism,' and 'faith without ideology.' It is clear that its dualistic indifference to history conceals an ideology of its own.[97]

While these approaches exclude the socio-analytic mediation in one way or another, *semantic mix* accepts it but fails to criticize and properly assimilate the social theories it works with. Characteristic of many of the pronouncements of the Catholic magisterium on social issues, it does not define the relationship between theology and social science with any methodological rigor. The two languages are neither intrinsic nor extrinsic to each other but simply 'mixed,' not properly integrated and mediated. Yet the resulting mixture is always organized under the logic of religious language. Dualistic in its assumptions, it regards timeless truth as the only essential, important truth and denigrates historical reality and empirical existence as merely contingent and secondary, emptying the latter of their proper content so as to fill them with a spiritual one. When it makes judgements on historical reality, its analysis remains empiricist, its explanation moralistic.[98]

Bilingualism juxtaposes socio-analytic discourse and theological discourse and seeks to play two language games on the same field at the same time. This juxtaposition of two interpretations and approaches at first seems proper and fair; however, the possible tension and contradiction between the two interpretations will often lead to confrontation. One discourse may be eliminated by another, or, as in the case of semantic mix, a compromise may result. Sustained bilingualism is another form of compromise, in which "the contradiction is not dialectically resolved, yet the terms abide in mutual confrontation."[99]

What, then, is the proper relationship between the two discourses, between theology and social science? It is, according to Clodovis Boff, a constitutive relation between a "material" and a "formal" object. TL seeks to interpret and transform concrete historical praxis, and as such, it has to do not so much with the abstract nature of power or society, the concern of traditional theology of history, as with "that altogether determinate power or society in or under which Christians and human beings generally live, struggle, and die."[100] The theologian as such, however, does not know this concrete history and its specific challenges to praxis. It is the province of the social sciences to investigate and critically analyze social reality in its concrete dynamics of actuality and possibility, and thus to "prepare the text for theology to read, the raw material for it to transform."[101] Without this mediation, theology would remain ignorant of what it is supposed to reflect on, guilty of *ignoratio elenchi*, and prone to a religious–political rhetoric which may sound pious but which is ultimately empty and irrelevant. This socio-analytic mediation is an integral part of the theological process.

The social sciences provide the raw material or "material object" for theology to assimilate according to its own theological perspective or form and thus to transform into its "proper object." This relationship is not an extrinsic relation of "application" between two separate things but one of "constitution," which consists of "an organic interchange in which each of the terms of the relationship shares in a vital way in the whole of which it is a part,"[102] not one of "affixation or superimposition" but one of "vital assimilation, a kind of metabolism."[103] The articulation of this relationship should occur under the regime of theology; otherwise, it would not be theology. The gathering of social-scientific information does not, as such, constitute theology. Such information remains pre-theological until it has been reworked "by procedures proper to theologizing, in such wise as to issue in a *specifically* theological product."[104] The sociological and the theological do not exist in the same continuum. The transition from the one to the other constitutes a qualitative, "epistemological breach or rupture."[105] At the same time the theological assimilation of the social sciences must proceed with both respect for their autonomy and their own rules and methodologies and a critical attitude towards the implications of those claims and conclusions which often go beyond their particular sciences, especially their tendency towards reductionism.[106]

Which social theory, among the numerous existing theories, should a theology of liberating praxis choose? More importantly, by what criteria should such a choice be made? These questions have already been broached in the discussion of the preference of TL for Marxian analysis in the preceding chapter ("Why Marxism?"). Given that the value of a theory lies in its capacity to shed light on concrete problems proposed for its explication, the logically prior question is: What are the concrete problems demanding explication and resolution? The choice of a theoretical explication and of practical means—such as programs, strategies, and actions—is dependent on a prior determination of the concrete problems to be solved.

Here the criterion is clearly ethical. Is the primary problem one of maintaining the order and harmony of a social system or one of resolving basic social conflicts and raising the poor and oppressed majority to a level of social existence in which they too can enjoy liberty, equality, and justice? On the level of the content of Christian faith, there is also the evangelical criterion—i.e. Jesus' own identification with the plight of the poor and oppressed. From this ethical and evangelical perspective, then, the only problem to be resolved is not how to maintain the harmonious functioning of a social system as given, along with its inequitable distribution of privileges and powers, but how to improve the lot of the poor and resolve the basic social divisions and conflicts. It is this ethical and evangelical option which has led TL to prefer a dialectical theory of society to a functionalist one, the former stressing the idea of conflict, tension, and struggle in a vision of society considered as a complex, contradictory whole, the latter stressing order, harmony, or equilibrium and considering society as an organic whole with complementary parts. This does not imply that the ethical option of a social theory necessarily validates every particular conclusion of the theory; the validation of a conclusion depends on the validity of the analysis, a task which cannot be substituted for by the ethical option and which must proceed according to the intrinsic criteria of the social science itself.[107]

By the very nature of the case, TL does not and cannot provide a precise technique or a manual of technical rules for conducting this socio-analytic mediation of theology. Instead, it suggests two things for its actual implementation. The first is the development of socio-analytic *habitus* as an intellectual virtue, which implies not only critical social consciousness but also possession of a significant amount of social-scientific knowledge in its own right. The theologian must know enough about the dynamics of society to overcome sociological naivete, unmask current ideologies, and evaluate the validity and implications of new theories. Preferably, the theologian must be able to produce, not merely consume, social-scientific knowledge. The second is the practice of inter-disciplinary collaboration. Theology is neither a total science nor a complete guide to action. If it is to avoid abstract generalizations, often merely verbal, ineffective, and demobilizing, it is imperative that the theoretical elaboration of political programs and strategies be done by a team of those who, Christian or not, share a common front in the struggle for liberation.[108]

Scripture and Historicity

Let me now turn to the hermeneutic mediation or theological assimilation of the socio-analytic mediation. How does TL interpret Scripture and the Christian tradition and relate that interpretation to the demands of contemporary history, thus giving theological form to the matter of the social sciences? What does the phrase "in light of the Word of God" mean when TL typically defines itself as "a critical reflection on Christian praxis in the light of the Word?"[109] It is interesting to note that in this regard TL has been accused by its critics of everything from arbitrary interpretation to arbitrary selection of themes to a fundamentalist reading innocent of the historical–critical method.[110] Let me begin, therefore, with the approach of TL to biblical interpretation.

Christian faith is objectively bound up with Scripture as its *norma normans*. This is the positivity of Christian faith, its objective givenness, which defines the limits within which an interpretation must remain if it is to be considered Christian. At the same time, it is clear that Scripture is the embodiment of the Word of God in *human* words, and as such it is not a brute fact without mediation. It is also a product, the literary objectification, of centuries of the lived experience of God under very determinate cultural, political, and economic conditions. This imposes on us the enormous task of hermeneutics, of bridging the distance of twenty centuries and more, of 'decoding' and reappropriating the original sense of the written Scripture. In this regard TL has been suggesting the method of a "hermeneutic circle" or dialectical interaction as guide to biblical interpretation.

According to Clodovis Boff, the following circles occur: between the Word of God and Scripture; between creation of meaning and acceptance of meaning; between structure and meaning; between present and past; and between technique and interpretation.

Regarding the first circle, it is important to note that the Word of God is not simply identical with Scripture, the historically conditioned embodiment of the Word of God; they are on two different levels. The divine meaning of Scripture does not interpret itself to us, and this is why the Christian tradition invests the norm of faith, the *regula fidei*, not simply in Scripture but in Scripture as read in the church. The sense of Scripture can be apprehended only in relation to the *sensus fidelium*, the living spirit of the living community. Scripture is not only *norma normans* but also in some sense *norma normata*, i.e., authenticated as the Word of God by the community of the faithful, as witness the history of tradition criticism and the process of canonization. Strictly speaking, then, the Word of God is found neither in the letter of Scripture nor in the spirit of the hearing community. It is "precisely *between* these two, in their mutual, dynamic relationship, in a back-and-forth that is never perfectly objectifiable."[111]

The second hermeneutic circle is that of the creation and the perception of meaning. The meaning of Scripture cannot be created arbitrarily, as is the case with hermeneutic improvisation, or perceived purely passively, as semantic positivism would have it. Both of these tendencies are guilty of reifying and freezing one pole or the other of the interpretive relationship. The true meaning can be deciphered only in the sustained, dialectical relationship between creation and perception, between reader and text, between questions and answers. The same dialectic obtains between structure and meaning, the third hermeneutic circle. As in the case of any written text, the autonomous structure of the letter of the text must first be explained and grasped before one can comprehend or understand its sense and meaning. "Meaning needs structure for support. Structure serves meaning as its vehicle of communication, thus imposing upon it the confinement of its own determinations."[112]

The fourth circle is that between present and past. The meaning of a text is not exhausted by the 'original' meaning at the time of its composition. The text exists to be read and reread as a channel of a meaning through a succession of historical moments. The meaning of a text is in a real sense the history of its interpretations (its "tradition"). It is in relation to the present, the reader's contemporary history, that the meaning of a text comes alive, rejuvenates its vitality, and fulfills its *telos*.

> Although in a first moment, a basic one, to be sure, sense or meaning is obtained under sign, word under writing, spirit under letter—now, in another moment, sense is obtained in the present, word in time, spirit in history.[113]

Exegesis is a complex process bearing on the reader's present moment, in which "word ceases to be simply text to be interpreted, and itself becomes interpretive code. *Now word is no longer world to be seen but eyes to see, no longer landscape but gaze, no longer thing but light.*"[114]

The fifth and last hermeneutic circle is that of hermeneutic technique and interpretation. The essentially dialectical nature of the preceding circles makes it plain that it is impossible to construct a technique of interpretation whose application to a text would uncover and exhaust once and for all its ultimate meaning and foreclose all further questions in advance, which is the dream and illusion of hermeneutic positivism. The meaning of a text cannot be fixed once and for all. By the same token, however, the meaning cannot be purely arbitrary, and it is the function of a hermeneutic technique to "fix the spatial limits of the appearance of meaning or sense,"[115] beyond which an interpretation would become purely arbitrary and unfounded. Within such limits the discernment of the right meaning also requires an act of creation or *Sinngebung*, "a decision and determination of meaning in the space that 'hermeneutic reason' has opened and circumscribed."[116] For example, in the relationship between Scripture and the reading community, Boff notes that

> Scripture evokes an appeal, an invitation, a provocation, and interrogation. Its text is persuasive. It persuades acceptance, openness, availability. But there remains the task of the one invited—personal response, for meaning is realized only in and by response. Further: it is only in concrete life that meaning unfolds, and "comes to itself." And here hermeneutics flowers into ethics.[117]

The essential reference to the historical present of the reader as a constitutive moment of biblical interpretation requires further observations, especially in view of the unique (*ephapax*) character of the salvific events described in Scripture and the traditional notion of the 'closure' of revelation. In order to understand this reference of Scripture to the historical situation of the reader, consider three things. The first is the general anthropological condition, namely, the historicity of human existence which governs all human praxis including the activity of interpretation. The interpreter always and necessarily brings along the presuppositions and expectations of his or her historical present to the work of interpretation, just as the written text remains essentially open to future readings. It is an illusion to think that one has direct, unmediated access to the 'original' sense of Scripture. "The present is not only that which is read, it is also that *by which* the reading is done."[118]

In addition, as contemporary biblical research has shown, the formation of the books of Scripture was a function of the historical present of the various communities, their contemporary cultural presuppositions, their historical crises and needs, their *Sitz im Leben*. The Scripture is itself "the result of an 'updating,'

a going-beyond the 'letter' in favor of a free amplification of the 'spirit'."[119]
There are also specifically theological or dogmatic reasons. One of the central
messages of the New Testament is that of the risen Christ present in the
community of his disciples in the generations to come as the inspiring and
directing Spirit of that community. The meaning of Scripture, by its own message,
is not confined to the generation of the first disciples. In this sense, the texts
of Scripture

> cry out in every word for their own effacement, erasure, *Aufhebung*,
> sending us back to the Risen One, whose currency renders the sense of
> these scriptures current as well. They send us to the voice of the Spirit
> present in the community.[120]

In this sense, then, revelation is never closed. The Word of God continues
to speak to each new generation. At most, it is canonized, and canonized
precisely as a model, exemplar, or code for interpreting the Word of God,
which indeed rules out certain meanings but by the same token does not freeze
any one meaning as the definitive and ultimate one. Scripture is a model
interpretation, *"an interpreting interpretation, a norma mormans ut normata."*[121]
As a hermeneutic paradigm Scripture grows richer through the very interpretations it permits and engenders, which, in turn, in some sense, further
determine its "letter." Tradition is precisely the totality of these interpretations
and meanings historically generated by the hermeneutic paradigm. To be
taken up and given historical contemporaneity and relevance in each new generation, then, is "a principle woven into the very writing of Scripture itself."[122]
The hermeneutic circle of past and present is not a "vicious" but a "virtuous"
circle.

In this view, the living historical present has a certain primacy over the
past, which also necessitates a certain hermeneutic "vigilance" against the
ideological and manipulative uses—in view of present needs—to which Scripture is always prone. For this reason, a rigorous scientific exegesis which respects
the "actual density" of the texts will always remain indispensable. Nevertheless, the Word of God continues to speak to each new generation, demanding
fresh interpretation and realization of its message in the ever new historical
present. Scientific exegesis, oriented to the past, therefore, is not enough.
There is no 'essence' of Scripture which is given once and for all and which
can thus be definitively uncovered by scientific exegesis. If there were, there
would be no need for ongoing theological reflection. The text of Scripture,
then, is more a spring of meaning than a cistern, more a focus of energy
than a traffic light. It is pregnant with all the "virtual senses that will come
to light upon contact with historical currency" and which must be taken
as an "integral part of the text itself, a demonstration of its kairological
virtuality."[123]

The Hermeneutic Mediation

How does this dialectical hermeneutic bear on contemporary praxis? How does theology reflect on such praxis "in light of the Word of God"? How does one draw a dialectical correlation between Scripture and contemporary history? Here Clodovis Boff rules out two models, the Gospel/politics model and the correspondence of terms model, and opts for the correspondence of relationships model as the most appropriate.[124]

The *Gospel/politics model* posits an immediate correspondence between Scripture and our political situation. It seeks to apply Scripture without hermeneutic mediation to contemporary political situations without socio-analytic mediation. It thus ignores the internal complexity of both Scripture and politics. In its uncritical naivete, this model is open to the ideological manipulation of the Gospel as well as to the mystification of political reality. In hermeneutics it wavers between improvisation and positivism. Historically, this model has led to the justification of theocracy and the medieval ideal of Christendom, using Scripture as a kind of map for social organization, or, as in modern theories since Machiavelli, to the dismissal of the Gospel as politically impracticable. The basic flaw of this 'application' model is its historical innocence, its insensitivity to the historical context of each of the terms of the relationship.

The *correspondence of terms model*—also called *parallelism*—is more sophisticated and richer than the application model in that it includes the historical context missing in the latter. It seeks to establish correspondence between Scripture and contemporary theology and draw political inferences based on that correspondence. Theology today must be in *our* political context what Scripture was in *its* political context. On this basis the model goes on to draw correspondences or parallels between the Exodus and contemporary liberation, the enslavement of the Hebrews and the oppression of the peoples of the Third World, the Roman power and contemporary imperialism, the power of the Sadducees and that of dependent bourgeoisies, the Zealots and the revolutionaries of today, and of Jesus and Christians. The Christian community must do today what Jesus did in his poltical context. Thus, if Jesus could be shown to have been a Zealot, as Brandon argued, this would justify our participation in revolutionary movements, If Jesus could be shown to have been a pacifist, as Cullman and Hengel argued, this would rule out such revolutionary politics. If Jesus could be shown to have had no interest in politics whatsoever, as the eschatological interpretation would have it, it would necessitate the withdrawal of all Christians from the arena of politics.

For all its popularity, however, this model lends itself to a number of criticisms. Regarding the figure of Jesus, it fails to pay sufficient attention to the uniqueness of his human destiny, the religious, political, and cultural conditions which influenced him, and the degree of politicization of his human consciousness. It also too readily assumes similarity between his political context and our own and tends to take the figure of Jesus in a mythical, ahistorical way.

Regarding the parallelism between his political stance and ours, it assumes that Jesus is a model for us today in the sense of an example to be copied in every detail, and seeks to deduce a model of political conduct valid for today exclusively from an analysis of Jesus' own conduct. In assuming a term-for-term correspondence between Scripture and our situation, it does not take seriously enough the extreme complexity of contemporary society or the degree of political consciousness, at the level of both analysis and ideology, which has developed during the twenty centuries separating us from the events of the Gospel.[125]

The alternative model advocated by Boff is that of *correspondence of relationships*, bound to one another by 'creative fidelity' (Marcel). This model takes its inspiration from the manner in which the primitive church dealt with the words and deeds of Jesus. As various forms of biblical criticism have demonstrated, the primitive church did not look for or merely repeat the *ipsissima verba* of Jesus but tried to interpret them in view of the concrete situations and the needs of the various communities, the *Sitz im Leben* of the New Testament in its final form. In doing so they were guided by creative fidelity to the Jesus tradition and attributed to Jesus even the later developments and interpretations of his original message and work, fully convinced of the identity of the Christ of glory with the historical Jesus. This sort of development has been repeated by the post-biblical communities in their changing historical contexts, and continues to occur in the everyday hermeneutic practice of contemporary communities, as witness the content of homilies, catecheses, liturgy, and other symbolic or discursive practices. Scripture continues to be lived and commented on by successive generations of Christians, in a dialectic in which the text and the situation are not reduced to each other, each instead being taken in its respective autonomy.

According to this model, the relationship between the message of Jesus and his context corresponds to the relationship between the message of the New Testament church and its context, which in turn corresponds to the relationship of the post-biblical tradition and its varying historical contexts, to which the relationship between our message and our context should correspond. The correspondence or identity posited in this model is not one of context or one of message; it does not imply that the context of Jesus is the same as our context or that the message for the New Testament church is the same as the message for us. The correspondence refers to the relationship between context and message, which remains the same in different historical periods. This identity is not a mechanical identity but one of creative fidelity to the Gospel in a diversity of historical situations.

What accounts for and guarantees this creative fidelity to the Gospel? It is not fidelity to this or that particular text of Scripture corresponding to a particular situation with a resulting obligation to act in a particular way. It is fidelity to the "global, and at the same time particular 'spirit'" of the Gospel.[126] What is to be looked for in Scripture is not formulas to copy or techniques of application.

What Scripture will offer us are rather something like orientations, models, types, directives, principles, inspirations—elements permitting us to acquire, on our own initiative, a "hermeneutic competency," and thus the capacity to judge—on our own initiative, in our own right—"according to the mind of Christ," or "according to the Spirit," the new, unpredictable situations with which we are continually confronted. The Christian writings offer us not a *what*, but a *how*—a manner, a style, a spirit.[127]

This kind of "pneumatic" hermeneutic—similar to Rahner's "instinct of faith"—presupposes our "compenetration with the meaning that informs Scripture, and a sustained familiarity with the Word indwelling in it."[128] That this sort of hermeneutic practice is not immune to abuse and manipulation is quite clear, but by the same token it should be accepted as an invitation and a challenge. It goes without saying that this pneumatic approach does not dispense with the normal application of exegetical methods and social-scientific analysis.

On the basis of these methodological reflections we are now in a better position to understand the dialectical character of TL's self-definition as "critical reflection on Christian praxis in the light of the Word of God." TL is necessarily involved in a hermeneutic circle with an inner dialectic between the socio-analytic and the hermeneutic mediations, between what is reflected *on* and the perspective or horizon *from* which it is reflected on. What is reflected on—the object of theological reflection—comprises the traditional forms and interpretations of faith, the actual empirical praxis of faith, and the historical contexts of that praxis as analyzed by the social sciences. The perspective from which the theologian carries on this reflection comprises the living Word of God and Scripture, the history of its interpretations, and the prophetic sensibility to the plight of the poor and their perspective acquired through participation in their struggles. The relation between object and perspective is always fluid and self-reversing: object becomes perspective, and perspective becomes object, in a dynamic interaction. To put this circle in simpler terms, as Gutierrez does:

> This is the basic circle of all hermeneutics: from the human being to God and from God to the human being, from history to faith and from faith to history, from love of our brothers and sisters to the love of the Father and from the love of the Father to the love of our brothers and sisters, from human justice to God's holiness and from God's holiness to human justice, from the poor person to God and from God to the poor person.[129]

To put it in another way, following Segundo, the hermeneutic circle is hermeneutic in that "it is the continuing change in our interpretation of the Bible which is dictated by the continuing changes in our present-day reality, both individual and societal," and circular in that "each new reality obliges us to interpret the Word of God afresh, to change reality accordingly, and then to go back and reinterpret the Word of God again, and so on."[130] Segundo elaborates on this circle in terms of four stages: (1) "our way of experiencing reality, which leads us to ideological suspicion"; (2) "the application of our ideological suspicion to the whole ideological superstructure in general and to theology in particular"; (3) "a new way of experiencing theological reality that leads us to exegetical suspicion, that is, to the suspicion that the prevailing interpretation of the Bible has not taken important pieces of date into account"; and (4) "a new hermeneutic, that is, our new way of interpreting the fountainhead of our faith (i.e., Scripture) with the new elements at our disposal."[131]

TL often speaks of praxis, the commitment to the poor, as the 'first act' or 'initial experience,' and of theology as the 'second' act. In light of the basic circularity of the hermeneutic situation, it should be clear that the word 'first' or 'initial' does not signify a blind commitment or experience without the mediation of thought; it is meant to stress the primacy and impact of praxis over mere theory, a praxis which preserves its own dialectic with Scripture, tradition, and critical social science. The four stages of Segundo form a circle precisely in that they are *dialectically internal* to one another, and denote the essential components of such a circle, not self-contained, mutually discreet atomic entities that merely succeed one another chronologically.[132]

RESPONSES TO CRITICS

Transcendence, Existence, History

Let me now turn to the critics. Could theology link itself so closely with praxis, especiallly with the political praxis of and for a particular group, without being "partisan" and "classist"? Is the critical distance between praxis and perspective, between reflection *on* praxis and reflection *in* praxis, great enough to ensure the objectivity and universality appropriate to theory? Isn't there a *via media* between the ahistorical universality attributed to traditional theology and the historical particularity insisted on by TL? Doesn't TL rule out all dialogue with other points of view in too dogmatic a fashion?

First, regarding whether TL is critical enough as theory, it seems caught between two horns of a dilemma. The Vatican charges that TL turns praxis into the "supreme criterion" for theology, "re-reads" its traditional content, and denies the transcendence of the truth of faith. This is so by virtue of its historical and ideological critique of tradition. TL is too critical. Ogden and McCann and Strain, on the other hand, accuse it of uncritically assuming the truth of the particular contents of faith and the normative basis of such contents and thus failing to inquire into their truth, the primary task of theology. To them, TL is not critical enough.

TL does not deny the transcendence of the truth of faith, nor does it consider the perspective of the oppressed the only or supreme criterion of theology, as I think the preceeding discussion should have made quite clear, although some statements of TL, taken out of the total context, might create such an impression. Faith as praxis is not blind activism but contains truths—*fides quae*—as its objective content and referent, truths whose meaning is indeed universal, not reducible to their meaning for contemporary history. This is precisely why theology is a reflection on praxis "in light of the Word of God." In addition to the historical perspective of the oppressed, TL includes the truths of faith as part of the horizon of theological reflection, the horizon of transcendence proper to theology *as* theology. It is precisely out of respect for this transcendence and universality of faith that TL, unlike many other theologies, self-consciously recognizes its own 'transitional' character: TL does not exhaust the universal meaning of the truths of faith. By the same token, it also insists that this very universality and transcendence of faith requires that it become concrete and effective in the particularities of history: the Christian faith in the Kingdom poses an inherent demand for historical actualization. Likewise, the faith at issue is not angelic but human faith, and as such must be understood in its concrete historical actuality and thus against the historical conditions of the development of its self-understanding, which often involves ideological distortions. A universal which is only transcendent and in no way concretely embodied in historical particularity would be not only, like Hegel's 'bad infinite,' a lifeless, abstract, empty universal, but also inaccessible to humans as concrete historical beings. The task of theology is to find the appropriate historical mediation of this universal and transcendent faith.

Does this mean, then, accepting Ogden's charge that TL uncritically assumes the truth of the traditional content of faith in its universality and transcendence? If Ogden's point is that TL fails to institute a transcendental critique of the very meaning of God, Christ, and faith in the manner of existential and transcendental hermeneutics, he is quite right. In another sense, however, TL does engage in a more radical critique of the basic content of faith than the existentialist and transcendental theologies; this is precisely the reason why the Vatican finds TL too critical. The political hermeneutic of TL inquires not so much into the transcendental conditions for the possibility and meaning of Christian faith in relation to *existence*, in its search for authenticity and transcendence towards God in the midst of sin, mortality, and finitude, as into the sociohistorical possibility and meaning of that faith in relation to *concrete historical existence,* which suffers precisely that very sin, death, and finitude in the most concrete and painful ways, and apart from which there would cease to be *human* sin, *human* death, and *human* finitude. (I think it is safe to assume that these alone are at issue in human theology; I confess ignorance of what the sin, death and finitude of angels would be like and thus of the a priori condition for the possibility of angelic theology.) After all, the theologies of Bultmann, Tillich, Rahner, and

Ogden do not ask why human existence as transcendence, not as a historically concrete totality, should be the anthropological, transcendental condition and correlative of faith, nor are they critical of the very basis of theory, including existentialist theology, in the historical conditions of human praxis. They simply assume the validity and telos of theory and truth independent of their concrete historical contexts.[133]

Ogden's own procedure is an excellent illustration of this pre-critical stance. He is aware of "modern historical consciousness" and claims that contemporary theology in its *content* must become a theology of liberation in the Latin American sense in order to make the Christian witness to God's boundless love "credible" to that consciousness. He thus introduces historicity into the content of faith as an *object* of theological reflection, that *on* which theology reflects. He fails, however, to introduce historicity into the *act* of theological reflection itself, as though theology as theory could be so independent of the historical situation, or into the *content* of human existence as the correlative of faith, as though existence were separable from historical praxis.[134] TL, on the other hand, institutes a transcendental–historical critique of the very basis of theory in praxis and seeks to reconstitute the whole of theology, including the initial anthropological starting point, on that basis. In doing so, however, TL proceeds dialectically. It is not a question of "reducing" the universal content of faith to the particular demands of immediate praxis or to its perspective, but one of subjecting both the content of faith and the historical perspective to a mutual critique. The received content of faith and the perspective of the oppressed constitute the horizon of theology in such a way that there is a dialectic internal to the horizon itself.

The Poor as Concrete Universal

The question remains, however, why a prior preferential—although not exclusive—commitment to the oppressed is a necessary condition of *contemporary* theology. Isn't such a commitment another form of bondage? What gives the oppressed such an epistemological privilege and makes their perspective a norm for the theologian? What about the charge of classism? Given the basic historicity and historical task of theology, it should not be too difficult to construct an argument in defense of such a prior commitment. The challenge to theology, it was pointed out, is to reflect from within history, not from outside, and it is essential, therefore, to find, not just any perspective but that perspective which in some way captures the essential crises and conflicts of the time. Whose perspective, then, would fulfill this function and provide the necessary access to history for theology? Whose perspective, moreover, would do so without an ideological class bias and self-interest, as the Vatican rightly insists? Insofar as all human perspectives are necessarily concretized in a particular group, the perspective we are seeking must be particular. Insofar, however, as that perspective embodies the essential human crisis of the time in which all groups are involved, it is also universal, at least within the limits of that epoch or society. The perspective must avoid both sheer particularism and ahistorical universalism; it must be concretely universal.

The quest for objectivity in historical knowledge has been the classic problem in sociology of knowledge. It is informative to contrast here the approach of Karl Mannheim, one of the founders of that sociology, and that of TL. Mannheim locates such an objective perspective in the intelligentsia. The intellectuals certainly belong to particular classes, as does everyone else, and to that extent their perspective is likewise historically conditioned, partial and limited. At the same time, however, they have an advantage over non-intellectuals by their common education, which both makes possible certain reflective distance towards class interests and makes them open to the interests of the diverse classes from which they originate, whereas non-intellectuals are generally preoccupied with the immediacy of their lives and tied to the interests of the classes to which they respectively belong. The intellectuals, therefore, are capable of a perspective which is at once rooted in the particular classes of their respective individual origins and sensitive to the plurality of conflicting class interests in society—thus, a concretely universal perspective. It is important to add here, however, that this search for objectivity is motivated by the desire for a comprehension of history and its dynamics as a possible basis of "a science of politics." The search is for the historical bearer of the intellectual synthesis of diverse ideologies and perspectives, with Hegel as the historical model. The point of Mannheim is not so much to 'change' reality as to 'understand' its dynamics.[135]

TL, on the other hand, is not so sanguine about the capacity of the 'free-floating' intellectuals for historical objectivity, and is much more interested in changing the oppressive structures than in comprehending their dynamics, although neither TL nor Mannheim denies the intrinsic connection between changing and comprehending. As the preceding discussion makes clear, social sciences are not neutral, and the perspective from which they carry on their empirical research is crucial to the result. The question still remains, therefore, whose perspective comes closest to being concretely universal.

TL locates such a perspective in that of the poor and oppressed, who, as victims of the injustice of the social structure, embody and suffer in their own life the universal human crisis of the time. The poor embody the universal theologically, ethically, and structurally. Theologically, they are, as even the Vatican recognizes, the object of God's preferential love, to which the rest of us are summoned in faith. Ethically, the universal dignity of humans *as* humans—which is the viewpoint of the ethical and thus the concern of us all *as* humans—is most at stake in the poor. The degradation of the poor, furthermore, is not the result of merely 'natural' poverty or accidental exploitation on the part of isolated individuals, but that of 'artificial' poverty rooted in structural injustice—both regional and now, increasingly, international, an injustice in which, therefore, *all* are involved directly or indirectly. This poverty is due to the unjust structural monopoly of the major means of production of the basic needs of life, and the resultant inequitable distribution of power and opportunity which also leads to political oppression and cultural deprivation.[136] The perspective rooted in the objective life situation of the poor, then, is universal: in *their* suffering is also at stake *our* contemporary human destiny, regardless of all our contingent differences in status, race, sex, profession, and so forth. It is not exclusive. Insofar as the universal human destiny is concretely embodied in the particularities of the poor and commands special attention from all of us, it is also preferential.

If this description of the poor as a concrete universal is correct, and we do well to remember that the poor make up the absolute majority of humankind today, and if, as TL insists, theology must enter into the crisis and challenge of comtemporary history and reflect from the horizon or perspective of that crisis, it seems difficult to deny the poor their 'epistemological privilege' as a group through which theology can gain concrete access to contemporary history. As a historically situated being, the theologian is bound to reflect, implicitly or explicitly, from a particular historical perspective; the only question is whether he or she does so consciously, as a result of reasoned choice, and whether the perspective can indeed claim universal significance. The alternative would be either an ahistorical conception of theology or a frankly relativistic pluralism which accords equal ethical value to all experiences and equal epistemological value to all viewpoints rooted in such experiences. To opt for the perspective rooted in the experience of a particular group is not necessarily partisan and classist. To think so and to thus demand transcendence of all particular group experiences and perspectives would be to deny the sociohistorical origin of human knowledge and revert to the ahistorical conception of human perspectives; the latter, however, is not without its own—although unacknowledged and hidden— ideological content and consequences.[137]

Praxis as Transcendental Horizon

What, then is the exact epistemological value of this perspective of the poor, referred to earlier as prophetic sensibility? Here I think it is essential to introduce a distinction, not always clearly made by TL, between the two senses of 'praxis'—between praxis in the empirical sense of particular actions and opinions and praxis in its "disclosive" function, i.e., in the relatively a priori or quasi-transcendental sense of the perspective or horizon of the oppressed that is generated in the process of praxis in the empirical sense. It goes without saying that there is an intense inner dialectic between the transcendental horizon and empirical praxis. It is through the empirical praxis of liberation that one may acquire the perspective of the oppressed, as it is in light of that perspective that the truth, validity, and effectiveness of empirical praxis is to be evaluated.

Ever since Plato, and much more self-consciously since Descartes and Kant, there has been a general recognition of the relational character of human knowledge: true knowledge is a function of the conformity or agreement between subject and object, and thus depends on the nature of the subject as well as of the object. In the language of the Thomist tradition, whatever is known is known according to the mode of the knower; this sets an a priori condition and limit to the knowledge of the object or objective knowledge. How one understands the nature of the knower, therefore, is crucial. Does one understand the human subject as a soul (Plato), a synthesis of body and soul (Aristotle and Aquinas), a thinking ego (rationalism), a subject of sense perception (empiricism), a transcendental subject (Kant and idealism), a subject of existence (existentialism), a being-in-the-world (Heidegger), a subject constituted by intersubjectivity (phenomenology, personalism of John Paul II and Cardinal Ratzinger), or a concrete totality of sociohistorical existence (Hegel, Marx, Dewey, TL)? If the object is not given except in relation to a subject, whose structure constitutes the a priori condition for the possibility of objective knowledge, it is essential to be clear about the anthropological presuppositions of any epistemological discussion. The emphasis of TL on involvement in history at its most critical and on the need for acquiring the perspective of the poor as the condition of objective knowledge of the historical situation must likewise be understood in this anthropological–epistemological context. It is the logical extension of the classical relational view of human knowledge in accordance with its own anthropology of concrete historical totality—a conception of the human subject who can know only through praxis in history and society.[138]

The important thing to note here is that the horizon of the poor fulfills the same transcendental or critical function in TL as the a priori categories of the understanding in Kant and the understanding of being-in-the-world in Heidegger. The difference is that in Kant those categories are ahistorical and asocial, and in Heidegger the understanding of being is indeed historical but historical only in its subjective, existential significance as temporality, whereas in TL the horizon of the poor is derived from our involvement in concrete history and its social conflicts. For the latter, it is an understanding of acting-in-the-world precisely *as* a world ridden with class conflicts and demanding the sublation (*Aufhebung*) of such conflicts for the sake of the humanity of all, along with the hope in the possibility of such sublation. In this quasi-transcendental sense, then, the horizon includes the global experience of oppression, a generalized pre-understanding of its social causes, the collective will to sublate it, and the hope in the real possibility of its sublation. It is a critical counterpart of ideology, which also functions as an a priori horizon, except that ideology is used to maintain the status quo and exclude the hope of structural change.

As a transcendental condition, this horizon, as TL fully admits, does not guarantee either the truth of our empirical judgments or the efficiency of our empirical praxis, any more than the transcendental category of causality in Kant assures the infallibility of our empirical judgments concerning particular causal relations. In this sense, then, the particular judgments and actions of the poor and of the theologians who participate in the praxis of their liberation may be quite fallible and ineffective. The possession of the horizon is not a sufficient condition to guarantee the infallibility of our empirical judgments and the efficiency of our practices; this is precisely the reason why TL so insists on the necessity of empirical social analysis and interdisciplinary cooperation with the social sciences. However, the latter would be impossible without the horizon. Just as, for Kant, it is only the a priori category of causality which makes it possible for us to perceive or recognize anything *as* cause or effect at all, and therefore without it no empirical judgments are possible in the first place, still less true or false, so, for TL, it is the moral perspective of the oppressed alone that enables us to perceive the moral dimension of oppression with something more than an abstract pity, assess the social reality in terms of the possibility and urgency of its elimination, and propose solutions and answers relevant to the situation of the poor.

Without that perspective, the moral crisis of poverty is not recognized as moral or critical, the social reality is studied from the purely technical, instrumental point of view, and attention is diverted from the structural sources of social injustice in the name of anti-utopian "realism." The relevant issues are not even raised or recognized; hence, no solution is proposed which then might be either true or false in relation to the issues. By the demand of their objective situation, not always because of conscious ill will or hypocrisy, the privileged members of society do not see the moral urgency or social necessity of structural change. The oppressed and the privileged see different things in the same social situation because their transcendental horizons are different.

This distinction between empirical judgments and the transcendental perspective both justifies and invalidates the Vatican's critique that TL absolutizes the "partisan" consciousness as the only "true" consciousness, denies the objectivity of truth, and makes impossible all dialogue between TL and other theologies. If we take praxis in the empirical sense and thus partisan consciousness in its immediacy and claim it as the criterion of truth, we do fall into egregious nonsense. Every partisan would be right, in that case, by definition, and the inevitable result would be an impossible subjectivism. This would indeed make all dialogue impossible, not only between a partisan and others but also among the partisans themselves. And yet it is also a fact that liberation theologians do disagree and dialogue, as do Marxists, among themselves as well as with others.

By the same token, it is also true that a meaningful dialogue is not concretely possible between different transcendental horizons. Such dialogue is not a matter of the truth or falsity of a particular opinion, or even of a set of opinions, but one of the very perspectives in which particular opinions assume their meaning precisely as true or false. That the difference in perspective and priorities leads to different assessments of the historical situation and its challenges and sets a definite limit to the possibility of dialogue should be quite clear from the debates between capitalists and socialists, Continental philosophers and British analysts, Thomists and Whiteheadians, theists and atheists, and indeed the Vatican and TL itself. A dialogue only becomes concretely possible either if one party converts to the horizon of the other or both parties rise to a 'higher' horizon which they can share. In either case, it is a matter of conversion, as TL rightly insists.

The Limits of Pure Reason

Finally, McCann and Strain's charge is that TL fails to institute a transcendental analysis of the conditions for the possibility of authentic public discourse, a discourse among free, unbiased, rational agents committed to the values of pluralism and tolerance and intent on achieving a consensus with regard to the courses of political praxis to be taken. It is this failure which, for McCann and Strain, leads TL to theological totalitarianism in theory and blind activism in praxis. TL does not allow a genuine dialectic between theory and praxis because it does not allow theory, in its independent integrity as intersubjective, public, democratic rationality, to inform the political praxis of the community.

The basic problem with McCann and Strain's criticism is their conception of the relation between theory and praxis, which they consider "dialectical" but which turns out to be anything but that. They assume the existence of theory and praxis each independent of the other and construe the dialectic as the inter-action between the two subsequent to such independent constitution. Thus, they postulate an ideal speech situation and the conditions of such a possibility according to the demands of pure theory, out of which will emerge, they hope, democratic consensus which in turn will guide praxis. A genuine dialectic, however, would consist in the mutual constitution—*perichoresis*—of theory and praxis, their mutual opposition—*chorismos*—and the process in which such opposition is *aufgehoben* into reconciliation, however partial and provisional.[139] Human theory is anything but pure; it is always conditioned by the needs, con-texts, and horizons of praxis, just as praxis is never blind action but is always mediated by some theory. McCann and Strain take theory out of this living contact with praxis and seek to impose the demands of pure theory on praxis from out-side, as though the empirical reality of praxis could be reduced to such demands. Their reason is pure reason divorced from praxis altogether, outside of all history, not empirical reason or reason in history.

Consider the ideal speech situation of McCann and Strain and Habermas, where humans gather for a dialogue, each of them an autonomous and responsible self committed to no particular tradition but only to "a partisanship on behalf of reason," to a norm of social praxis "transcendentally presupposed in the struggle of all persons and groups to see and say what is true, to do what is right, and above all, to remain truthful to themselves and to their fellows."[140] These are, of course, admirable ideals—ideals, in fact, shared by TL. I am even willing to accept the validity of their transcendental deduction. In a world increasingly fragmented and incapable of any consensus on substantive issues yet anxious to avoid violence and dictatorship, there is an understandable temptation to retreat into the purely formal and procedural conditions of genuine dialogue to be respected by all parties despite all their substantive differences; John Rawls's *A Theory of Justice* is one of the recent examples.

However, what if not all the parties to the dialogue agreed to those procedural conditions or were capable of committing themselves to either such conditions or the conclusions of such a dialogue? What if these disagreements and inabilities were themselves products—to a great extent at least—of a social interaction "distorted" by the conflicting political and economic interests of a particular society, from which speech should not be isolated and reified? What if, in short, our empirical reason operates under conflicting horizons, at odds even with its own transcendental conditions? Do we wait until these conflicts have been reconciled—i.e., until we have achieved justice and equity in politics and economics—i.e., until we no longer need such dialogues? How can parties with radically different horizons engage in a real dialogue, not merely the appearance of one?

Habermas and McCann and Strain, of course, are aware of the fact that such an ideal speech situation is precisely an "ideal," nowhere fully realized. Nevertheless, they insist that it is an ideal worth striving for. But on what basis? Is there any basis for the actualization of such an ideal in the historical world with all its ideological and class divisions? If there is no such basis, is it still meaningful as an ideal? Are they not in fact, if not in intention, defending the status quo by insisting on an ideal that is in principle incapable of realization as the condition for any social change? Basically, their difficulty is derived from postulating the existence of a human being who is purely rational, ahistorical, and universal *à la* Kant, a total abstraction from the concrete historicity and particularity of real human existence, and trying to impose such an abstraction, demanded by pure theory, as a condition for transforming the world of concrete historical praxis, which has a logic and rationality of its own.[141]

Of course, I do not mean to reject the value and necessity of dialogue altogether. I reject dialogue or public discourse only and precisely in its claim to be *the* foundation of practical theology. Once a basic horizon is shared on the basis of a common commitment to praxis, there is room for dialogue, and this is precisely what is going on among the theologians of liberation in matters of theological construction and social analysis. Indeed, the shared horizon of the preferential option for the poor does not dictate any particular political stategy or action; these can be determined only empirically. The socialist option shared by theologians of liberation is the result of longstanding debate, analysis, and observation regarding the particular historical situation of Latin America. The charge of dogmatism and exclusivism regarding this option, therefore, is a totally misplaced one. It is, of course, not a result of a dialogue with the generals, landlords, and the multinational corporations, any more than capitalism is a result of a dialogue with blacks, the unemployed, or those living under the poverty line. Should Cardinals Lorscheider and Arns have entered into dialogue with Cardinals Trujillo and Obando, the Somozas and the Pinochets?[142]

CHAPTER IV

Dialectic of Salvation and Liberation

At the heart of Christian faith is the reality and hope of salvation in Jesus Christ. Christian faith is faith in the God of salvation revealed in Jesus of Nazareth. The Christian tradition has always equated this salvation with the transcendent, eschatological fulfillment of human existence in a life freed from sin, finitude, and mortality and united with the triune God. This is perhaps *the* non-negotiable item of Christian faith. What has been a matter of debate is the relation between salvation and our activities in the world. What is the salvific meaning of our existence and activities in this world? On this matter options have ranged from straight dualism, which *opposes* the sacred and the profane; to duality, in which the natural and the supernatural coexist side by side, each with its own autonomy; and then to a unity of intrinsic relation, which sees all experience in this world as in principle salvific by virtue of the Incarnation.

TL is the latest and certainly the most radical attempt to integrate and unify salvation and our secular experience, faith and our praxis of life in this world. Clodovis Boff puts the perspective of TL as follows:

> The theology of liberation seeks to demonstrate that the kingdom of God is to be established not only in the soul—this is the individual personal dimension of the kingdom—and not only in *heaven*—this is its trans-historical dimension—but in relationships among human beings, as well. In other words, the kingdom of God is to be established in social projects, and this is its historical dimension. In sum, liberation theology is a theology that seeks to take history, and Christians' historical responsibility seriously.[1]

Like the two natures of Christ within the hypostatic union according to Chalcedon, salvation and liberation are neither to be confused nor to be separated. They are not to be confused and simply identified, for salvation transcends liberation. Nor are they to be separated, for salvation includes liberation. Partially identical with salvation, liberation is nonetheless subordinate to salvation.[2] This position of TL has come under attack, notably from the Vatican, and has been accused of harboring Pelagianism, politicizing faith, and reducing the transcendence of faith and salvation.

In this chapter I begin, as in the preceding chapter, with criticisms of TL, especially those of Joseph Cardinal Ratzinger, Stanley Hauerwas, and John Cobb. In the second section I discuss the dialectical relation—unity in difference—of salvation and liberation, of transcendence and history, as elaborated in the works of liberation theologians. In the third section I go on to develop my own concept of social sin, in accordance with the spirit of TL. The concept of social sin and its theological correlative, the conversion and liberation of social structures, have been among the distinguishing charcteristics of TL; and yet, judging by the literature available in English, it seems clear that the notion of social sin is more assumed than elaborated, which is not necessarily to the discredit of TL. The concept of the social, of social structure and structural contradiction, has long been elaborated and become familiar in the intellectual tradition of Hegel, Marx, neo-Marxism, and critical social science, which is also the intellectual milieu of TL; liberation theologians may therefore see no compelling reason to belabor the familiar. In the North American milieu. however, which is still burdened with the legacy of atomistic individualism, such a concept still seems to be in need of elaboration and defense. Responses to the critics will be integrated into the second and third sections. This chapter, then, deals with the much-debated, often attacked theological substance of TL, which involves issues of critical importance.

CRITICISMS OF THEOLOGY OF LIBERATION

The Vatican

According to Cardinal Ratzinger in his 1984 Instruction,[3] TL is guilty of the denial of the integrity of salvation in its three dimensions; transcendence, individuality, and wholeness. First, we will examine the first charge—the denial of the transcendence of salvation. For Ratzinger, "some are tempted to emphasize, unilaterally, the liberation from servitude of an earthly and temporal kind" and to "put liberation from sin in second place and so fail to give it the primary importance it is due" (Introduction).

> To some it even seems that the necessary struggle for human justice in the economic and political sense constituted the essence of salvation. For them, the Gospel is reduced to a purely earthly gospel. (vi, 4)

In denying the distinction between salvation history and profane history and affirming "only one history," TL falls into "historicist immanentism," which tends to "identify the Kingdom of God and its growth with the human liberation movement" (ix, 3) and to "misunderstand or eliminate" "the transcendence and gratuity of liberation in Jesus Christ. . .the sovereignty of grace, and the true nature of the means of salvation, especially of the Church and the sacraments" (xi, 17). It makes "history itself the subject of its own development, as a process of the self-redemption of man by means of the class struggle" (ix, 4). In short, TL is a "temporal messianism," "one of the most radical of the expressions of secularization of the kingdom of God and of its absorption into the immanence of human history," and in giving such priority to the political dimension it is also led to deny the "specific" character of salvation, which is "above all liberation from sin" (x, 6, 7).

The second error of TL is its denial of the interiority and transcendence of personal existence. TL tends to "localize evil principally or uniquely" in "social sin" or "structural evil," and ignores "the full ambit of sin" or the totality of effects of sin, of which social sin is only one dimension. It fails to recognize that sin, which is always primarily personal, not evil structures, is the source of all evils (iv, 14, 15). It demands "first of all a radical revolution in social relations" and "criticizes the search for personal perfection," but this is to deny "the meaning of the person and his transcendence, and to destroy ethics and its foundation" (iv, 15). Considering that the source of social injustice lies in the human heart, truly humane social change can be brought about only by the search for personal perfection, "only by making an appeal to the moral potential of the person and to the constant need for interior conversion" (xi, 8). Instead, TL resorts to "the systematic and delibarate recourse to blind violence (xi, 7). By the same token, TL is guilty of a double illusion. It believes that "these new structures will of themselves give birth to a 'new man' in the sense of the truth of man," and forgets that "it is only the Holy Spirit" "who is the source of every true renewal" (xi, 9). It also believes that the revolutionary overthrow of an old structure is "*ipso facto* the beginning of a just regime" and forgets the threat of totalitarianism, which is "a major fact of our time" (xi, 10).

This reduction of transcendent salvation to political liberation on the one hand and of personal sin to structural, social sin on the other also leads to the third error, which sums up the essence of the first two, namely, the destruction of the "wholeness" of salvation. Ratzinger does not deny the necessity of political structural liberation: in his own way, he insists on it. What he does find unacceptable, he states, is that TL selects this one aspect of salvation—political and social liberation—and makes it the "uniquely" or "exclusively" important dimension, which reduces the whole essence of salvation to the political and temporal, or else makes it the "principal" dimension of the whole, distorting the proper hierarchy of order and rank. TL subordinates the transcendent agency of God to the Pelagian effort of autonomous humans and places what is "fundamental" and "primary," sin and personal interior conversion, after what is only "secondary," political servitude and structural change. Sin, the cause of all evil, is subordinated to structural evil, which is only a consequence and result of sin; what is "higher", the religious and spiritual, is placed below that which is "lower," the temporal and political. This process postpones the theologically essential—evangelization, the Word of God, the sacraments—for the sake of material 'bread' and the satisfaction of temporal needs (vi, 3).

In order to appreciate the logic behind the rather bald assertions of the Instruction, it would be useful to take note of a lecture given by Ratzinger at the Rheinisch-Westfälische Akademie in July of 1985, in which he presents a more systematic critique of Gutierrez's *A Theology of Liberation*.[4] Ratzinger begins by admitting Gutierrez's "personal" orthodoxy, acknowledging that Gutierrez does *not* personally intend to reduce the Kingdom of God to a new society on earth or Christian salvation to the process of political liberation in history. For Gutierrez, the "one" history of salvation is a complex unity with differentiation of three levels—historical liberation in its economic, social, and political aspects; creation of new humanity in a utopian society of solidarity; and liberation from sin as condition of communion with God and other humans—to which correspond three distinctive types of rationality respectively, the scientific, philosophical, and theological. Despite the orthodoxy of Gutierrez's personal or subjective intention, however, Ratzinger questions whether Gutierrez objectively preserves the unity in difference without falling into reductionism, whether he really preserves both the logic of the whole and the distinctive rationality of each level. Objectively, Gutierrez ultimately reduces both the empirical rationality of historical liberation and the theological rationality of faith to a utopian philosophy of history on the model of Saint Simon and Marx. How is this so?

First of all, Gutierrez reduces the proper claims of faith and theological rationality to nothing by preempting theological content and transferring it to the utopia. The forgiveness of sins and the reconciling communion with other humans are comprehensively anticipated in the utopian vision of new humanity and a society in solidarity; forgiveness of sins effects nothing and adds nothing to this vision. Faith provides no ethical criteria, which are already contained in the utopia of a classless society, as God too is encountered in the engagement in the process of historical liberation towards such utopia. To hope in Christ is only to believe in the adventure of history. Nothing specific is reserved for God, faith, and theology, which are rendered "totally functionless."[5] Likewise, Gutierrez fails to provide any empirical analysis of society, something one would expect of someone who interprets faith in political terms and suggests concrete directives for political action. Instead, he replaces concrete social analysis with a general, abstract philosophical sociology based on a utopian conception of human existence. There is no concrete, empirical content to economic, social, and political liberation. Thus, only the second plane, the utopia of cultural liberation, remains as both the methodological justification and the real content of the entire project. Both historical liberation and theological rationality are subordinated to the historical project of utopia, which becomes the motivating and unfiying power of the whole.[6]

Second, Gutierrez fails to give any justification of this utopian principle itself. Although the utopia is made to serve as a synthesizing principle of theology and politics and to provide a new content and a new praxis to the doctrine of salvation, he merely takes it as a presupposition of the whole accepted in faith, which, however, appeals to history, not to God. History becomes the divinity of utopia, claiming not only the attributes and power of the divine but also the divine right to unconditioned obedience and promises. It stands for the totality. Behind this historicist immanentization of God lie Marxian presuppositions which are taken over without question; however, the real father of such a faith in history is Saint Simon, who saw history as an irreversible process of necessary progress and of messianic political projects based on such faith. He also saw religion as the basis of social organization and enlisted its power in the service of social progress, refusing to see any separation between temporal and spiritual power. It is no wonder that this political messianism has found strong welcome and support in the soil of Latin America, a continent itself burdened with a long history of a theopolitical tradition. The theology of Gutierrez, eschewing both scientific and theological rationality, merely utilizes the power of popular religion as justification of the irrational faith in the utopia of history; the utopia then becomes totalitarian, creating a world where there exists only one right politics. Politics orders not only the political but also the cultural revolution, the factory of new humanity. In short, Gutierrez's theology is philosophically irrational.[7]

Third, Gutierrez is also guilty of a properly theological error. This error consists in inserting the political–social problem into the doctrine of redemption where, theologically speaking—in terms of the logic and possibilities of theology—it has no proper place. He understands redemption as ontology or metaphysics of hope, of the not-yet-being, which under the presuppositions of Saint Simon becomes the physics of the not-yet-being. This degeneration of metaphysics to physics is unavoidable as long as redemption is closely bound up with politics. For if redemption lies on the plane of being and must become concrete in the domain of the political, then being must be controllable, and human affairs must contain a necessity that can be designed and manipulated. Metaphysics must be capable of being transformed into the physics of humans. Thus, the insertion of the political problem into the doctrine of redemption intrinsically leads to such systems of thought as Saint Simonism and theologized Marxism. There is an intrinsic, systematic connection between them which arises from an original relationship and which is unavoidable.[8]

Stanley Hauerwas

From a different perspective, Stanley Hauerwas objects that the concept of liberation in Gutierrez's theology is at best sociologically and theologically inadequate and at worst "profoundly anti-Christian."[9] The concept is derived from the ideal of individual autonomy in Kant and the Enlightenment. Sociologically, it abstracts from the notions of power and equality, and leads to the liberal capitalist justification of the power of some and the powerlessness of others. Unless the concept of freedom is made concrete in the context of the equalization of power, both political and economic, and unless this equalized power is enlisted not so much in the service of making each individual "an artisan of his own destiny" as in the service of making the individual more capable of cooperating in the creation of a fraternal society, the ideal of liberation remains an abstraction liable to ideological manipulation. When used as the single dominant category of social analysis and strategy, it is antithetical to the values of equality and fraternity. Theologically, such liberation distorts the Christian concept of liberation in Christ, which is precisely a means to service and fellowship, not a pretext for individualism and domination. The function of the Christian churches is to be "a body of people who have found freedom through learning to serve one another and the world."[10]

John B. Cobb, Jr.

A third source of objection to TL is John B. Cobb, Jr., whose basic objection, from the Whiteheadian perspective of ecological theology, is directed to the "anthropocentrism" inherent in the political theology of Johann Metz in particular but also in any sociological theology in general, and whose criticism, therefore, may be considered relevant to TL as well. For Cobb, the basic problem of any sociological theology is its anthropocentrism, the heritage of Kant and German idealism, which makes too sharp a distinction between "nature" and "history" and subordinates the former to the latter. Nature is understood only within the horizon of history, only in its appearance to human subjectivity and its utility to human purposes, not in its own right and independence. It ignores the fact that humans are only part of nature, which as such transcends human subjectivity.

The result of the preoccupation with and the exaltation of the human species is the exploitation of nature, leading to ecological deterioration and the constant threat of nuclear suicide. The transformation of oppressive social structures is indeed necessary and urgent, but "changing the structures of human society and the attitudes of human beings to other human beings in itself is unlikely to solve the environmental problem."[11] What is required is a fundamental break with the Kantian tradition and the recognition of the "inherent reality and worth of our fellow creatures," of the fact that "the rest of the creation should also be treated with respect and recognized to have reality and value quite apart from usefulness to human beings," for "other creatures are of value in themselves and for God." To do otherwise would be "profoundly false to the Biblical vision."[12] In short, we need a shift to a wider cosmological or ecological horizon for the "indivisible salvation of the whole world."[13]

DIALECTIC OF SALVATION AND LIBERATION

Is TL guilty as charged? Regarding Ratzinger's criticisms the anwser, I think, requires more than a simple yes or a simple no, more than even a partial yes and a partial no. This sort of answer presupposes the existence of a common horizon of understanding between the disputants, which alone makes agreements and disagreements possible and meaningful. Between Ratzinger and TL no such horizon seems to exist. Instead, we have two different horizons, two radically different modes of thinking, hence two different theologies in conflict. This radical difference of horizon should become quite evident in the next chapter where I present Ratzinger's—and Pope John Paul II's—"authentic" or "integral" theology of Christian freedom and liberation, and in the concluding chapter where it will be the subject of extended reflection and commentary. In this chapter let me respond to the charges as simply as possible, without further commentary on the deeper implications, as I present the positive doctrine of TL along with the underlying horizon of its thinking regarding the relationship between salvation and liberation.

Transcendence and History: The Charge of Reductionism

Perhaps the best place to begin is the charge of reductionism, which has burdened TL from its very inception. Does TL reduce salvation to political liberation in history? Is it guilty of denying the transcendence of the Kingdom and the sovereignty of grace, of temporal messianism and historicist immanentism? On this matter the response of TL, I think, has sometimes been cavalier. Clodovis Boff, for example, calls it "a precipitant, simplistic—and terrified—interpretation to "read 'political too' as 'political only,' 'earth too' as 'earth only,' or 'also, and especially, the poor' as 'only the poor,' and so on."[14] He goes on to state:

It would be an interesting experiment to respond to the allegation of reductionism with the classic riposte: What about the reductionisms of classical theology, especially in a later, essentialistic scholasticism, that great, vaunted "total theology"? What about *its* reduction of major biblical themes, such as physical poverty, physical liberation in history, social transformation, justice for the laborer, and the like, to "spiritual" poverty, liberation, righteousness, and so on?[15]

It is all very true, of course, that 'also' or 'too' is not the same as 'only,' and that classical theology was reductionistic in its own way. There is likewise a certain partiality in picking on TL for its alleged reductionism while remaining blind to or at least not as concerned with the reductionism of the classical theology of the Church. In light of the crucial importance of praxis in relation to discourse discussed in the preceding chapter, Boff's appeal to the praxis of the basic communities, I think, also deserves serious attention:

When this imputation of "reductionism" is subjected to verification in the living practice of the theology of liberation in the communities—of which, after all, this theology seeks to be the reflex and reflection—there can no

longer be any doubt. One need only watch the people reading the Bible
and praying their faith to realize that this allegation is pure myth. Never
in the history of Latin America has there been as much praying as in today's
basic church communities.[16]

The relationship between salvation and liberation "is not always worded in a
perfectly satisfactory manner" in TL; nevertheless, Boff asserts:

> this means that we in Latin America are better at practice than at theory.
> But after all, does life not "say" more than discourse does? On our conti-
> nent transcendence is practice, not rhetoric.[17]

It is clear, however, that the emphasis of TL on political liberation in history
also affirms far more than what might be implied by the connective 'also.' It does
not merely affirm—nor equally—the three dimensions of salvation—personal,
historical, and transhistorical. After all, the emphasis on the sociohistorical
dimension is the most distinctive aspect of TL, in contrast to other theologies.
It does not merely say that there is "also" a historical dimension to salvation
as there is "also" a personal and "also" a transhistorical dimension to salvation. It is not enough, therefore, to insist on the truism that "also" does not mean
"only." It is incumbent on TL to demonstrate the systematic connection and unity
among the three dimensions, the specific importance of the political dimension
within that unity, and how this unity does not reduce the personal and the transhistorical dimensions of salvation. As I shall try to show, TL on the whole—
and certainly Boff—does try to demonstrate these. I am here only referring to
certain polemically motivated simplifications, of which opponents of TL are certainly not less guilty.

The position of TL on the irreducible transcendence of the Kingdom and
the sovereignty of grace, I think, has been unambiguously affirmative. According to Gutierrez, the Gospel is

> a message that can never be identified with any concrete social formula,
> however just that formula may seem to us at the moment. The Word of
> the Lord is a challenge to its every historical incarnation and places that
> incarnation in the broad perspective of the radical and total liberation of
> Christ, the Lord of history.[18]

Christian hope "keeps us from any confusion of the Kingdom with any one
historical stage, from any idolatry toward unavoidably ambiguous human achievement, from any absolutizing of revolution."[19] In the same vein, Enrique Dussel
recognizes that "some day, we may have to demythologize the notion of the 'new
man' too, lest it oppress us and prevent us from continually moving ahead in
the process of liberation."[20] As Ignacio Ellacuria writes:

the Liberator God, who transcends history, has been made present in history in a signifying way by man, and now man proclaims and affirms in history something that goes beyond history. History and that which lies beyond history are not identical.[21]

Regarding sin, TL agrees with Ratzinger that salvation from sin is not simply identical with political liberation, and that it is, in fact, only in the theological perspective of salvation and sin that the true dimension and meaning of political liberation and oppression can be disclosed and appreciated. For Gutierrez, "sin—a breach of friendship with God and others—is according to the Bible the ultimate cause of poverty, injustice, and the oppression in which men live."[22] It is the "fundamental alienation" "present in every partial alienation."[23] "Liberation from sin is at the root of political liberation. The former reveals what is really involved in the latter,"[24] and thus "the very meaning of the growth of the Kingdom is also the ultimate precondition for a just society and a new man."[25] This coming of the Kingdom, however, "is above all a gift," "the gift which Christ offers us."[26]

The charge of reductionism, then, seems groundless, but Ratzinger is certainly justified in asking whether TL—Gutierrez in particular—does justice objectively to the transcendence of the Kingdom, whether it merely affirms such transcendence subjectively while betraying that transcendence in the actual elaboration of its theology. This question is only fair. After all, it is a common phenomenon in intellectual history for a thinker to affirm something only to negate it in practice either by neglecting it altogether or by failure to accord it the weight or importance it deserves in his or her actual reflection and elaboration. How seriously does TL take the transcendence of the Kingdom and the sovereignty of grace? Does it preserve that transcendence, and what role does the transcendence play in its actual theological reflection?

What is at stake here, however, is not simply whether TL does or does not preserve the transcendence of God, as though there were only one simple concept of transcendence given once and for all, but also—and more importantly—what conception of transcendence is more in accord with the normative tradition of Christian faith and is philosophically more consistent and adequate. For TL, it is indeed essential but not sufficient to stress, as does Ratzinger, the irreducible transcendence of God and salvation over history and human liberation; it is also necessary to show a positive connection, an inner mediation between the two, if we are to avoid an impossible metaphysical and theological dualism and to remain true to the historical and incarnational conception of God so pervasive of Scripture. For TL, God is transcendent precisely as the totality, and all the distinctions between divine transcendence and historical immanence, eschatological salvation and historical liberation, are posited and mediated within the unity of God's salvific will and by virtue of the totalizing function of the Kingdom. The position of TL in this regard is shaped by two things—the Hegelian conception of God as self-differentiating and self-unifying totality, as discussed in chapter 2, and the historical, incarnational conception of God in Scripture.[27]

First, we will discuss the Hegelian conception. The basic issue here has to do with the concept of divine transcendence itself and the way one can do justice to that transcendence. Does one promote the true transcendence of God by constantly stressing God's irreducible difference from history, that God is not human? Is this not in fact in danger of reducing the divine to one pole of the relation and thus to an object at the same level as creatures to which it is only negatively related? Does it still maintain, or in fact only reduce, the sovereignty of grace when it excludes the whole realm of history from the scope of its power and activity? For Hegel, as, in a similar although different way, for the later Barth, the apostle of "radical otherness,"[28] an infinite being which is only opposed and external to the finite is not truly infinite or absolute, because it still has something outside itself and thus remains limited by the latter, just as a finite being which is external to the infinite and not intrinsically dependent on it ceases to be finite. The infinite must be conceived as the totality which differentiates itself into itself, the infinite, and its Other, the finite. The difference is real, but it is something posited by the infinite itself and thus ultimately subject to the unity and totality of the infinite and its transcendent finality. It is the result of the *internal* self-differentiation of the divine, not an autonomous power external or opposed to it. The divine infinite thus unifies both infinite and finite, both transcendence and history in itself. The alternative would be a metaphysical dualism to which even the divine is subject. Furthermore, such self-differentiation of the divine, for Hegel, is the result of divine "activity," which always means both "actualizing" and "expressing" the divine finality. If a 'real symbol' means for Rahner a reality which at once expresses an Other constitutive of its essence and realizes what it expresses, the finite, for Hegel, would be precisely such a real symbol of the infinite.[29]

Now we come to the historical and incarnational interpretation of the God of Scripture in TL, for which this Hegelian dialectic of the divine totality is an essential background. For TL, the God of the Bible is God who acts in history and thus unifies transcendence and history in his own historical action. According to biblical faith, "God makes himself known in his *works*."[30] "The very essence of Christian revelation" is not "some abstract knowledge of God or some doctrine" but "a manifestation of God in *action*," "the historical and historicized love of God."[31] The God so revealed is

> a God who not only governs history, but who orientates it in the direction of justice and right. He is more than a provident God. He is a God who takes sides with the poor and liberates them from slavery and oppression.[32]

The work of creation is "the first of God's salvific deeds," which reveal him as "the liberator of human existence in its *totality*."[33]

Furthermore, "in Jesus God not only reveals himself in history, he *becomes* history."[34] As a result, "the liberating action of Christ" "is at the heart of the historical current of humanity."[35] It is also the history and historical praxis of Jesus of Nazareth that reveals the divinity of the Son and through it the divinity of the Father. "The historical life of Jesus is the fullest revelation of the Christian God."[36] TL stresses the historical Jesus not because it wants to reduce Jesus to a revolutionary symbol, as Ratzinger claims, but because it is precisely through his historical praxis that God chose to reveal who he is. The alternative would be a subtlely disguised docetism and monophysitism and the introduction of alien (i.e., Greek) conceptions of the divine into the Christian conception of God. It is in light of "the historical Jesus who is the key providing access to the total Christ"[37] that we have to understand the Christ of faith and the risen Christ as well.

God's relation to history is best captured in the central biblical symbol of the Kingdom or Reign of God, where 'reign' is to be taken in the verbal sense of the activity of reigning. There are two elements to this potent symbol. The first is its *historicity*. It symbolizes God's will to transform history and his empowering presence in history. The Kingdom of God does not mean God's rule *over* history from an ahistorical point of view but his transforming and empowering immanence *in* history. The relation between God and history is not external but internal, and it is God himself who posits this internal relation, who mediates himself through history to his own transcendent agency and finality, "overreaching" history as his own other (Hegel). It is through God's own initiative, not because of some 'immanentist' attempt to 'reduce' God's transcendence and deify history, that the liberating transformation *of* history as such becomes an intrinsic dimension of salvation itself.

The second element is its *totality*. God is the sovereign, the Lord of all history. No area of human life is exempt from God's sovereign demand for transformation. God is not only the God of the sanctuary, the Sunday worship, or the interiority of the believing heart, but also of the marketplaces, factories, and capitol hills. *All* areas of human existence stand under God's judgment and God's call for transformation. As an impediment to salvation, sin means rejection of God and others, but it is not a purely interior but a concretely historical reality, part of the daily events of human life. The removal of sin and its consequences in history, therefore, is an essential condition of salvation. As a "totality," salvation "embraces *all* human reality, transforms it, and leads it to its fullness in Christ."[38] It "embraces *all* men and the *whole* man."[39] The Gospel proclaims "total" liberation in Christ, which "includes a transformation of the concrete historical and political conditions that men and women live in," but also "leads this same history beyond itself, to a fullness that transcends the scope of all human doing or telling."[40] The true "sovereignty of grace" requires nothing less than this "radicality" and "totality" of the salvific process, that "nothing is outside the pale of the action of Christ and the gift of the Spirit."[41] The Kingdom is indeed "an eschatological *totality,*" but "precisely because of that it is encountered in history,"[42] "in its historical mediations."[43] The Kingdom is not only "not yet" but also "already" operative in the world. The eschatological Kingdom begins in and through the embodiment of its values in history, not apart from it. To exempt history from God's salvific activity would be in fact to deny his sovereignty. "If an absolute is unwilling to immerse itself in the relative, it ceases to be absolute; indeed it fails to attain even the value of that which is 'relatively' alive and operative."[44]

From the standpoint of faith, then, history is no longer merely profane history externally opposed to sacred history. It is itself an inner moment of the Kingdom, the divine agency and finality which as such transcend it, an intrinsic dimension of sacred history. The meaning of historical liberation can be "grasped in all its depth only when one knows that this liberation leads this same history out beyond itself."[45] The salvific process "gives human history its profound unity,"[46] and "faith reveals to us the deep meaning of the history which we fashion with our own hands."[47] By the same token, "salvation history is not some history different from human history; it is history as interpreted by the message which enables us to comprehend its profundity and destiny"; in fact, "the elevation of grace is the most profound dimension of human history itself."[48]

The relation between salvation and liberation, then, is a thoroughly dialectical relation. The order of creation and history, as mentioned, is distinct from and thus irreducible to the order of salvation; each has its own agency and finality distinct from that of the other. Still, the relation is internal, not one of two merely juxtaposed, parallel, or even convergent paths which still remain mutually external. History has been overtaken, assumed, or overreached by the salvific agency and finality of God herself/himself, immanent in history, and thus become an inner moment of salvation history. The Kingdom of God unifies transcendence and history in an intrinsic, mutually mediating relationship, and as such it is "a single unifying reality," "a unifying unity," or "the unity that unifies and is not itself only subsequently united."[49] The distinction, therefore, strictly speaking, is not between historical liberation and transcendent salvation as two mutually external spheres but between liberation and salvation within *the unity of salvation itself.* They are internally united, but the principle of that unity is not, contrary to Ratzinger, liberation or utopia but salvation, not history but God. It is God herself/himself who posits the history of liberation with its autonomy, which as *created* autonomy could never be total, and subjects it to her/his own transcendent agency and finality. In Hegelian terms, God posits the *otherness* of human history yet also "sublates" (*aufhebt*) it, that is, purifies, preserves and elevates it to the level of her/his own intentionality. God posits history in its autonomy, purifies it of every idolatrous self-absolutization, and transforms it into a symbol which at once concretizes and points to the Kingdom.[50]

Salvation, then, transcends liberation as a totality transcends its parts, and in this sense liberation is only partial, not total, salvation. Insofar as liberation is internal to salvation, however, this *partial* salvation is still partial *salvation* or has an intrinsically salvific significance. TL seeks to maintain "the correct 'partial' identification of social liberation with salvation, and the correct subordination of the former to the latter," and "to maintain the unity of the history of God *with,* and *within,* its vehicle, the history of men and women, in the spirit of Chalcedon: 'without confusion, yet without separation.'"[51] For there is

> only one human destiny, irreversibly assumed by Christ, the Lord of history. His redemptive work embraces *all* the dimensions of existence and brings them to their fullness. The history of salvation is the very heart of human history.[52]

Thus "the growth of the Kingdom is a process which occurs historically *in* liberation," and "the historical, political liberating event *is* the growth of the Kingdom and *is* a salvific event," although "it is not *the* coming of the Kingdom, not *all* of salvation."[53] In this sense, "those who reduce the work of salvation are indeed those who limit it to the strictly 'religious' sphere and are not aware of the universality of the process,"[54] just as, for Hegel, those who reduce the transcendence of the infinite are precisely those who separate the infinite from the finite in a purely external relationship and are not aware of the totalizing power and function of the 'true' infinite.

Three Dimensions of Liberation: Their Distinction

This unity and totality of the history of salvation, however, is not an undifferentiated unity. It is a single process, with inner differentiation. Within this unity of salvific history, TL generally distinguishes three distinct dimensions or levels. The first level is that of the historical praxis of social, political, and economic liberation; the second is that of the transformation of culture, of human self-consciousness based on a utopian philosophical anthropology which sees history as a process of human self-liberation for the realization of the possibilities of authentic existence; and the third is the theological dimension of faith, liberation from sin, and reconciliation with God and other humans.[55] How, then, are these dimensions distinct from one another, and how are they also mutually related? Furthermore, does TL relate them without, as Ratzinger suspects, reducing their distinction to nothing?

First, consider the real difference or distinction among the three dimensions. The first dimension is the political praxis of liberating and transforming oppressive structures—social, economic and political—and creating a just society. Here 'liberation' serves as a key concept, as is clear from the very naming of "Theology of Liberation." Originally derived from the various phases of the modern Enlightenment—Kantian, Marxian and Freudian—it is also used as an antithesis to the concept of 'development,' which has been much touted as a solution to the problems of the Third World since the fifties.[56]

There are three aspects to the concept of liberation which must be noted. The first is that it is revolutionary, in the sense of structural change. In contrast to the notion of development, which implies gradual, evolutionary improvement of the standard of living within the structure of capitalism while maintaining the oppressive dependence of the poor on the wealthy, of the Third World nations on the First World, liberation stresses the necessity of changing the structure of dependence and creating a new social order free of oppression and injustice. Second, unlike the reified and individualistic notion of freedom in capitalist societies, liberation implies a constant and ongoing process of collective struggle against the forces of oppressive structures. Liberation is not something given once and for all when it receives legal recognition, as are the freedoms of bourgeois capitalism; it is something to be fought for and deepened ever anew through social collaboration. Third, while developmentalism assumes a harmonistic vision of society and conceals the existence of social divisions and contradictions, liberation is predicated on an explicit recognition of such divisions and conflicts and seeks to create a classless society, which necessarily implies struggle against the privileged class that has a vested interest in the maintenance of the status quo. In this struggle neither pious exhortations to moral conversion nor rhetorical appeals to the common good will do. What is needed is political action—i.e., mobilization of the poor masses in confrontation with the powers that be.

If political liberation has to do with the transformation of conditions and structures, the second dimension, cultural revolution or liberation, is concerned with the transformation of our self-consciousness as humans—i.e., our basic attitudes towards ourselves and others and our vision of what it means to be human. Capitalism and socialism are themselves embodiments of a basic human option regarding the ideals of authentic human existence and human relations. Human liberation is not completed with the liberation of structures; it also requires the liberation of enslaving and oppressive mentalities and the creation of a new image of humanity and humane social existence. The goal of liberation for TL is not, as in the vision of "developmentalism" or as Ratzinger seems to charge, the production of an economically affluent and politically legitimate society. For Gutierrez, "beyond—or rather, through—the struggle against misery, injustice, and exploitation the goal is the *creation of a new man*."[57] Humans must appropriate new attitudes, new outlooks, and new ideals, in particular the ideals of autonomy instead of dependence, of fraternal solidarity instead of divisive individualism. Here it is essential to stress the importance of *self*-liberation—not, of course, in the sense intended by paternalism and reformism, that individuals should seek their own liberation in an individualistic way and afterwards perhaps struggle for the liberation of others, as though liberation of some individuals *as* individuals were possible in a generally oppressive society. Self-liberation is stressed in the sense that one must become aware of the fact that one cannot be truly liberated as an individual when society as such remains alienated and oppressive, and that one should identify with those who bear the brunt of oppression. The self to be liberated from dependence to autonomy is not the isolated and individualistic self, but the self conscious of itself as a member of an interdependent humanity and therefore in solidarity with others.[58]

Humans must be liberated from naive consciousness, which takes the oppressive status quo as given, to politically mature, critical consciousness, which sees the status quo as a *product* of a process of interaction among human interests and groups. They must be liberated from passive consciousness, which takes their present condition as an immutable fate, to active consciousness, which sees human history as something made by humans and therefore as something that *can* be humanized by self-conscious, collective human effort. What is required, in Hegelian language, is a transition from consciousness to self-consciousness, from a despairing acquiescence in history to a hope and confidence in the liberating possibilities of history. History is not the past, the repetition of the same, but the future open to qualitatively new and different possibilities of being human.[59] This cultural liberation, of course, is no more a 'once and for all' affair than is political liberation; it is just as much a process to be ever renewed and deepened. This is all the more so given the historical fact that liberators often turn into oppressors once the revolution is over. The temptation to domination and oppression is always present, and so is the necessity of constant vigilance against the possibilities of new modes of oppression.[60] In this sense, the goal "is not only better living conditions, a radical change of structures, a social revolution; it is much more: the continuous creation, never ending, of a new way to be a man, a *permanent cultural revolution*."[61]

The third dimension is that of faith, the realm of human relationships with God and one another as interpreted in light of God's gracious self-revelation in Jesus of Nazareth. It is the realm of sin and grace, of rejection of God and neighbor and salvation from sin and communion with God and others, of the eschatological finality of human existence, the horizon of transcendence from which everything human and historical must receive its ultimate interpretation and judgment. It is the realm of the Kingdom of God, God's free initiative in creation and redemption, God's judgment and promise regarding the ultimate destiny of the human creature. The dimension of faith is a dimension beyond all human knowledge and achievement. "The Kingdom must not be confused with the establishment of a just society."[62] Just as "a social transformation, no matter how radical it may be, does not automatically achieve the suppression of all evils,"[63] so historical liberations "do not establish the eschatological state."[64] As sin, alienation from God, is the ultimate root of all injustice and evil in the world, so salvation or liberation from sin is "the ultimate precondition for a just society and a new man," a precondition available "only through the acceptance of the liberating gift of Christ, which surpasses all expectations."[65]

Regarding the real distinction between the theological dimension of faith and human experience, which must always be understood in the context of the basic unity mentioned earlier, Jon Sobrino brings out another aspect of the distinction from the perspective of an anthropology of concrete totality. For Sobrino, there have been three ways, throughout history, of affirming the transcendence of God, each of which presupposes a different kind of anthropology. The classical, metaphysical approach, based on an intellectualist anthropology, consists of a theoretical affirmation of God's otherness by way of analogical predication. It seeks to know God "in himself" by means of metaphysical attribution. The 'other' to which God's otherness is addressed is the human being taken as an intellect. The second, existentialist approach, that of Kiekegaard and his followers, is based on an anthropology which takes human life as personal existence responsible for itself and to be accepted in commitment amid the ambiguities of life. Reason is not independent of but a dimension of this existence, which as such transcends it. God's transcendence, then, is not so much to be intellectually affirmed as to be accepted and experienced in existence, and thus as a scandal to human reason demanding a 'crucifixion of the understanding.' God is 'other' not to theoretical reason but to the personal subject of existence as an individual totality.

The third approach to divine transcendence, that of TL, is different from both the classical metaphysical and the modern existentialist approaches. For TL the human subject is neither the cognitive nor the existential individual but a concrete totality, a subject who must pursue his or her cognitive and existential transcendence to God only in and through concrete society and history, amid social contradictions and historical conflicts. The negativity to be overcome in transcendence is not primarily that of intellectual ignorance, or of existential ambiguity and personal suffering, but precisely that inherent in the historical situation of poverty, injustice, and oppression. What is required, therefore, is not merely the acquisition of knowledge—even through revelation—or the sacrifice of the intellect, but the crucifixion of human life as a concrete totality: the transformation of oppressive structures, in accordance with the demand of the Kingdom, and the suffering entailed in the following of Jesus in political praxis. God's otherness or transcendence is not addressed primarily to the intellect or personal existence but to the subject of concrete totality and praxis, which is to affirm that transcendence not only by changing our knowledge or personal existence but most importantly by transforming, i.e., concretely transcending, the oppressive status quo of contemporary history. The transcendence of God is not simply an object of theoretical contemplation or a call to personal repentance; it is primarily a call to concrete historical transcendence of sin and evil on the basis of the eschatological hope in the definitive Kingdom of God of the future.[66] As Clodovis Boff put it earlier, in TL, "transcendence is practice, not rhetoric."

Each of these three dimensions, political, cultural, and eschatological, whose distinction is clear enough, likewise has a distinctive rationality of its own to guide and evaluate our actions and experiences in each dimension. The praxis of political liberation is to be guided by scientific rationality, the rationality of the social sciences, political, economic, and sociological, with emphasis on the critical analysis of social structures. I have already elaborated on this socioanalytic mediation in the preceding chapter.

To respond briefly to Ratzinger, who criticizes Gutierrez for not providing any empirical analysis despite his talk about its necessity and for not giving concrete empirical content to liberation, it can be said that both charges, while they may seem factually true, are unfair. It is true that there is not much empirical social-scientific analysis of the situation in Gutierrez and TL in general, but this is not to say that they reduce the autonomy of empirical rationality to nothing. They generally presuppose the results of the social analyses already given by many Latin American social scientists, notably the theorists of dependence. Furthermore, they are primarily theologians, not social scientists: they do not presume to substitute for the work of the latter, precisely out of respect for their autonomy. In general, TL tries to integrate the results of critical social science to a degree never attempted by any traditional theology. In this regard the relation between TL and social science is analogous to the relation between contemporary European theology, such as that of Rahner and Ratzinger himself and philosophy. Both Rahner and Ratzinger stress the necessity of philosophy in and for theology, but neither of them would consider it an absolute condition for doing theology to engage in explicit philosophical analysis of all the concepts and categories they do borrow—and simply assume—from contemporary philosophers; and yet no one would thereby think of accusing them of denying the autonomy of philosophy and reducing it to theology.

Nor is it fair to assail Gutierrez for not providing concrete empirical content to liberation. In general terms, the praxis of political liberation consists of mobilizing the poor so as to transform the structure of society such that all would be guaranteed basic human rights, political *and* economic, through a system of political representation and socialization of major industries. The system Gutierrez and TL favor, in this respect, approximates that of democratic socialism. Beyond this general outline of a future society, however, it would not be possible to give any more specific political and economic content to the idea of liberation. By its very nature, political praxis is always relative to the changing dialectic of the historical situation, and to demand more than such an outline would be to demand the gift of prophecy regarding the future yet to be shaped and to lack a sense of the contingencies of history, as though political praxis ever claimed to eliminate such contingencies. Strategies and programs are meant to be elaborated in a constant dialectic with the changing situation, not predetermined for all situations.

The praxis of cultural liberation is to be guided by the rationality of philosophy, especially a philosophical anthropology which not only spells out the essential structures and constitutive relations of human existence but also integrates these into a "utopian" philosophy of history that views history as a process of the actualization of the ideals and hopes of human liberation. This dynamic, historically oriented anthropology sees a dialectic between essential structures and sociohistorical developments, and thus avoids the ahistorical, asocial, and static essentialism so characteristic of traditional philosophical anthropology, as well as the latter's fatalistic, conservative reification of history as something simply independent of collective human efforts and aspirations.

What is and is not possible for human existence is not something simply *given* once and for all; it is something ultimately to be decided by history. There are possibilities of transformation in history—as witness the many epochal and revolutionary transitions—which are usually unsuspected and often covered up by reigning ideologies, and which become actualities in times of critical change. To explore the liberating possibilities inherent in history, therefore, requires the mediation of creative imagination which is rooted in the unsuspected potential of the present yet transcendent and subversive of its reified phenomenality. This is the sort of creative imagination found in all genuine sciences; it is also present in the utopian element that underlies the rationality of liberating anthropology. The ability to project new possibilities is not contrary to rationality but constitutes the dynamic and mobilizing element of true rationality.[67]

Regarding this philosophical anthropology, Ratzinger accuses Gutierrez of simply assuming, not justifying the utopian principle; of having an irrational faith in history; and of reducing the metaphysics of human beings to a physics of mechanistic necessity. That Gutierrez assumes the utopian principle, I believe, must be granted; he did not produce a metaphysics of hope à la Marcel, a theology of hope à la Moltmann, or a grand historical speculation on the role of hope à la Bloch. Nevertheless, he does elaborate his anthropology at some length, in dialogue with traditional thought and drawing on the insights of Hegel, Marx, Marcel, Moltmann, and Bloch. Again, it is to be wondered whether it is fair to ask someone who is primarily a theologian to produce a fresh justification of the philosophical insights he or she borrows from professional philosophers. Of course, some theologians, such as Tillich and Rahner, do this, but most do not. As far as I know, Ratzinger has not produced an independent justification of the dialogical personalism underlying his own theology. The issue, therefore, is not whether a theologian does or does not provide his own justification of the philosophical foundations of his theology, but whether the philosophical tradition he borrows from enjoys certain validity and relevance.

Regarding this validity, Ratzinger seems to be raising two issues: that faith in history is irrational and that Gutierrez reduces metaphysics of human being to a physics of mechanistic necessity. The two issues are in fact one. Ratzinger assumes that history as history of human freedom is so contingent that no speculation or hope regarding history is rationally possible, or that it is possible only on condition that one denies freedom, reduces metaphysics to physics, and renders history a succession of mechanistically determined events. The choice is between freedom and utter contingency on the one hand and determinism and necessity on the other.[68] He is not aware of a third possibility, the construction of a new future which depends on two things: free collective human effort to shape history according to desirable ideals and the hope that such shaping of history is truly, not just abstractly, possible.

This need not mean that humans can plan or predict every detail of history; after all, as Hegel pointed out, there is such a thing as unintended consequences, not only of individual action but also of collective action. It does mean that insofar as history is a product of collective human action, it is possible to try to shape at least its outline in the direction of liberating ideals according to the best scientific insights available regarding the concrete dynamics of history and the real possibilities of change latent in it. This sort of attempt, in turn, would not be possible without hope in the future, a hope which, unlike mere 'wish,' does not dispense with the need for concrete action. Such action is in part based on the past experience of actual achievements of human hopes while also projecting itself towards the future. This hope need not be predicated on the assumption that there are no retrogressions, failures, or defeats in history—past history invalidates such an assumption, as Hegel himself knew; by the same token, it is precisely hope which sustains human struggles in the midst of the setbacks and failures—some temporary, some protracted—which are inevitable in any attempt for structural change, as history amply shows. The alternative would be to leave our common future not just to neutral chance or accident, but to the forces of oppression, who are indeed always planning and manipulating the course of events to maintain themselves in power.

The praxis of faith is to be guided by the rationality of theology, which, as also discussed in the preceding chapter, consists not only of interpreting the data of faith and revelation but also of reflecting on the *contemporary* demand and meaning of those data—the dialectic between the Word of God in Scripture and contemporary experience.

Three Dimensions of Liberation: Their Relation

How are these three distinct dimensions of liberation mutually related? For TL, as elaborated earlier, in a general way, in this and the preceding chapters, their relation is one of mutual intrinsic mediation as moments of an essential totality, not one of contingent, extrinsic connection as among parts of an accidental totality. The distinctions of the dimensions arise from the basic unity of one history, a 'Christo-finalized' history, and must be understood on that basis: "the salvific action of God underlies *all* human existence. The historical destiny of humanity must be placed definitively in the salvific horizon."[69]

Consider, first, the relation between political liberation and cultural liberation. The praxis of political liberation which seeks to transform and humanize oppressive structures is pregnant with the future in a number of ways. The commitment to such praxis presupposes negation of present reality and denunciation of the existing order by affirming and announcing new, alternative possibilities and ideals of human existence, which serve as both the criterion for the criticism of the present and the goal to be achieved by present praxis. It is the affirmation of these critical norms of new and alternative modes of existence which makes it possible to recognize the present as dehumanizing, unmask its ideology, and mobilize human action to transform it. Such affirmation, however, presupposes a creative hope in the future or utopia (Ernst Bloch) in the sense of an imaginative break with the reified present in favor of new, creative possibilities and of a confidence in the future as capable of actualizing such qualitatively different possibilities. Without this utopian hope, political praxis would lack the existential energy to sustain it in the midst of conflicts and protect it against the ever-present temptations to despair. It would remain in the grip of the present, evolutionary and reformist at best, and at worst always liable to a lapse into reactionary nostalgia for the past or a closed ideological dogmatism which absolutizes a particular historical achievement. Without that hope and the concurrent implementation of that hope in the cultural liberation of new human and social consciousness, the political liberation of structures alone is likely to betray its original purpose and turn into the creation of a new structure of oppression, an inhuman bureaucracy. Cultural revolution must inform, guide, and be pursued simultaneously with, not postponed until after, political liberation.[70]

If the utopian principle of cultural liberation mediates political liberation as a dynamic and mobilizing factor, as a principle of critical, historical transcendence, concrete political praxis in turn mediates the utopia as a principle of concretizing realism. In order to fulfill its subversive, mobilizing funtion, the utopia must maintain its orientation not only to the future but also to the present. After all, it is the present which must be transformed. The utopia is effective only to the extent that it transforms the present, and thus must be verified in terms of present political praxis. Likewise, the possibilities of transformation the utopia projects into the future must be rooted in the historical present; not everything is possible at all times. Present political praxis thus concretizes the utopia by testing its efficacy in the realities of the present and by plumbing its unsuspected yet real possibilities of transformation. Without this concretizing mediation by political praxis the utopia would become 'utopian' in the usual, pejorative sense—the empty and ultimately evasive idealism dismissed by Hegel in the *Phenomenology of Spirit,* the "utopian," not "scientific," socialism in Engels's sense, a futuristic illusion—of which Moltmann's hope tends to be guilty.[71]

What, then, is the mutual mediation or contribution between the utopian anthropological vision and Christian faith, between the hopeful projection of ever more authentic possibilities of human existence within history and the experience of God? First, we consider the utopian mediation of faith. Perhaps the best way of defining this mediation, not as clearly presented in TL as are the mediations between political praxis and utopian hope and between political praxis and faith, is to use an analogy with the concept of 'transcendence' in the theology of Karl Rahner. For Rahner, whose concern has been to avoid traditional dualism and extrinsicism, transcendence—in the sense of the ontological drive towards the 'more,' absolute being or mystery—is both an 'existential' of human existence and the point of contact with divine revelation and grace. It is the human correlative and the human condition—itself posited by God—for the possibility of the "supernatural existential" or God's offer of grace. It is through this existential transcendence that humans can "hear" the Word of God, that God is known and anticipated.[72]

TL, of course, works with a different anthropology. For TL the human subject is not, as for Rahner—at least the early Rahner—primarily the subject of cognitive ontological transcendence but that of a concrete totality, i.e., transcendence towards God through concrete history. Nevertheless, transcendence through history, symbolized by the utopia—i.e., the striving towards ever more authentic possibilities of existence in history which is at the same time aware of its own limits and points beyond itself towards the transhistorical—is the human correlative and condition for the possibility of divine revelation and faith. The utopian hope in a society of solidarity and love is an implicit yearning for the eschatological Kingdom of justice and love and a historical, not merely cognitive, anticipation of that Kingdom. It implies a yearning for total liberation, liberation from all that alienates humans from one another, and thus also from sin and death. At the same time, just as, for Rahner, transcendental theology keeps Christian revelation from lapsing into mythology so the utopia, a critical principle of self-transcendence in history, prevents eschatological salvation from falling into idealism and escapism, as it also keeps political praxis from the danger of ideology and political messianism. Thus, as the inspiring and critical *telos* of political liberation within history but also by pointing to the transhistorical fulfillment of the human hope in the eschatological Kingdom, the utopia mediates between political praxis and Christian faith.[73]

Contrary to Ratzinger's charge that TL renders Christian faith "totally functionless," it is faith that in turn mediates the utopia by opening up a horizon that gives salvific meaning, moral motivation, self-critical principle, and transcendent hope to the utopian struggles for political liberation. To be sure, the Gospel does not provide a recipe for a utopia or norms and criteria for particular political options at a particular time. The utopian projections must be guided by philosophical rationality, political actions and strategies by rational analysis of the structural dynamics of a particular society. In this sense, the relation between faith and the utopian struggle for liberation is not a direct or immediate relation, which would ignore the mutual autonomy or 'otherness' of faith and politics and only result in dangerous politico-religious messianism or 'pre-critical' sacralization of politics. This does not mean, however, that they are merely juxtaposed or unrelated, which would often lead to opportunistic alignment of faith with *any* political option.[74] Rather, the relation lies at a deeper level, the level of ultimate meaning and transcendent motivation. Through the mediation of the utopian dimension, the horizon of faith, the unifying, totalizing dimension of the three as mentioned earlier, transforms the profane meaning of liberation struggles into events with transcendent, salvific significance. "Faith reveals to us the deep meaning of the history which we fashion with our own hands."[75] The salvific process "gives human history its profound unity,"[76] and "seeing human history as a history in which the liberation of Christ is at work broadens our outlook and gives the political commitment its full depth and genuine meaning."[77]

More specifically, faith provides theological, moral motivation to political praxis. The ultimate motive for participating in the struggle for liberation is "the conviction of the radical incompatibility of evangelical demands with an unjust and alienating society."[78] The promise of the Kingdom "reveals to society itself the aspiration for a just society and leads it to discover unsuspected dimensions and unexplored paths," and thus "the political is grafted into the eternal."[79] After all, the basic obstacle to the Kingdom and our eschatological salvation is sin, the selfish rejection of God and neighbor, which is not an abstraction but manifests itself in historical realities concretized in unjust and oppressive institutions and structures, and which constitutes the ultimate source of injustice and oppression. "Behind an unjust structure there is a personal or collective will responsible—a willingness to reject God and neighbor."[80] "For freedom Christ set us free" (Gal. 5:1), and "the freedom to which we are called presupposes the going out of oneself, the breaking down of our selfishness and of all the structures that support our selfishness."[81] "All struggle against exploitation and alienation," therefore, "in a history which is fundamentally one, is an attempt to vanquish selfishness, the negation of love."[82] In this sense, the struggle to build a just society "has an indirect but effective impact on the fundamental alienation. It is a salvific work, although it is not all of salvation."[83] It is "not simply a stage of 'humanization' or 'pre-evangelization'" but "part of a saving process which embraces the whole of man and all human history."[84] "Every human act which is oriented towards the construction of a more just society has value in terms of communion with God—in terms of salvation," just as, inversely, "all injustice is a breach with him."[85]

Faith also provides a self-critical principle to the praxis of liberation. It not only makes us critically sensitive to the presence of sin in oppression and injustice; it also makes the praxis of liberation critical of its own motives, strategies, and the temptation to absolutize itself. It makes sure that "evangelical motives preside over that praxis,"[86] and "keeps us from any confusion of the Kingdom with any one historical stage, from any idolatry toward unavoidably ambiguous human achievement, from any absolutizing of revolution."[87] Thus, faith "simultaneously demands and judges" our political praxis.[88]

The eschatological perspective of faith likewise gives transcendent support to the utopian hope in the possibilities of historical liberation. The divine promise of the eschatological fulfillment of human existence is indeed a projection

towards the future, the end of history; however, as studies of Old Testament pro-
phets make clear, it is not merely a future event, a "not yet," which has inspired
so much escapism and historical pessimism in the past, but also an "already,"
with a demand on the present to begin to conform to the values and expectations
whose complete realization doubtless lies in the future. Prophetic messages are
proclaimed in the present and for the present even while projected beyond the
present. The future promised by God demands and inspires actions in the present. This attraction of what is yet to come constitutes the driving force of history,
its constant mobility. God's action in history and God's action at the end of history
are inseparable. As Gutierrez puts it:

> The full significance of God's action in history is understood only when
> it is put in its eschatological perspective; similarly, the revelation of the
> final meaning of history gives value to the present. The self-communication
> of God points towards the future, and at the same time this Promise and
> Good News reveal man to himself and widen the perspective of historical
> commitment here and now.[89]

This eschatological hope in the Lord of history, of the present as well as of the
future, provides divine support to the utopian hopes of historical liberation. It
protects against despair, and inspires the conviction that a just society is something
"possible," that the struggle for liberation "is not in vain," that "God calls us
to it and assures us of its complete fulfillment."[90] Thus, "to hope in Christ is
at the same time to believe in the adventure of history, which opens infinite vistas
to the love and action of the Christian."[91]

The praxis of political liberation, in turn, mediates faith by "concretizing"
in history the demand and perspective of faith. As mentioned earlier in this
chapter, this is not a question of "external" mediation of faith by political praxis
as though the two were originally (*ursprünglich*) mutually independent realities,
but one of internal "self-mediation" of faith through a praxis internally demanded
and inspired by it. For faith, or its object, God, remains the unifying, totalizing
power of all the dimensions of human existence and history. Within this divine
totality the role of political praxis, as elaborated in some detail in the preceding
chapter, is to "respond" and "attest" to the eschatological values and demands
by concretizing, incarnating, and "symbolizing" them in concrete historical
situations.[92] For God's love for all humans, especially the poor, "must be given
substance in history and must become history," and in this sense "the political
dimension is *inside* the dynamism of a Word which seeks to become incarnate
in history."[93] It goes without saying that this concretizing praxis, as mentioned
in the preceding chapter, also "discloses" new meanings and dimensions of faith
even while illumined by it.[94]

In TL, then, the theological dimension of salvation and faith mediates the
historical dimension of the utopian struggles for political and cultural liberation

as the unifying or *totalizing* principle of the latter, while the latter mediates the former as its *concretizing* principle, which makes salvation historically effective. If the conceptualization of salvation as transcendent yet also inclusive of historical liberation is due, at least in its *Denkform,* to Hegel's dialectical conception of God *in* history, not to speak of the biblical tradition, the utopian conception of history as a process of collective self-liberation of humanity and the imperative to make human liberation real and effective in concrete history are clearly traceable to Marx. If the emphasis on salvation as total liberation is a reaction to the traditional tendency to 'spiritualize' salvation by limiting its scope to the 'religious' dimension, the emphasis on political praxis as a means of making salvation historically and socially concrete is a reaction to the tendency of tradition to stress the importance of ulitimate ends— transcendent salvation—and neglect that of concrete ways and means to make such ends effective and actual.[95]

Perhaps another way of putting this mediation between the historical dimension of politics and the transcendent dimension of faith is to compare TL and Ratzinger in their respective interpretation of the event of the Exodus. Ratzinger recognizes that the Exodus is a political event ("represents freedom from foreign domination and from slavery," iv, 3), but insists that this political content is not its "specific" significance, which comes from "its purpose," "the foundation of the people of God and the covenant cult" (iv, 3) and ultimately "a figure of baptism" (x, 14). Thus, "the liberation of the Exodus cannot be reduced to a liberation which is principally or exclusively political in nature" (iv, 3). Ratzinger thus opposes the historical political "content" of the Exodus to its salvific "purpose" and insists on the specificity and irreducibility of the latter to the former. He ignores the fact that precisely that "purpose" became concrete and actual *through* that "content," and fails to state the positive connection between the two, which he leaves merely juxtaposed.

As if to anticipate this charge, as early as his *Theology of Liberation,* Gutierrez agreed with Ratzinger that throughout the whole process of liberation from Egypt "the religious event is not set apart," that this religious event is "its deepest meaning," namely, that "Yahweh liberates the Jewish people politically in order to make a holy nation," that "the Covenent gives full meaning to liberation from Egypt."[96] Yet Gutierrez does not merely juxtapose the political content of the Exodus and its religious meaning. Rather, he sees a mutual inner mediation between the two: "one makes no sense without the other," and they are "different aspects of the same movement."[97]

> The Exodus affords a grasp of the perspective in which the covenant is *situated,* and the covenant in turn gives full *meaning* to the liberation from Egypt. Liberation leads to communion. This is the *process* by which the "people of God" is built.[98]

For TL the question is not one of keeping the political and the religious separate for fear of reductionism, although such separation would result precisely in reducing total salvation to the religious, but one of accentuating the respective significance of *both* within the *unity* of the event. To ask whether the exodus is "principally" or even "uniquely" either "political" or "religious" in nature would be to commit the "category mistake," reducing the internally unified totality of the event to an entity of mutually separable dimensions or parts to which one may then selectively assign "principal" or marginal significance. For TL the event of the exodus is both *wholly* political and *wholly* religious—the former as the concretizing, the latter as the finalizing principle of the whole. Without the political liberation in the order of historical efficacy, the religious meaning of the Covenant in the order of transcendent finality would have been only an abstraction imposed on concrete historical existence from outside, just as the political liberation would have lost its ultimate significance without the religious meaning. To separate or merely juxtapose them would be to do justice neither to the politics of the exodus nor to its theology, reducing all the pain of political liberation to a mere show at best accidental to the covenant, and the Covenant itself to an event which is in history yet without significance for that history. Segundo puts the relationship succinctly: "the God of liberation revealed and transmitted his word *through* his activity of freeing the Hebrews from Egyptian imperialism."[99]

It is important at this point to stress the kind of unity TL attributes to the three dimensions or levels. Enough has been said about the theological dimension of salvation as the unifying principle of the three. It is likewise necessary to point out that they are not to be taken as merely parallel or chronologically successive dimensions, which would lapse into idealism and immediatism.[100] The three dimensions are not three separable realities but one and the same reality considered from three formally different points of view. What is oppressive inequality from a sociological point of view is the moral vice of injustice from the philosophical and the sin of hubris and hatred from the theological perspective, which looks at all reality *sub ratione salutis et peccati,* as symbols of grace and sin. The political act of educating and mobilizing the poor is a concrete embodiment of both a philosophical vision of authentic existence and a theological virtue of charity. In this sense, the three dimensions are formally distinct but materially identical.[101]

Likewise, the unity of the dimensions does not imply either mechanical necessity or absolute agreement. The theological dimension of salvation and faith depends on God's free and gratuitous act and free human response, as the political dimension has to take into account the contingent facticities of history, which is precisely why TL insists on the need for empirical studies. The utopian vision of history as a history of freedom certainly does not assume a mechanistically determined linear development. It is an expression of both a protest against the fatalistic reification of history, which is itself a kind of determinism, and a hope in the openness of history and the possibility of shaping it according to human aspirations under the providence of the Lord of history. By the same token, there is no absolute agreement among the three dimensions in the sense of a one-to-one correspondence. As the lower dimensions are concretizing symbols of the higher, and as symbols are always multivalent and multidimensional, so they symbolize the higher in an open form. The perspective of faith is not exhausted by any one utopian vision of authentic existence in history, any more than it could be exhaustively realized by any one political action, strategy, or system, just as it does not dictate any one political option, although this does not mean that *all* options are equally legitimate or prudent.[102]

DIALECTIC OF SOCIAL AND PERSONAL SIN

The Social and the Personal

If salvation thus transforms the very meaning of history into an inner moment of salvation history, it is through historical liberation that salvation becomes historically effective. If salvation is the totalizing principle for the unity of salvation and liberation, liberation is the concretizing principle of that unity. TL calls special attention to social sin and to the praxis of political liberation as a central, although not the only, dimension of this liberating process. In this regard it is worth recalling Ratzinger's charge that TL wholly forgets the transcendence of human dignity and personal freedom and the need for interior conversion, reducing them to the social and political as something antithetical to the personal.

Regarding this charge, I think two things must be said. On the one hand, it is simply not true that TL ignores the transcendent claims of personal dignity and freedom or the need for personal conversion. What it does is to place such concerns in the concrete social context of personal existence in which they arise; only there can they be effectively met, if at all. On the other hand, it is true that TL does ignore or at least has nothing important to say about the existential problems that have so preoccupied Kierkegaard, Dostoevsky, the early Heidegger, Bultmann, and Tillich. Insofar as the problems of "existence" are not *simply* reducible to those of "history" it remains incumbent on TL to show their inner relationship and mutual mediation. What will not do is merely to juxtapose existence and history side by side and to ignore the concrete inner unity of the person, the subject of both.

Despite this difference between Ratzinger and TL, however, what is really at stake in the dispute is a more fundamental difference in the way of conceiving the very relation between the individual and society. For Ratzinger, sin is primarily an affair in the inwardness of the individual, and social sin only a "consequence" or "effect" of individual sins. By the same token, the inward conversion of individuals, it is assumed, will necessarily result in the reform of social structures as its effect. What is implicit in this view, then, is a conception of society as, in Segundo's expression, "the end result of juxtaposing already constituted individuals,"[103] a mere collection of individuals with no antecedent relations constituting the conditions of their existence. Social sin is not greater than the sum of individual sins. It is sin only in an analogous, not a proper sense. (See the following chapter for a fuller discussion of Ratzinger's position.)

For TL, on the other hand, as for much of contemporary thought in the tradition of Hegel, Marx, and Dewey, society is "from the very first a system of human reactions and interrelationships that constitute the individual and form part of his total human condition."[104] Individuals neither come into existence nor shape their existence in isolation; at all stages they are dependent on their fellows and are *internally* constituted by these relations of interdependence already there as the very condition of their individual existence. 'Being-with' *(Mitsein),* not in the abstract, ahistorical phenomenological sense but in the sense of always and already being involved with others in a particular society at a particular time as the inner environment of one's own life, is an "existential" of all human existence. By the same token, society is not an impersonal thing opposed to the personal; it is precisely "a system of human reactions and interrelationships" of individuals in their constitutive interdependence which has been objectified— often, indeed, reified—into political, economic, and cultural institutions and structures. It is individuals themselves, not in isolation but in their togetherness, who constitute the subject of society, its relations and objectifications, and who are therefore collectively responsible for both its good and evil. The proper contrast, then, is not between individuals on the one hand and society on the other, but between individuals considered in their (relative) isolation and individuals considered in their concrete association. By the same token, society and its institutions should not be seen as merely a "means" external to the individuals, to be exploited for private ends, as bourgeois individualism would have it. Such institutions are actualizing expressions, however dialectical and ambiguous, of the very ends and social subjectivity of the associated individuals who remain the ultimate subject of society.[105]

Personal freedom, whether civic, intellectual, or existential, is always situated in this sociohistorical context. The transcendence of the person in the inwardness of his or her free act is always a transcendence within this society and history. The relation to transcendence and the relation to society are not merely juxtaposed and external; they are mutually mediating, although not reducible, dimensions within the unity of the person. It is the whole person who is transcendent as a free being, and it is likewise the whole person whose existence is concretely mediated by the historically given social relations, ideologies, and institutional structures. Both the freedom to sin and the freedom to reform one's life are acts of the whole person as a concrete totality of transcendence and history, not of some purely spiritual, angelic interiority but of concrete subjects already immersed in and reacting to the pull and push of existing social conditons; these conditions generate the need for such free acts, challenge them positively or negatively, and in any case determine their limits. The anxiety in the presence of death, condemnation, and meaninglessness, respectively the absolute forms of ontic, moral, and spiritual experiences of non-being and finitude according to Tillich, is itself mediated and qualified by the relative forms of fate, guilt, and emptiness, each varying according to the dominant conflicts and contradictions of a particular society.[106]

This is not to deny the possibility of free self-determination or metaphysical and religious transcendence, but simply to recognize the sociohistorical limits of human freedom and human transcendence as a finite being. Human finitude means not only that our existence depends on the creative causality of God but also that it depends on others in history and society. This sociohistorical interdependence is but a relative expression of the absolute dependence on God. In this sense individuals and society, or, more accurately, individuals as individuals and individuals in their organized social interdependence, are not coequal powers. The freedom of the individual is conditioned by society, whose impact far surpasses that of the individual as such.

The Concept of Social Sin

For TL, two consequences follow from this. First, as "a human, social, and historical realilty which originates in a socially and historically situated freedom,"[107] sin

> cannot be touched in itself in the abstract. It can be attacked only in concrete historical situations—particular instances of alienation. Apart from particular, concrete alienation, sin is meaningless and incomprehensible.[108]

That is to say, even though there is indeed a transcendent dimension to sin as a distorted relation to God, the subject of that relation and sin is the concrete human subject, and it is imperative to understand sin as a reality expressive of and affecting the concrete sociohistorical *totality* of human existence, not to reify it by isolating it as a phenomenon of pure inwardness. Whether one isolates sin from God, as in true secularism, or from history, as in true 'spiritualism,' the result would be reifying reduction of sin to an abstraction. For Gutierrez, sin

> is not something that occurs only within some intimate sanctuary of the heart. It "always" translates into interpersonal relationships. . .and hence is the ultimate root of all injustice and oppression—as well as of the social confrontations and conflicts of concrete history.[109]

Sin, while the primary source of all evils, as Ratzinger rightly insists, is not a phenomenon of pure interiority but a reality of situated freedom in the concrete totality of existence. By the same token, the fundamental alienation which is sin cannot be removed either in toto or as a purely interior reality. It

can be removed only in the form of its concrete historical and thus partial mediations, just as the Kingdom is "not found in its totality but in its historical mediations."[110] To oppose the "radical slavery to sin" as of "fundamental" and
"primary importance" and servitudes of an "earthly" and "temporal" kind as
"secondary" (Introduction) and to fault TL for "reducing" the former to the
latter, as Ratzinger does, would be to commit a "category mistake" at best, and
at worst to fall into an inhuman dualism. It would be a category mistake in viewing
sin and oppression as two entities on the same level to which one must assign
differential importance, rather than as two dimensions of one and the same
reality—sin as the dimension of transcendent meaning, oppression as the
dimension of its historical concretion; it would be dualistic in ignoring the
concrete totality and unity of the subject of sin, ultimately reducing sin to an
abstraction and depriving oppression of its theological significance.

The second consequence is the primacy of social sin among sins and of the
praxis of political liberation among the means of salvation. Sin does involve the
abuse of human freedom and does call for interior conversion, but it is also
necessary to distinguish between personal and social sin, in accordance with
the structure of the human subject of freedom and sin. The subject of personal
sin is an individual in his or her (relatively) separate existence, and so is its object,
the victim. The consequence of personal sin is private, in the sense that it does
not seriously affect the life of individuals in their interdependence as a community. The extent of responsibility for personal sin is defined by the limit of
the subject's personal knowledge and his or her power to affect the course of
events. The subject of social sin, on the other hand, is any number of individuals
as associated, interdependent beings with power over the destiny of their community, regardless of whether they are government officials or not. Individuals
as citizens are also responsible for the social sin of their government insofar as
the latter depends on their democratic consent, as private businesses can be subjects of social sin to the extent that they control and exploit the mode of economic
interdependence or structure in the community for their selfish ends. The object
of social sin is the community of individuals and the structural and institutional
objectifications of that community. The extent of responsibility for social sin,
therefore, is defined by the extent to which individuals, as members of an organized community and thus together with others, can know and control the consequences of their communal actions.

As social life becomes increasingly interdependent and enables even
(relatively) separate individuals to affect the communal destiny of others, it is
likewise difficult to draw a sharp distinction between personal and social sin.
Nonetheless, such a distinction is crucial in assigning proper agency and responsibility for different kinds of action. Social sin is committed by individuals in their
associated existence who *together* produce consequences that go beyond their
separate individual intentions and wills and thus their separate individual responsibilities. The mere fact that individuals are not responsible for such sins as

separate individuals, however, does not mean that they can simply disown their responsibility. What they are not responsible for as separate individuals they are responsible for as associated individuals, for they remain the subject of social sin, which expresses their "collective will"[111] and which is objectified and often reified into degrading institutions and oppressive structures. This also means that social sin is sin in the most proper sense of the term, not merely by analogy with personal sin, with its own subject of freedom and responsibility.

Similarly, social sin is not merely, as Ratzinger claims, the "consequence" and "effect" of a sin which is primarily that of the individual in his or her separate existence. It lies in the rejection of God through the abuse and perversion of freedom—commissions and omissions, actions and passions—on the part of individuals precisely in their communal existence. Individuals are responsible for and guilty of what they do or fail to do communally, not only what they do or fail to do separately. Social sin likewise transcends the mere sum of individual sins and as such is a cause and source of sin in its own right. Just as a social structure is more than the sum of its component individuals, so its evil outweighs by far that of merely personal sin or even a collection of such sins in its scope, duration, and penetration. The structural evils of unjust economies and totalitarian political structures, as Ratzinger himself so well recognizes (without, however, drawing the logical conclusion), are more devastating than personal greed or personal ambition taken in isolation.

Structural sin and personal sin, then, are not two coequal realities; rather, structural sin functions as the totalizing context and condition within which personal sins occur. Contrary to Ratzinger's accusation, TL fully recognizes that structural change does not automatically abolish all personal sins, but it does abolish the effect of social, collective sin and provides a positive incentive and wholesome pressure for doing good as well as a negative pressure for avoiding evil. In this sense, "changing social and cultural structure is a way of changing the human heart,"[112] and "the individual can only be liberated within the total human condition, within his social context."[113] Total liberation requires the conversion not only of individuals but also of "the whole network of their active relationships that keep them bound to socioeconomic and political realities and their structured sinfulness."[114] In a continent such as Latin America, where the majority remain in a state of 'non-persons' and lack the minimum material and political conditions of 'personal' existence, a genuine concern precisely for the dignity and freedom of persons will make all the more imperative this struggle against structural sins with all their degrading and depersonalizing consequences.

The Meaning of the Political

If structural evil is more than the sum of individual sins, it also follows that the responsibility for it is the collective responsibility of a community of individuals, not that of isolated individuals, and that the action required is a collective, organized action, not the private, separate action of individuals. What individuals cannot accomplish as individuals, they can and must try to as a community. A true community, however, presupposes a shared perception of a common good and a shared willingness to engage in cooperative action for it. In existing societies, however, this is precisely what is lacking, as they are based on class antagonisms. What passes for the 'common good' is in reality a cover for the self-interest of those in power. The agency for the liberation of oppressive structures, therefore, necessarily falls on the oppressed class as a class, who can liberate themselves only by abolishing the structure of power and thus also by liberating the oppressors as well from that structure. The agent for social transformation, for TL, is not Hegel's 'world-historical' individuals and states or Marx's 'industrial proletariat,' but the oppressed poor of the Third world— the poor as a class, the collective victim of global capitalism.[115]

This collective action for the removal of social sin and the creation of structural conditions worthy of human dignity—the 'polis' of free persons—is precisely 'political' action in the best, classic, and salvific sense of the word. Just as Ratzinger seems to fail to appreciate the gravity of social sin, so he also fails to understand the true meaning of the political, as when he speaks of "the merely political." For TL, politics is not something one does occasionally as when one goes to the polls or out on the campaign trail. It is not an activity reserved for a particular occasion or a particular class, the professional politicians and lobbyists. It certainly does not mean the use of manipulative techniques, as in 'dirty politics.' To think of politics in this way would be precisely one of the bourgeois mystifications which renders the majority apolitical and thus serves the interest of the ruling class by immunizing and protecting it from all challenges from below.

The political sphere is a sphere in which the distribution and use of social power, power over others, is at stake, where the basic quality of human relations and self-determination is decided. Politics ultimately decides whether humans will live in reconciling solidarity or in sinful antagonism, whether they will treat one another as subjects of dignity or as objects of exploitation. As Gutierrez argues;

> it is within the context of the political that the human being rises up as a free and responsible being, as a truly human being, having a relationship with nature and with other human beings, as someone who takes up the reins of his or her destiny, and goes out and transforms history.[116]

In this sense, politics is "a dimension that embraces, and demandingly conditions, the entirety of human endeavors," "the global condition, and the collective field, of human accomplishment."[117]

That is, the political is not simply one particular dimension alongside of other dimensions of human existence, as Ratzinger seems to assume when he accuses TL of stressing "only" the political dimension, but a dimension which at the same time overreaches all others, a totalizing condition and context to which other dimensions and spheres of human life are subject although not simply reducible to it. The spheres of material and cultural production also both embody and affect the relations of power and can be humanized only through organized, collective action—i.e., political action. The emphasis of TL on politics thus highlights the pervasive influence of the relations of power, of domination and subjugation, in all spheres of human life, its consequences for human dignity, and the necessity and possibility of transformation through political action. As the cooperative action of the poor as a class, aimed at the creation of liberating structural conditions, then, the praxis of political liberation is the principal means of making the salvation of concrete human existence real and effective in history: it seeks to convert the principal, i.e., structural, social source and consequence of sin.

In assigning priority among the "means of salvation," Ratzinger wavers between two alternatives. On the one hand he seems committed to both the sacramental life in the Church and the praxis of social justice and liberation, seeing them as two "equally" important means. On the other, he leans in favor of the sacramental practice as something "special." In either case, the connection between the two is not clearly stated; they are merely juxtaposed. TL, on the other hand, does consider the praxis of liberation as the principal means of salvation without denying the importance of orthodoxy, cultic worship, and participation in the life of the Church as a whole. The praxis of discipleship through participation in political liberation is

> the most original and *all-embracing* reality, far more so than cultic worship and orthodoxy. Rather than being opposed to these latter, however, the following of Jesus *integrates* and *crystallizes* them.[118]

In other words, the praxis of political discipleship is the unifying and concretizing principle of which the sacramental life is an inner moment, into which it is meant to be integrated, and which it must serve by encouraging the concrete praxis of love and in turn expressing and celebrating that love. The Church and the sacraments are not ends in themselves; these are valuable precisely and only as the "effective sign" of concrete praxis, inspiring the faithful towards efficacious action and sacramentally celebrating that action of which it is meant to be a sign. They should not be reified as entities in themselves, apart from the service of the praxis of faith, the praxis of love and reconciliation in concrete history. This would indeed be, as Ratzinger charges, "a challenge to the sacramental and hierarchical structure of the Church" (ix, 13), but only if one would reify and separate such a structure from its historical mission of service "willed by the Lord himself" (ibid.).[119]

A word of clarification is in order at this point. In the preceding section of this chapter I called salvation the unifying, totalizing principle of salvation and liberation. In this section I used the same concept to describe the function of the political in relation to other spheres and dimensions of human existence. In what sense are both the dimensions of salvation and political praxis the totalizing principles of human existence? The answer, I think, is that the salvific action of God in history is the totalizing principle from the theological perspective of ultimate meaning and efficacy, which gives meaning and efficacy to the relative sphere of human history, whereas the political is the totalizing principle from the anthropological perspective of our historical participation in God's own meaning and efficacy. God's meaning and efficacy remain the totalizing principle in the absolute sense, while politics may be so only in the relative sense, only on condition that it is overreached, elevated, and empowered by God to share in God's own meaning and efficacy.

Responses to the Critics

What, then, can be said in response to the critical concerns raised earlier by existentialism, Hauerwas, and Whiteheadian ecological theology? Regarding the existentialist objection, TL does not deny the subjectivity of the subject, the irreplaceable responsibility of the subject for the authenticity of his or her own existence, or the reality of the experience of sin and finitude. The question is not whether humans are subjects but what they are to do precisely to actualize their subjectivity in authentic existence in a world of sin and finitude, given the historicity and sociality of existence and the Christian emphasis on self-sacrificing love and the hope in the Kingdom.

From this historical and theological perspective, TL is indeed critical of the tendency of existentialism to individualism, its indifference to the fate of fellow humans, and its historical and political pessimism.[120] TL argues that it is precisely in shifting the center of our life from our own existence to that of the other that we attain true authenticity, that it is in the concrete response to the needs of the marginalized Others of history that we realize our responsibility for ourselves, and that the proper Christian response to sin and finitude is not to dwell on one's own theological guilt and ontological impotence or on the universal futility of human effort ("vanity of vanities, and all is vanity"), which would only lead to un-Christian despair and repressive tolerance of historical injustices, but to sublate them (*Aufheben*) into active responses to the demands of the Kingdom in the overcoming of the historical sources and consequences of sinful finitude, sustained by hope in God's own absolute future. In concrete imitation of the crucified yet risen Lord, the Christian is to die to one's own self and live to the divine Other by living to the human Others in history in which God is especially present. We search for our own perfection not by commitment to our own existence but by commitment to the liberation of oppressed sisters and brothers. The ontic, moral, and spiritual anxiety inherent in sinful, finite, and mortal existence (Tillich) cannot be overcome by a retreat into ahistorical inwardness or a preoccupation with the asocial self; it can only be overcome by accepting it as a burden of a concrete totality and by struggling to save and redeem that totality under God's liberating grace.

In light of the preceding discussion, it should be easy to see that Hauerwas's critique of Gutierrez is based on a misreading of *A Theology of Liberation*. For Hauerwas, the notion of 'liberation' is too individualistic, innocent of the reality of the struggle for power, and unworthy of the Christian notion of freedom at the service of fraternal love and fellowship. For Gutierrez, on the contrary, the human subject of liberation is not the egoistic self of bourgeois individualism but the social and historical self who shares a common structural destiny and solidarity with others and who can be fully liberated only when others are liberated as well. Gutierrez, along with other liberation theologians, is also only too painfully aware of the reality of power in society; this is precisely the reason why he so insists on the necessity of political struggle in the midst of conflictual history for the transformation of power relationships and the creation of a classless society. Furthermore, the true meaning of Christian freedom does lie in the service of fraternal love and fellowship, not in the enjoyment of self-sufficiency, still less in the domination of others or anarchistic "rule of caprice" with which Ratzinger identifies the notion of liberation in TL.[121]

Basically, Hauerwas's misreading, I think, is due to his hasty and exhaustive identification of the notion of liberation in Gutierrez with the ideal of individual autonomy in the Kantian phase of the Enlightenment, which leads him to overlook the broadening integration of the notion of freedom into both the sociohistorical conceptions of the Hegelian–Marxian phase of the Enlightenment and the Christian theological conception of freedom as service. Hauerwas erroneously directs against Gutierrez precisely the same critique that Gutierrez directs against 'developmentalism' and its individualistic, harmonistic, and economistic assumptions.

Finally, it must be conceded to Cobb, Ogden, and other Whiteheadian ecological theologians that TL, along with other sociological theology, does not have much to say about the ecological crisis posed by environmental pollution and nuclear threats. TL has, thus far at least, been preoccupied with the redemption of history and society and concerned with nature only insofar as it enters into human concerns in the economic process of production and distribution. Its philosophical perspective has largely been anthropological, in the tradition of Hegel and Marx, not cosmological in the sense in which process theology is.

Does this mean, however, that TL is so wedded to anthropocentrism that it could neither recognize the intrinsic and autonomous value of nature nor say something relevant about the liberation of nature? I don't think that there is any incompatibility, theoretically at least, between TL and a concern with ecology and the intrinsic value of nature. After all, TL fully recognizes the creatureliness of human existence and the basic idolatry—absolutization of selfishness and rejection of God—inherent in human sinfulness: God, not humans, is the Lord of creation and history. There is no reason why the call to repentance and conversion, from selfishness to selflessness, which underlies the transformation of oppressive relationships and structures into liberating ones, could not be extended to the liberation of nature from the human will to domination. As Cobb himself recognizes, the oppression of fellow humans and the exploitation of nature "deeply influence each other."[122] Both are rooted in the same source, the self-absolutizing adolatry of selfishness. It is true that the dominant horizon of the philosophical sources of TL, Hegel and Marx, is anthropocentric, although the young Marx did show an appreciation of nature as a value in itself and criticized capitalism precisely for subordinating even nature to utilitarian domination.[123] As Christian theology, however, TL is also determined by the transcendent horizon of faith with its emphasis on the sovereignty of God as creator and redeemer and the relativity and creatureliness of human existence. Such philosophical sources are themselves to be integrated and sublated into this transcendent horizon of faith. That this integration has not occurred is a fact, but is it also evidence enough that such integration is in principle impossible?

This question, however, presupposes another question—namely, must a theology be comprehensive, as Cobb seems to assume when he talks about the need for the integration of sociological and ecological theology in "a truly comprehensive political theology"?[124] Historically, of course, comprehensiveness has been the driving ideal of all systematic theologies, and yet we also know that such comprehensiveness not only is historically relative but may also suffer from abstractness and irrelevance to the concrete problems of historical existence. What we need is not comprehensiveness for its own sake but comprehensiveness relevant to historical existence. As pointed out in the preceding chapter, TL does not claim to be a universal theology valid for all time; its modest claim is to serve the praxis of faith by enlightening it with a critical reflection which, of course, must include all relevant considerations but must also remain within the limits of historical knowledge and practical relevance. The question, then, is whether ecological concern should be part of any 'relevantly comprehensive' TL and what place such concern should have in the hierarchy of relevant concerns.

Here, I think, we have to consider the difference in the *Sitz-im-Leben* of Latin American TL and the First World theologies. A First World theology which also seeks to be a theology of liberation should indeed have a horizon comprehensive enough to include ecological concerns. After all, the First World must assume the main responsibility for the pollution of the environment and the threats of a global nuclear suicide, often exporting them to the Thrid World. It is the capitalism of the First World and its exploitative ethos which have dominated not only human relationships and social structures, in the First World and increasingly in the rest of the world, but also our attitude toward nature as such. The problem originates in the First World, and it is also there that a real solution must be found. A 'relevantly comprehensive' political theology of the First World, then, clearly must integrate the ecological concerns.

The problems of environmental pollution and nuclear suicide, of course, are not irrelevant to Latin America and the Third World in general; these too are involved in them, at least as victims and often as collaborators. It is clear, however, that in terms of both impact and the capacity to do anything about them they are not the most urgent problems confronted by the countries in the Third World. These countries are faced with the more elementary problem of creating a social structure that can guarantee the basic minimums of humane existence. The main problem indeed remains that of social change, which would also have the side effect of putting restraint on capitalist greed, the source of both social and ecological exploitation, not—primarily at least—that of the protection of nature. In terms of relevant comprehensiveness, then, it is not self-evident that the lack of ecological concern in TL should be such a paramount issue, given its sociohistorical situation.

Furthermore, even assuming that TL is crucially deficient because of its lack of ecological concern, it must be conceded, I think, that such concern can rise above empty moralism and impotent idealism only if it can be concretely and effectively implemented—that is, only through political praxis. Implementation of such concern requires consciousness-raising on a large scale and mobilization of pressure groups against the reified structures of exploitation, as does the struggle against racism and sexism. To be effective, ecological theology needs the mediation of TL.

To conclude, through the mediation of Hegel's dialectic of concrete totality as its organizing principle, TL tries to produce an integral synthesis of Christian faith in salvation and the Marxian dialectic of liberating praxis. In this synthesis faith serves as the totalizing principle within the unity of salvation and liberation, while political praxis, itself an inner moment and demand of salvation itself, serves as the concretizing principle of that unity. As Clodovis Boff puts it, "it is the faith that assimilates or subsumes elements of Marxism, then, and not the other way about," and "the elements assimilated are profoundly transformed in the very assimilation, in such a way that the result is no longer Marxism but simply a critical understanding of reality."[125] To put the matter a little differently, one could say that TL is no more or no less Marxian— and Hegelian—than, say, Rahner's transcendental theology is either Kantian or Heideggerian. In both instances, I submit, it is the theological horizon of faith which subsumes and sublates the philosophical sources from which they borrow.

The resulting relation between salvation and liberation in TL is no longer one of two juxtaposed planes or orders of creation and redemption, profane history and salvation history.[126] It is one of mutual immanence requiring "mutual enlightenment and reciprocal demands."[127] As a causality derived "from the strength of God himself who promotes it," liberation has a "genuinely causal character with respect to the definitive Kingdom of God. This causality is partial, fragile, often erroneous and having to be remade," but it is more than "anticipations, outlines or analogies of the Kingdom." What is at stake in the struggle for liberation "is the eschatological Kingdom itself."[128] To see sin in structural evil is "not horizontalizing sin," but on the contrary, "transcendentalizing what others want to maintain on a purely horizontal level, thus bringing it into relationship with God."[129]

Through this mutually internal yet non-reductionistic relationship, TL seeks to avoid all the conventional dualisms as well as one-sided reductionist monism. It seeks to avoid "both the reductionism of a disincarnate spiritualism masquerading as 'religion,' and the reductionism of a political action approach that ignores the reality of the people's faith."[130] The approach of TL is neither "secularism" nor "spiritualism," neither "horizontalism" nor "verticalism."[131] Salvation is neither a "purely immanent process" nor a "purely transcendent process," as it could not be identified with either "subjectivist interiority" or "ahistorical transcendentalism."[132] It does not remain passive and interior on the ground that all historical achievements are merely 'relative.' It seeks to make itself effective in the midst of historical struggles and its ambiguities by coming to grips with the structural sources of oppression and injustice and the necessity of political action. It does not withdraw into the impotent inwardness of Hegel's 'beautiful soul' in order to remain pure from the taint of action. By the same token, it does not, like Prometheus, 'absolutize' the relative and the human, but subjects them to the eschatological reservation.[133]

CHAPTER V

The Vatican's Theology of Liberation: A Critique

That a new theology on the horizon should face criticisms is both an entirely normal and a constructive phenomenon in the history of human thought. Ever since its inception in the 1960s, TL too has had its share of criticisms from its opponents. In this regard it is safe, I think, to single out the Vatican, represented by Pope John Paul II and Joseph Cardinal Ratzinger, as the most important among the critics. The Vatican's position on TL deserves special attention for a number of reasons. It has been the most persistent critic of TL from a well-defined theological position since 1978, the inauguration of Cardinal Wojtyla as Pope John Paul II. It has also proposed an alternative theology of liberation, a way, according to some, of "coopting" and "preempting" the voice from Latin America.

The significance of the Vatican position, however, goes beyond the merely theoretical merit of its criticism and its proposed alternative. The theological position of the Vatican is not simply one position among other positions, at least for Roman Catholics. It expresses not only ideas and arguments, which may be judged like any others on the basis of their intrinsic merit, but also the practical institutional weight of the highest teaching authority of the Church, an authority with enormous power to impose its own position on the rest of the Church and even to eliminate all competition and dissent within it. This goes far beyond the normal "ecclesial" constraint facing any Christian theology, Catholic, Orthodox, or Protestant, which is always rooted in a particular community whose life it is meant to serve and whose response, therefore, is decisive, in the long run, for the life of a theology. The significance in this regard of the Vatican position on liberation cannot be overestimated. As Leonardo Boff's 1985 compliance with the Vatican ban on his public activities amply suggests, it is often a matter of the very survival of a theologian.[1] The future of TL and the kinds of tribulation it may face depend, at least to a significant degree, on the position the Vatican has taken and will take in the years ahead.

It is with this practical institutional as well as its theoretical significance in mind that I have decided to devote a full, independent chapter to an analysis of the theology of the Vatican on the subject of freedom and liberation. I have already commented on its position on the relationship between theology and praxis (chapter 3) and that between transcendence and history (chapter 4). In this chapter I begin with a brief discussion of whether there was indeed, as the media speculation would have it, a change in the Vatican attitude toward TL between its two Instructions (1984 and 1986) on the subject, then go on to an exposition of its own theology of sin and salvation, its anthropology of personal existence, and its conceptions of social sin and social doctrine, and finally point out the inherent limits of the Vatican's personalist theology as a theology of liberation (which it claims to be), largely on the basis of a philosophical critique of its personalist anthropological presuppositions. It is important to note in this regard the difference between the Vatican and TL in their respective philosophical presuppositions. The difference is one of basic horizon, not of particular opinions within the same horizon, and the relation between TL and the Vatican, therefore, is not simply a matter of some dissident theologians in conflict with their ecclesiastical superiors but a conflict of two irreconcilably opposed theologies.

HAS THE VATICAN CHANGED ITS MIND?

The Vatican has issued two Instructions on the subject of liberation theology. The first, called "Instruction on Certain Aspects of the 'Theology of Liberation'" or *Libertatis Nuntius* (LN), was issued on August 6, 1984. The second, promised in the introduction of LN, was issued on March 22, 1986 under the title, "Instruction on Christian Freedom and Liberation" or *Libertatis Conscientia* (LC).[2] Each time an Instruction appeared, reactions varied.[3] What is interesting is that soon after the publication of LC, there also appeared Pope John Paul II's Easter letter to the Brazilian hierarchy with his comments on various aspects of TL along with his "explicit approval" of the two Instructions,[4] significantly adding to the media speculation about a possible change in the Vatican attitude towards TL. Was there indeed a change between the two documents? If there was, was it a substantial change, a change in matters of basic theological and anthropological perspectives and assumptions, or only an accidental change, a change in matters of tone and purpose?

Clearly, there are some minor or accidental differences between the two. The basic underlying difference is that of purpose. The purpose of LN was to "warn" against "deviations" from the Christian faith and thus was basically negative, while that of LC was to "detail in a positive fashion" a theology of freedom and liberation, to "highlight the main elements of the Christian doctrine on freedom and liberation" and to indicate "its principal *theoretical* and *practical* aspects" (LC, 2). By its very nature LN was full of warnings, criticisms, and accusations bordering on condemnation. By contrast, LC contained fewer such negations and concentrated more on elaborating what the Vatican considers an "authentic" TL to be. Apart from the first paragraph, which reaffirms the earlier "warning" against "deviations" as "ever more timely and relevant" (LC, 1), LC's negative remarks seemed more general and more brief than those of LN and directed to adversaries whose names remained unmentioned. It seemed even to go out of its way to say something positive about the basic Christian communities, calling them a "treasure for the whole church" (LC, 69), and described the theological method of praxis as "a very positive contribution, inasmuch as it makes possible a highlighting of aspects of the Word of God, the richness of which had not yet been fully grasped" (LC, 70).

The tone of John Paul's Easter letter to the Brazilian bishops was also conciliatory and encouraging, so much so that when the letter was read, so reports Peter Hebblethwaite, "the Brazilian bishops sang joyous alleluias and shed tears."[5] John Paul even went so far as to say that "the theology of liberation is not only opportune, but useful and necessary."[6]

This, however, is also the extent of the difference and change of attitude between LN and LC. To show how minor and in fact superficial such change really was, I must hurry to add that those apparently encouraging remarks about the basic ecclesial communities, the method of praxis, and the theology of liberation as such, came loaded with so many limiting conditions that they in fact died "the death of a thousand qualifications." Consider the remark about the base communities being "a source of great hope for the Church" or "a treasure for the whole Church." In a short paragraph containing four sentences, three have to do with the conditions under which alone the communities could become such a source and treasure:

> The new basic communities or other groups of Christians which have arisen to be witnesses to this evangelical love are a source of great hope for the Church. *If* they *really* live in unity with the local Church and the universal church, they will be a real expression of communion and a means for constructing a still deeper communion. Their fidelity to their mission will *depend* on how careful they are to educate their members in the fullness of the Christian faith through listening to the Word of God, fidelity to the teaching of the Magisterium, to the hierarchical order of the church and to the sacramental life. *If this condition is fulfilled*, their experience, rooted in a commitment to the complete liberation of man, becomes a treasure for the whole Church. (LC, 69; emphases added)

These, it must be noted, put in much stronger terms the concern for "the quality and the content of catechesis and formation" in the base communities (xi, 16) and the invitation to theologians to "welcome" the "word" and "directives" of the magisterium "with filial respect" (xi, 4) expressed in the earlier LN.

Likewise, "a theological reflection developed from a particular experience can constitute a very positive contribution," but

> in order that this reflection may be truly a reading of the Scripture and not a projection on to the Word of God of a meaning which it does not contain, the theologian will be careful to interpret the experience from which he begins in the light of the experience of the Church herself. This experience of the Church shines with a singular brightness and in all its purity in the lives of the saints. It pertains to the pastors of the Church, in communion with the Successor of Peter, to discern its authenticity. (LC, 70)

Again a comparison with the earlier criticism of the method of praxis in LN (x, 3; xi, 13) reveals no change in the Vatican's position. In speaking of "an important and delicate role" of the Brazilian church in "creating a space and conditions" for developing a theological reflection as a response to the challenge of our time, John Paul also insists that such reflection must be "in *perfect* accord with the rich doctrine contained in the two above mentioned *Instructions* [LN and LC]" and

> *fully* adherent to the constant teaching of the Church in social matters, and at the same time apt to inspire an efficient praxis in favor of social justice and equality, the defense of human rights, of the construction of a human society based on fraternity, harmony, truth, and charity.[7]

For John Paul, the theology of liberation "is not only opportune, but useful and necessary" and "should constitute a new stage" of theological reflection, but this is so only on condition that such a theology remain "*consonant* and *coherent* with the teaching of the Gospel, of living tradition and of the perennial magisterium of the Church" and

> in strict connection with earlier stages of that theological reflection begun with the Apostolic Tradition and continued with the great fathers and doctors, with the ordinary and extraordinary magisterium, and in most recent opochs with the rich patrimony of the Social Doctrine of the Church, expressed in documents that go from *Rerum Novarum* to *Laborem Exercens*.[8]

He goes on to urge the pastors

> to keep constant vigil so that the correct and necessary liberation theology will be developed in Brazil and in Latin America, in a *homogenous* and *not heterogenous* way, with relation to the theology of other times, in full fidelity to the doctrine of the church, with a preferential and not exclusive or excluding love for the poor.[9]

Along with LC's reaffirmation of LN, its dismissal of the Latin American TL as a "deviation," and John Paul's "explicit approval" of both LN and LC, these remarks should make it clear that the TL which is "useful and necessary" is anything but the Latin American TL, which certainly is not in "perfect accord" with either LN or, as will be shown, LC. Certainly, the concept of praxis still evident in the remarks quoted remains a far cry from that of the Latin American TL. For John Paul and LC as for LN, praxis remains subsequent and external to theory, i.e., the magisterial doctrine of the church, which must be affirmed prior to and merely "applied" in "practice." It is more "practice" than "praxis," whereas praxis, for TL, is itself a source of disclosure and actuality and enters into a mutually mediating, dialectical relation with theory. Likewise, the concept and function of the basic ecclesial community in LC and LN are not those of TL. Both LC and LN see the community only as a good example of communion and even this much on condition of strict obedience to the hierarchy, whereas TL sees it as a living model of what the church as a whole should be—a church of the people, a popular and democratic church, which does not deny the need for authority in the church but by the same token does not absolutize or reify such an authority either, seeing in the authority a means which *serves* the poor and is open to their praxis as constitutive of its own theoretical magisterium.

A comparative look at the Vatican's interpretation of the Exodus in LN (iv, 3) and LC (44) also clearly shows what little change or difference there had been between the two documents. Superficially, there is some difference between the statement of LN that "the specific significance of the event comes from its purpose, for this liberation is ordered to the foundation of the people of God and the Covenant cult celebrated on Mount Sinai" and that of LC that "the major and fundamental event of the Exodus therefore has a meaning which is both religious and political." The first, as discussed in the preceding chapter, stresses the 'religious' meaning of the Exodus, while the second seems to affirm *both* the 'religious' and the 'political' meaning. A warning against political reductionism, however, is sounded in both documents. "The liberation of the exodus cannot be reduced to a liberation which is principally or exclusively political in nature" (LN), and "one cannot therefore isolate the political aspect for its own sake" (LC). Furthermore, LC likewise takes pains to subordinate the "political" to the "religious": "God sets his People free and gives them descendents, a land and a law, but within a Covenant and for a Covenant." The political aspect itself "has to be considered in the light of a plan of a religious nature within which it is integrated," i.e., "communion with their God." And just as LN was critical of the "inversion of symbols," i.e., turning the Exodus, "a figure of baptism," into "a symbol of the political liberation of the people" (x, 14), so, two years later, commenting on LC, Ratzinger expressed exactly the same fear that "baptism is becoming a symbol of the Exodus and the Exodus a symbol of political and revolutionary action in general," that "Jesus is interpreted backwards with reference to Moses. Moses, however, is interpreted forwards with reference to Marx."[10] The fear of reductionism and the concern with preserving the distinction between the political and the religious are equally evident in LN and LC.

Theology of Sin and Salvation

After all the controversies of recent years on TL it should be clear by now that the heart of the issue has to do with the relation between salvation, in the transcendent, eschatological sense, and liberation, in the immanent, historical sense, or, more precisely, with the transcendent, theological meaning—or lack thereof—of historical liberation. Both TL and the Vatican insist on the theological necessity of liberation, but they differ as to the basis of such necessity and the subsequent relation between salvation and liberation. In this regard, which concerns the theological center of the controversy, I think it must be said that there is no change, not even an accidental one, between LN and LC. We have to take seriously Ratzinger's statement soon after the second Instruction that "the two Instructions together form an indissoluble unity that one only understands if one reads and considers them as a coherent whole."[11] The mode of thinking in LC, as will become clear, remains essentially as dualist as in LN, in contrast to the dialectical thinking of TL.

LC is just as anxious, as was LN, to distinguish between transcendent salvation and historical liberation, or, using the term 'liberation' in a broad sense, between "salvific" and "temporal" liberation. For LC, the "first" and "fundamental" meaning of liberation is the "salvific" one: "man is freed from the radical bondage of evil and sin" (23); just as, for LN, the "specific" character of salvation or "true" liberation (xi, 16) means "first and foremost" liberation from the "radical slavery to sin" (Introduction). "Liberation in the strongest sense of the word" means the "redemption" brought about by Christ through his cross and resurrection, because "it has freed us from the most radical evil, namely sin and the power of death" (LC, 3). The "primary" meaning of liberation is "salvific" (LC, 99). The "essential" mission of the Church lies in evangelization, i.e., "the proclamation of salvation," which is mediated "through the Word of God and the sacraments" (LC, 63).

To be distinguished from this "radical liberation" (LC, 71) in the "transcendent" (LC, 62) and "supernatural order" (LC, 80) of salvation is the "temporal" order of human life (LC, 80); "temporal liberation," i.e., "all the processes which aim at securing and guaranteeing the conditions for the exercise of an authentic human freedom" (LC, 31); "integral liberation from everything that hinders the development of individuals" (LC, 63); or "human promotion" in the "temporal order" (LC, 64). In the words of LN, this is liberation from servitude of an "earthly" and "temporal" kind, whereas liberation from sin is liberation from "the most radical form of slavery" (iv, 2), which remains of "fundamental" and "primary" importance (Introduction). It is "important to make a careful distinction between earthly progress and the growth of the Kingdom, which do not belong to the same order" (LC, 60), just as the latter "cannot be confused with the progress of civilization, of science, of human technology" (LN, Conclusion). The "salvific" dimension of liberation "cannot be reduced to the socio-ethical dimension" (LC, 71). Commenting on this passage of LC, John Paul insists:

> liberation is, above all, *soteriological*, (an aspect of salvation fulfilled by Jesus Christ, Son of God) and *ethico-social* (or *ethico-political*). If we reduce one dimension to the other—practically suppressing both—or if we put the second before the first, we subvert and distort true Christian liberation.[12]

Despite this "distinction," LC likewise insists on the "unity" of the two dimensions and claims that liberation in the temporal order is part of the mission of the Church, which "takes great care to maintain clearly and firmly both the unity and the distinction between evangelization and human promotion" (LC, 64). The "distinction" of the dimensions is "not" meant to be a "separation" (LC, 60). The work of "salvation" is "*indissolubly* linked to the task of improving and raising the conditions of human life in this world" (LC, 90; emphasis added). Thus, the Church is "firmly determined to respond to the anxiety of contemporary man as he endures oppression and yearns for freedom" (LC, 61). This is quite consistent with the earlier position of LN, which reconfirmed Medellin's "preferential option for the poor" (Introduction), recognizing "the acute need for radical reforms of the structures which conceal poverty" (xi, 8), and issuing "a great call" to "all the church" to "hear the cry for justice" and "to respond to it with all her might" as "a matter of the highest priority" (xi, 2 & 3). Liberation from sin, "as a logical consequence," "calls for freedom from many different kinds of slavery in the cultural, economic, social and political spheres" (LN, Introduction). In the Old Testament "justice as regards God and justice as regards mankind are inseparable" (LN, iv, 6), just as in the New Testament "the commandment of fraternal love extended to all mankind" "provides the supreme rule of social life" (LN, iv, 8).

The question to ask, however, is not only whether the Vatican affirms the "unity" of salvation and liberation, but, more importantly, on what grounds may such a unity be affirmed and what kind of relationship can result from such grounds. Given the Vatican's constant emphasis on their "irreducibility," what would be the grounds for their unity? Would such a unity be consistent with their "irreducible" distinction? In order to answer these questions it is necessary to consider in some detail each of the two key concepts, salvation and liberation, focusing especially on the theological and anthropological assumptions both implicit and explicit in the two documents.

First, we examine the concept of salvation. Salvation means "the most radical liberation" (LC, 22) or liberation from "the most radical evil, namely sin and the power of death" (LC, 3) or from "the radical bondage of evil and sin" (LC, 23) through the cross and resurrection of Jesus Christ. What, then, is sin? Sin means "breaking away from God" (LC, 37). How does this come about? By the abuse and perversion of personal freedom in the "hearts of men" (LN, xi, 8). Humans are created free with a destination to communion with God and sharing in God's divine life. Human freedom is essentially the limited, dependent freedom of the creature created in the image of God, which constitutes the "truth" of the human being (LC, 27). Authentic freedom lies in harmonizing the will with this truth and observing the moral limits of that nature.

The actual history of human freedom, however, shows the "tragic paradox" of that freedom: "God calls men to freedom. In each person there lives a desire to be free. And yet this desire almost always tends towards slavery and oppression" (LC, 37). Why this paradox? Because of sin. Humans are indeed called to be like God, not through total self-sufficiency and arbitrary caprice but by respecting the truth of their being as creatures loved by God. In sinning against God the person succumbs to the "temptation to deny his own nature," forgets his or her finitude, and claims to be a god. This is the "profound nature of sin": "man rejects the truth and places his own will above it. By wishing to free himself from God and be a god himself, he deceives himself and destroys himself. He becomes alientated from himself" (LC, 37). This "alienation from the truth of his being as a creature loved by God is the root of all other forms of alienation" (LC, 38). For the Vatican, as for Augustine, sin is *contemptus Dei*, false attachment to creatures, *conversio ad creaturam* now substituted for the infinite. In this "disordered love of self" one tries to rely on oneself alone, to "achieve fulfillment by himself and to be self-sufficient in his own immanence" (LC, 40). In "rejecting God" and seeking infinite happiness in himself or herself and in other creatures incapable of yielding such happiness, the person "destroys the momentum of his aspiration to the infinite and of his vocation to share in the divine life" (ibid.).

This conception of sin and freedom dictates a corresponding conception of salvation. Salvation means liberation from the slavery of sin and communion with God. It calls for "interior conversion" (LN, xi, 8), "conversion and renewal" "in the depths of the heart" (LN, iv, 7). How do we attain this salvation?

It is above all by the power of his Paschal Mystery that Christ has set us free. Through his perfect obedience on the Cross and through the glory of his Resurrection, the Lamb of God has taken away the sin of the world and opened for us the way to definitive liberation. (LC, 51)

Through Jesus Christ and in the Holy Spirit we are offered forgiveness and reconciliation with the Father. Through faith and the sacraments we experience the grace of justification. We receive "the new life of grace," which is "life in the Spirit" (LN, iv, 2), so as to "live and act as new creatures" (LN, iv, 15). Salvation is "an essentially religious experience: it is from God alone that one can expect salvation and healing," resulting in "spiritual" liberation and purification (LN, iv, 5). In Christ, therefore, we can conquer both sin and the power of death (LC, 52). The capacity "to love God above all things and remain in communion with him" (LC, 53), once taken away by sin, is now restored. "We are set free from disordered self-love, which is the source of contempt of neighbor and of human relationships based on domination" (ibid.). This freedom, of course, remains incomplete in this world and awaits its eschatological fulfillment "at the end of time with the resurrection of the dead and the renewal of the whole of creation" (LC, 58).

This, then, essentially (though briefly), is the concept of freedom, sin, and salvation evident in the two Instructions. The concept itself, of course, is quite traditional, and I do not mean this in any pejorative sense. Certainly, its content is basic to the identity of Christian faith, which would be inconceivable apart from the belief in human sinfulness and the need for transcendent salvation. The question is whether this basic content receives adequate conceptualization, especially whether its underlying anthropological assumptions are adequate. An examination of the Vatican's anthropology is important not only in itself but also in view of the fact that Ratzinger himself wants the "anthropological foundation" in the first four chapters of LC to be taken seriously, not neglected as by the media in favor of the fifth chapter dealing with the social doctrine.[13]

Anthropology of Personal Existence

The important question is not simply whether humans are sinful and in need of transcendent salvation. Equally important is the question of who these humans are who are sinful and in need of redemption, and that of how these humans, the subjects of freedom and sin, are conceived and characterized. Upon this question hangs the question of the relation between transcendent salvation and historical liberation. A dualistic conception of the human subject of sin and salvation would see only hostility between salvation and liberation; should it by any chance affirm a positive connection between the two, it would do so with great diffidence and have a difficult time justifying such a connection in any case.

Who, then, according to the Vatican, is the human subject who is free, sinful, and in need of redemption? The human subject is essentially a person, in the sense of an individual with the capacity of self-determination and a destiny which is transcendent, both the capacity and the destiny exercised and experienced chiefly in subjective inwardness. There are three characteristics of human subjectivity thus conceived: The true subject is basically *individual*, not social; *internal*, not external; *transcendent*, not historical. Let me consider these characteristics in some detail.

First, consider the individual and the transcendent conception of the human subject. The discussion of freedom, sin and liberation from sin in LC (25–42, 50–54) is conducted exclusively in terms of the relationship between the individual and God. The basic categories are "each person," "his will," "mastery of one's own act and self-determination," "his free action," "decides for himself and forms himself," "master of his own life," "his free personality," "disordered love of self," "free himself of God," and "alienated from himself." These categories, reflecting the personalism of John Paul's *The Acting Person,* understand the subject solely as "a person responsible for himself and his transcendent destiny" (LC, 32), i.e., solely in relation to oneself and to one's God. The subject of sin, freedom, and salvation is not the subject as a concrete historical totality of all the essential relations but the individual isolated from all relations except the relation to God, a transcendent, not historically concrete subject.

The anthropology of the Vatican in this regard is not significantly different from that of the Kierkegaardian 'individual before God' with its emphasis on the moral isolation of the individual and her or his direct relationship to God. I say "not significantly different" because, although the Vatican does possess an extensive 'social' doctrine, which Kierkegaard lacks, the basically individual conception of the essence of freedom, sin, and salvation remains the same in both. While references to the social dimension of human existence are not lacking, they are, as will be noted, chiefly concerned with the consequences, conditions, and other circumstances of freedom, sin, and salvation, not with their essence.

As John Paul put it in his Apostolic Exhortation on Reconciliation and Penance (RP) of December 2, 1984,[14] the essence of sin lies in the individual's "exclusion of God, rupture with God, disobedience to God" (14) without an intrinsic mediation by one's sociohistorical relations. "Sin, in the proper sense, is always a *personal* act, since it is an act of freedom on the part of an individual person, and not properly of a group or community" (16). A person may be conditioned and influenced by such "external" factors as structures and systems, which may attenuate one's freedom and responsibility, but "it is a truth of faith" that "the human person is free" (16). To deny this would be to deny not only such a truth of faith but also the dignity of the person, which, for John Paul, depends on the capacity to transcend such "external" factors and determine oneself for oneself.

The underlying anthropology of John Paul and Ratzinger is not only personalist or individualist—in the metaphysical, not psychological or ethical, sense—but also interiorist. The subject of sin and freedom is not the concrete subject of praxis in the historical world but the subject of the inner "heart," "spirit," or "conscience," the "inner man" of the Augustinian tradition. Freedom consists primarily in the "interior" mastery of one's own acts (LC, 27). The hardened "heart" is the "source" of repeated sins (LC, 46), just as the Spirit who dwells in our "hearts" is the "source" of true freedom (LC, 54). The cause of sin lies in the "hearts of men" (LN, xi, 8), not in evil "structures" (LN, iv, 15). The "heart full of evil" is the "source of man's radical slavery and of the forms of oppression which he makes his fellowmen endure" (LC, 39). Salvation from sin thus requires "interior conversion" (LN, xi, 8) "in the depths of the heart" (LN, iv, 7). Just as the "heart" is the efficient subject of sin, so

> sin has its first and most important consequences in the *sinner himself*; that is, in his relationship with God, who is the very foundation of human life; and also in his spirit, weakening his will and clouding his intellect. (RP, 16)

Sin destroys the individual's "internal" balance and generates contradictions "within himself" (RP, 15).

Freedom and sin in their essence, then, are traits and activities of the person as an individual in his or her inwardness, where he or she encounters the transcendent. Both Instructions and RP abstract altogether from the social, external, and historical relations in their account of the essence and origin of freedom and sin, just as John Paul deals with human "action" in total abstraction from the concrete sociohistorical context in his *The Acting Person*.[15] They include such relations only in their account of the "results," "consequences," and "effects" of freedom and sin. The sociohistorical dimension of human existence does not mediate the very essence or origin of freedom and sin in an intrinsic, constitutive way; it is only a "result" of such freedom and sin already constituted in their proper reality apart from society and history.

This is indubitably clear in the numerous statements of the documents. Temporal forms of slavery are "by-products" (LN, Introduction) and "effects" (LN, iv, 14) of sin, "the root of all other forms of alienation" (LC, 38). Evil structures are "the result of man's actions and so are consequences more than causes" (LN, iv, 15). Although "there are structures which are evil and which cause evil," we cannot locate evil "principally or uniquely" in them (ibid.). In both theological significance and causal efficacy, then, temporal forms of slavery are quite "secondary" to sin, sin as a phenomenon of the inwardness of transcendent subjectivity. Hence, "the first liberation, to which all others must make reference, is that from sin" (LN, iv, 12).

Personal and Social Sin

How, then, does sin in the inwardness of the individual bring about "the sin of the world"? According to LC, the sinner, by denying God, disturbs not only "his own order and interior balance but *also* those of society and even of visible creation" (38; emphasis added).

> Culpable ignorance of God unleashes the passions, which are causes of imbalance and conflicts in the human heart. *From this* there inevitably *come* disorders which affect the sphere of the family and society: sexual license, injustice and murder. (39; emphases added)

The causal sequence in the etiology of social disorder could not be clearer: *from* the sin against God *through* the passions of conflicts in the heart *to* the disorder in the family and society.

> *Having become* his own center, sinful man tends to assert himself and to satisfy his desire for the infinite by the use of things: wealth, power and pleasure, despising other people and robbing them unjustly and treating them as objects or instruments. *Thus* he makes his own contribution to the creation of those very structures of exploitation and slavery which he claims to condemn. (42; emphases added)

"Disordered self-love" is "the source of contempt of neighbor and of human relationships based on domination" (53). Poverty is "the result and consequence of poeple's sin and natural frailty" (67). The "social-ethical" dimension of liberation is "a consequence" of the "salvific" dimension, which, therefore, "cannot be reduced" to the former (71), just as a "cause" cannot be reduced to its "effect."

John Paul puts this hierarchical etiology of sin even more clearly: "the *result* of sin is the shattering of the human family" (RP, 15; emphasis added). The relation between personal sin and social disorder is a relation of "cause and effect" (ibid.). Social and historical alienations are "signs and effects of internal disorder" (*ibid.*). Every sin is "social, insofar as and because it *also* has social *repercussions*" (ibid.; emphases added).

John Paul elaborates further on the relation between person and structure, between personal and social sin, by distinguishing four meanings of 'social sin.' In the first sense, "by virtue of a human solidarity" "every sin" committed by an individual is a "social" sin in that "each individual's sin in some way affects others" (RP, 16). "There is no sin, not even the most intimate and secret one, the most strictly individual one, that exclusively concerns the person committing it," for every sin has "repercussions" on the entire world (ibid.). Here the subject of sin is an individual, but the consequence is social in that it affects others in some indeterminate way, in a "communion of sinners," a negative counterpart to the "communion of saints."

In the second sense, social sin refers to sins which "by their very matter constitute a direct attack on one's neighbor" (ibid.). It also includes every sin against "justice in interpersonal relationships," "the rights of the human person," "others' freedom," and "the dignity and honor of one's neighbor" as well as against "the common good and its exigencies in relation to the whole broad spectrum of the rights and duties of citizens" (ibid.). Among the subjects of sin in this sense John Paul does not distinguish between individuals in their private capacity and individuals in their public function, or, as I put in the preceding chapter, between individuals in their (relative) isolation and individuals in their organized interdependence, and thus includes within the same category private indivudals as well as "leaders" "who though in a position to do so do not work diligently and wisely for the improvement and transformation of society according to the requirements and potential of the given historic moment," and "workers" who "through absenteeism or non-cooperation fail to ensure that their industries can continue to advance the well-being of the workers themselves, of their families, and of the whole of society" (ibid.). Nor does he distinguish between actions whose consequences are temporary, limited, and thus "private" and those whose consequences are enduring, extensive, and thus "public."[16] He seems to include all the examples mentioned under the second sense because they are variations on "a direct attack against one's neighbor."

Social sin in the third sense refers to the evil attaching to the relationships between various communities—i.e., groups, classes, nations, and even blocs of nations. Here the situation is so general and often anonymous, and the cause of evil so complex, that it is difficult to assign moral responsibility to any particular person. For this reason social sin in this sense has only an "analogical" meaning, although this should not lead us to underestimate the responsibility of the individuals involved. What exactly is the subject and the object of social sin in this sense remains unclear.

In the fourth sense, social sin is used in contrast to personal sin with the purpose of watering down and even abolishing the latter. Derived from non-Christian ideologies and systems, it reduces every sin to social sin "in the sense that blame for it is to be placed not so much on the moral conscience of an individual but rather on some vague entity or anonymous collectivity, such as the situation, the system, society, structures, or institutions" (ibid.). This sense is both illegitimate and unacceptable. Such an anonymous collectivity "is not in itself the subject of moral acts. Hence a situation cannot in itself be good or bad" (ibid.). When various church documents in recent decades—Medellin, Puebla, LN, LC, and so on—speak of "situations of sin" or "social sins,"[17] they should really mean that "such cases of *social sin* are the result of the accumulation and concentration of many *personal sins*" (ibid.).

> It is a case of the very personal sins of those who cause or support evil or who exploit it; of those who are in a position to avoid, eliminate or at least limit certain social evils but who fail to do so out of laziness, fear, or the conspiracy of silence, through secret complicity or indifference; of those who take refuge in the supposed impossibility of changing the world, and also of those who sidestep the effort and sacrifice required, producing specious reasons of a higher order. (ibid.)

The real responsibility for social sins always lies with "individuals," who alone can be subjects of moral acts. The problem with the fourth sense of sin, then, is that it reifies situations, groups, and structures into independent entities apart from the individuals who compose them. "At the heart of every situation of sin are always to be found sinful people," so much so that a structural change "proves to be incomplete, of short duration, and ultimately vain and ineffective—not to say counterproductive—if the people directly or indirectly responsible for that situation are not converted" (ibid.). If the advocates of the fourth sense reduce every sin to social sin, John Paul reduces every sin to personal sin. All sins in the proper sense are "personal" sins, sins of "individuals," and when it becomes difficult to identify the individual subject of a sin as in the third sense involving the behavior of a group, it is a sin only in an "analogical" sense. The fourth sense is in fact only a variation on the social sins in the second sense.

The Vatican's insistence on the causal primacy of the individual in relation to the social and its reduction of the latter to the former may give the impression that it does not see any causal significance of the social for the life of individuals. The Vatican does recognize the social dimension of personal existence. LC acknowledges that the person is a "social" being. Social life is "not exterior" to a person, who "can only grow and realize his vocation in relation with others" (LC, 32). The person "belongs to different communities," and "it is inside these communities that he must exercise his responsible freedom" (ibid.). A just society provides "irreplaceable assistance" in realizing the free personality, while an unjust society is "a threat and an obstacle which can compromise his destiny" (ibid.). It is the task of the state to "create the conditions necessary for man to be able to achieve his authentic and integral welfare, including his spiritual goals" (LC, 84). Because the relationship between the person and work is "radical and vital," just work relationships are "a necessary precondition" for "the integral development of every individual," and can bring about "a profound and peaceful revolution in people's outlooks" (LC, 83). Just institutions and laws "are the guarantees of people's freedom and of the promotion of that freedom" (LC, 74). These statements would lead one to believe that social relations are not merely factual or accidental but the intrinsic ("not exterior"), "irreplaceable," "radical," "vital," and "necessary" conditions and components of personal existence as such, which would affect the origin, exercise and content ("outlook") of freedom itself.

Not so curiously, however, in light of the Vatican view of the primacy of the individual, LC immediately hedges these statements with reservations and qualifications. As cited earlier, "temporal liberation" has to do precisely with "all the processes which aim at securing and guaranteeing the conditions needed for the exercise of an authentic human freedom" (31). LC, however, hurries on to add:

It is not liberation which *in itself* produces human freedom. Common sense, confirmed by Christian sense, knows that even when freedom is subject to forms of conditioning it is not thereby completely destroyed. People who undergo terrible constraints succeed in manifesting their freedom and taking steps to secure their own liberation. A process of liberation which has been achieved can *only* create *better* conditions for the *effective* exercise of freedom. Indeed a liberation which does not take into account the personal freedom of those who fight for it is condemned in advance to defeat. (ibid.; emphases added)

Just as, for John Paul, "a situation cannot *in itself* be good or bad" (RP, 16; my emphasis), so, for LC, "structures established for people's good are *of themselves* incapable of securing and guaranteeing that good" (75: my emphasis). It is an "illusion" to think that "the abolition of an evil situation is *in itself* sufficient to create a more humane society" (LC, 78; my emphasis). Even "a radical revolution in social relations" does not create "new man" (LN, iv, 15). To give priority to structures over persons is "the expression of a materialistic anthropology" (LC, 75). Technical and economic conditions "cannot help but affect to some extent cultural and even religious life. However, by reason of his freedom man remains the master of his activity" (LC, 35). Unjust social structures "always depend on the responsibility of man, who can alter them, and not upon an alleged determinism of history" (LC, 74). The "root" of unjust structures is "sin," which "is in a true and immediate sense a voluntary act which has its source in the freedom of individuals" (LC, 75). The efficient causality of individual freedom is "prior" to that of structures, and likewise "personal" sin alone is sin in the proper and primary sense, "social" sin or sin of structures being so "only in a derived and secondary sense" (ibid.).

The Vatican's insistence on the primacy of individual freedom in one's interiority and transcendence also dictates a hierarchy of means in the pursuit of historical, social liberation. The individual is prior to the social in both finality and efficiency: the social must serve the transcendent dignity of the individual as its end and is itself only the "result" or "effect" of individual causality. In seeking the liberation of social relations and their structural objectifications, therefore,

the first thing to be done is to appeal to the spiritual and moral capacities of the individual and to the permanent need for inner conversion, if one is to achieve the economic and social changes that will truly be at the service of man. (LC, 75) (also cf. LN, xi, 8)

In the same section LC goes on to say that it is "necessary to work simultaneously for the conversion of hearts and for the improvement of structures," but it is clear that this "simultaneously" does not assign equal importance in either value or efficacy, only in chronology. Precisely because individual conversion is prior, and "moral integrity is a necessary condition for the health of society" (ibid.), liberation of sinful structures requires simultaneous changes in individual existence, apart from which structural change can not in itself be a true liberation at the service of human dignity and is in fact always in danger of merely substituting another form of oppression such as totalitarianism.

This insistence on the freedom and responsibility of the individual leads to the "ethical" approach of Catholic social doctrine, with its special emphasis on the role of education and culture (cf. LC, chapter V). In this regard Ratzinger poses a choice between two models of political philosophy, the mechanistic model of the utopian tradition from Saint Simon to Ernst Bloch and the ethical model of the realist tradition from Plato and Aristotle onwards, each with its own theological counterpart, represented by Eusebius of Caesarea on the one hand and Augustine, Aquinas, and Luther on the other. The mechanistic model links politics and metaphysics without any mediation and thus reduces metaphysics to physics, a determinate and determinable quantity. Politics is subordinated to the doctrine of being, and being is conceived on the model of a machine. Whoever speaks of collective historical projects as necessarily producing the "new man" denies human freedom and reduces politics to the determinism of a physicalist model. The tradition of Plato and Aristotle, on the other hand, subordinates politics to ethics, not metaphysics, and operates with a completely different understanding of human freedom and responsibility as basic components of political action.[18]

Which of these two models of political philosophy is more compatible with the biblical tradition is clear. For Ratzinger, only the ethical tradition of Plato and Aristotle could salvage the biblical image of the human being as an individual with freedom and dignity, which cannot be integrated into a "physics" of progress. Only that tradition can also preserve the rationality of politics from empty empiricism. The task of faith here is not so much to promise and undergird a historical future as to discover moral truth which cannot be derived from merely empirical analysis and which is at the same time the condition of authentically human and social action. True, this ethical approach cannot offer either exclusively valid political directives or promises of political salvation with necessity and finality. When politics rests on human freedom and moral responsibility, it rules out the prospect of necessary progress and the security of political salvation. Such politics requires constant renewal of education and moral effort: humans must learn to become human again and again and live by the power of their empirical and moral reason, which must be renewed with a sense of responsibility before God.[19]

Herein also lies the importance of the tradition of Catholic social doctrine. It seeks to relate the ethos of faith to economic and poltical reason and to develop models of action on the basis of such a synthesis, fully aware that such models "cannot produce redemption but can open up *conditions* of redeemed existence."[20] Such a social doctrine has been accused of political inefficiency and evolutionary reformism, playing into the hands of the status quo. Reform, however need not always be on the reactionary side. In fact, both evolution and revolution are categories of deterministic thinking, whereas reform presupposes ethics and freedom. Ethical politics is not concerned either with the finality of a system once posited or with the expectation of the totally other; it is content with the ever new effort towards a more humanly worthy form of political and social life. If Catholic social doctrine has historically been ineffective, which is only partially true, the reason lies in the fact that the dialogue between moral and empirical reason has not been pursued energetically enough and that the moral intuitions of faith have lacked the courage to face the challenge of empirical, quantitative reason. In this respect it is only fair to say that there is something valid about the attempt of TL to use the concept of utopia as the mediation of empirical reason and faith. However, it has been applied in the wrong way, devouring reason on the one hand and rendering faith objectless on the other. What is absolutely necessary today is to extend our concept of reason, recognizing both the limits of the merely quantitative approach and the reality of careful reflection on the data of faith.[21]

Models of action which emerge from such synthesis of faith and empirical reason no doubt have the weakness of not being exclusivistic and remaining open to pluralism in their prescriptions. They do not have the definitiveness and clarity of the political programs advocated by TL. Their promises are neither total nor final, for they are always subject to moral tension and the limits of the human. They have, however, the advantage of being honorable. They are predicated on the truth that humans are humans, not God, that history is not divine. The divinization of humans and their history only lead to the destruction of the human, a distorted image of redemption, and slavery. The human works of politics neither justify nor redeem. Faith, of course, needs works, but the works it needs are *paideia* in the Greek sense of the term, i.e., moral education or formation (*Bildung*), which alone, in the final analysis, can transform the human. This human work of education, however, needs to receive its directions and starting points from faith, the education which comes from God. It also needs dialogue with reason in its proper claims, without which moral formation would remain contentless. Thus, the work of moral formation enters into the conditions of redemption; it not only changes the human but also makes it possible for us to experience what transcends it.[22]

Social Doctrine of Liberation

Given the Vatican's conception of sin and salvation and its underlying individualist, interiorist, and transcendentalist anthropology, the question remains imperative: Why should the Christian also engage in the pursuit of historical liberation at all? What is the theological or salvific ground for such engagement, and what is the basis of the unity of salvation and liberation? If salvation is a matter of the religious and spiritual renewal and conversion of individuals in the inwardness of their personal subjectivity, why does the Vatican issue "a great call" to "all the church" to "hear the cry for justice" and to "respond to it with all her might" as "a matter of the highest priority" (LN, xi, 2 and 3)? Why is the work of "salvation" "*indissolubly* linked to the task of improving and raising the conditions of human life in this world" (LC, 80; my emphasis)? Why are the preaching and hearing of the Gospel, the frequent reception of the sacraments, meditation on the Cross and Resurrection, and other forms of piety aimed at the conversion of individual hearts not sufficient for Christian existence *as* Christian? If the demand for historical liberation is a "logical" consequence of salvation (LN, Introduction), what precisely is this logic?

In elaborating this logic the Vatican takes essentially three approaches— the appeal to God's will and love, the moral application of the causal relation between personal sin and social consequences, and the argument from unity, the unity of human existence and God's plan to recapitulate *all* things in Christ. Consider first the appeal to God's will and love. According to the Vatican, liberation from oppression and injustice is the will of God, who endowed humans with a transcendent dignity by creating them in God's image and calling them to the grace of divine sonship, "the foundation of justice" (LN, xi, 6). God and Jesus show special concern for those in need and distress (LN, iv, 9; LC, 46–47, 50, 67–68). Then there is the Great Commandment, the commandment to love God and neighbor (LC, 45, 55–57, 62, 71–72), the source of Christian moral praxis:

> By restoring man's true freedom, the radical liberation brought about by Christ assigns to him a task: Christian practice, which is the putting into practice of the great commandment of love. The latter is the supreme principle of Christian social morality. (LC, 71)

Liberation is an "ethical requirement" of evangelical love:

> It is from the most radical evil, from sin and the power of death, that he [the Redeemer] has delivered us in order to restore freedom to itself and to show it the right path. This path is marked out by the supreme commandment, which is the commandment of love. Liberation, in its primary meaning which is salvific, thus extends into a liberating task, as an ethical requirement. Here is to be found the social doctrine of the church, which illustrates Christian practice on the level of society. (LC, 99)

The "essential" mission of the Church is "the proclamation of salvation," which she does "through the Word of God and the sacraments," but

> in this mission, the Church teaches the way which man must follow in this world in order to enter the Kingdom of God. Her teaching therefore extends to the whole moral order, and notably to the justice which must regulate human relations. This is part of the preaching of the Gospel. (LC, 63)

Clearly, however, this is not so much an argument as a mere assertion of a fact: God commands us to love, which in turn imposes an obligation, a "task" to practice love and justice in social relations. This does not explain or argue *why* love of neighbor in either interpersonal or structural relations is "the touchstone of love of God" (LC, 56), why the great commandment should be practiced "on the level of society" and "regulate human relations," and why the task of historical liberation is "part of the preaching of the Gospel." It is basically a positivistic appeal to the mere fact of God's love and moral will. We have to love others because God says so. But why does God say so? Why does God make love of God instrinsically dependent on love of neighbor? Why should love of neighbor also take the form of structural justice? After all, the Great Commandment was there throughout the history of the Church, without awakening in its consciousness the need for structural change until very recently. What would be the theological justification for this shift of position?

Furthermore, why does God will in the first place that our salvific relation to God be mediated by our temporal concern for structural justice, when the Kingdom of God is not of this world in any event? Why is the commitment to concrete historical liberation an intrinsic necessity of salvation or "radical liberation" if it is primarily a matter of our individual relationship with God in the interiority of our hearts? Or perhaps such a commitment is not really intrinsic to the preaching of the Gospel, not, as the Synod of Bishops declared in 1971, "a constitutive" dimension of such preaching?[23] On the other hand, if there should indeed be an "indissoluble" link between salvation and liberation as the Vatican insists, one would also think that the work of liberation, "the way we must follow in this world in order to enter the Kingdom of God," also belongs *per se* to the order of "salvation," at least as much as do meditation on the Word of God and reception of the sacraments. The Vatican, however, insists on keeping the two "orders" of salvation and liberation "distinct" and forever warns against identifying the two.

In speaking of revelation, Karl Rahner once pointed out that traditional fundamental theology was guilty of extrinsicism and a positivism of revelation. We cannot say that humans have an obligation to listen to the Word of God when God speaks simply because we are finite creatures with a creaturely obligation to obey the creator. Such an argument is not only abstract because it is based on a *general* obligation of the creature *as* a creature, and positivistic because it appeals to the bare historical fact of revelation. It is also extrinsicist because it does not inquire into the a priori conditions for the specifically human possibility and necessity of hearing God's revelation in the very structure of human existence. What is there about human existence that would make the hearing of God's word spoken in history not only an imposition "from outside" but also a possibility and necessity on the part of humans, a response to and a fulfillment of something "intrinsic" to the human spirit while also preserving God's freedom to speak or not to speak the divine word in history? Rahner located such a possibility, our "obediential potency," in the dynamism of intellectual transcendence which, however, could transcend only in and through history.[24]

In a similar, non-positivistic, "critical" spirit, it is necessary to ask what there is about the very structure of human existence and our relationship to God which *necessarily* makes love of neighbor, interpersonal and structural, a touchstone of love of God. Perhaps God commands us to love one another as a concrete expression of love of God precisely because human existence is not primarily personal and transcendent interiority but a concrete totality with an intrinsic mediation between transcendence and historicity, personal interiority and social exteriority, transcendent salvation and historical liberation? Certainly, more is needed than the Vatican's positivistic appeal to the fact of God's commandment. We need a transcendental anthropological rationale for the unity of love of God and love of neighbor in its structural form in something like an anthropology of concrete totality. Such a rationale is all the more urgent because the entire social doctrine of the church depends on it.

The second part of the Vatican's "logic" lies in the moral application of the causal relation between personal sin and its social consequences. Having reduced all sin to personal sin and disregarded the reality of structural injustice and oppression as a source and origin of personal sins in its own right, the Vatican at the same time insists that personal sins do produce social "consequences" which "ridicule" and "scorn" human dignity (LN, i, 2) and "so often prevent people from living in a manner befitting their dignity" (LN, Introduction). In order to stress the "radical" character of salvation granted in Christ, "the New Testament does not require some change in the political or social condition as a prerequisite for entrance into this freedom" (LN, iv, 13). Nevertheless, "the new freedom procured by the grace of Christ should necessarily have effects on the social level" (ibid.). In other words, participation in historical liberation is not really "a prerequisite" or an essential condition of salvation, but insofar as personal sins, through their social consequences, do dehumanize human beings, we should also pay attention to structural injustice and oppression.

How logical and how strong is this "logic"? Does this justify concern for historical liberation as a "matter of the highest priority" or an "indissoluble" relationship between salvation and liberation"? I think not. Why should a Christian also be concerned with and engage in the liberation of unjust structures when these are basically "results," "effects," and "consequences" of sin, which is always personal in any event, when structures are at best extrinsic conditions of personal existence with only a marginal causality over the latter? Why is the individual's inward struggle to be liberated from sin, the root and cause of all forms of temporal slavery, not sufficient to bring about historical liberation as its "effect"? Wouldn't the elimination of the individual cause by definition also automatically eliminate its social effects? Isn't this precisely what the causal relation means? Why, then, not concentrate on the elimination of personal sin, the primary and radical cause of all social sins, through conversion of individual hearts?

Perhaps the Vatican would reply that if one were truly serious about conversion, one could not be indifferent to the necessary social consequences of one's personal sin and that there is a difference between interior sin and conversion and their social effects; that is, the removal of social effects does not automatically follow from, but requires a separate act in addition to, the interior act of repentance. This would amount to the recognition of the difference between personal interiority and sociohistorical reality, but only within the overall primacy of the personal over the social. This might perhaps justify the indissoluble relation between personal conversion and social liberation insofar as personal sin has a necessary social consequence, but would not amount to a recognition either of the transcendent, autonomous, causal reality of the social in relation to isolated personal existence or of an intrinsic relation between salvation and liberation. The "necessity" the Vatican recognizes is the necessity of the unilateral causal relation proceeding from the personal cause to its social effects, not also that of the reciprocal relation proceeding from the structural conditions of society to personal consequences.

While there is therefore an intrinsic relation between salvation and personal interior conversion, the relation between salvation and the conversion of sinful structures (the consequences of personal sins) remains extrinsic insofar as the cause remains external to and distinct from its effect. As mentioned earlier, the praxis of structural liberation cannot produce 'redemption,' which is a function of personal conversion under divine grace, but only the 'conditions' of redeemed existence. Moreover, these conditions in themselves neither produce nor destroy human freedom; they only facilitate its exercise. Freedom, and thus the possibility of personal conversion, remains fundamentally untouched by the conditions, no matter how oppressive these might be. The "indissoluble" relation the Vatican posits between salvation and liberation, therefore, is not really so indissoluble; even without structural change, humans still remain free. From the theological point of view, the necessity to remove the social consequences of the necessary causality of personal sin is at best a secondary necessity—i.e., through the mediation of the primary and essential relationship between salvation and personal conversion, which "also" requires removal of the social consequences of personal sins—not a primary necessity of an intrinsic relation between salvation as such and social liberation as such.

The third and perhaps the strongest part of the Vatican's logic, I think is found in its argument from unity, the unity of human existence and that of God's intention to recapitulate all things in Christ. It must be pointed out at the outset, however, that this argument occurs only in three passages which are rather of minor significance in the overall argumentation of LC and come rather late in the text. "The Church desires the good of man in *all* his dimensions, first of all as a member of the City of God, and then as a member of the earthly city" (LC, 63; my emphasis). There is "unity" between evangelization and human promotion "because she [the Church] seeks the good of the *whole* person;

distinction because these two tasks enter, in different ways, into her mission" (LC, 64: my emphasis). In exhorting the laity to involve themselves in social liberation as their specific vocation, LC states:

> the purpose of the Church is to spread the Kingdom of Christ so that all men may be saved and that through them *the world may be effectively ordered to Christ*. The work of salvation is thus seen to be indissolubly linked to the task of improving and raising the conditions of human life in this world. The distinction between the supernatural order of salvation and the temporal order of human life must be seen in the context of God's *singular* plan to recapitulate *all* things in Christ. (80; my emphases)

These passages, I think, contain the kernel of a solution to the problem of unity, but they are also inconsistent, I am afraid, with the underlying soteriology and anthropology of the Vatican. The passages invoke two principles of unifying totality, the theological principle of the Kingdom and God's "singular" plan to "recapitulate *all* things in Christ," and the anthropological principle of the totality of the dimensions of human existence, "the good of man in *all* his dimensions" and "the good of the *whole* person." The theological principle is inconsistent with the soteriology and the doctrine of sin discussed earlier. If indeed there is only *one* or "singular" divine plan for *all* things as part of the Kingdom, then, it would seem that neither salvation nor sin could be merely a matter of the relation between the interiority of personal existence and God: they must include the totality of human existence as concrete, social, historical beings, essentially and from the very beginning, which the Vatican does not acknowledge. It would also in principle abolish the distinction between supernatural salvation and temporal liberation and substitute total and partial salvation in mutual dialectic, as discussed in the preceding chapter.

The principle of the Kingdom should likewise include the anthropological principle of unity, "the good of man in *all* his dimensions" and "the good of the *whole* person," as a principle internal to the principle of the Kingdom and arising from its demand, for otherwise, the anthropological principle would remain outside of and implicitly coequal with the theological principle of the Kingdom. In LC, however, the anthropological principle is brought in purely ad hoc, merely added to the theological principle from outside; it is neither employed in the systematic elaboration of soteriology and the doctrine of sin nor generated by and intrinsically linked to the theological principle of unity. If indeed the person is a *whole* person, a unity of *all* one's dimensions and of transcendence and history, not merely the internal, individual subjectivity nor an external juxtaposition of contrasting "dimensions," one would also think that there is an intrinsic mutual mediation between internal and external, individual and social, transcendent and historical. The latter pole of the relation, then, would not be merely the result or effect of the former but also its reciprocating source and cause. The anthropological principle of unity, in this sense, remains inconsistent with the underlying dualism or, perhaps more accurately, personalist interiorist monism that reduces the social to the personal.

THE VATICAN'S ANTHROPOLOGY: A CRITIQUE

Reduction of the Social to the Personal

The preceding analysis of the Vatican's conception of freedom, sin, salvation, and the relation of personal existence to society and history makes it all too clear that its anthropology is essentially individualist, spiritualist, and transcendentalist. Its analysis begins and ends with this conception, introducing social and historical relations and structures only in its account of the sinful effects of actions which are basically personal and inward. God's relation to humans seems confined to transactions within the inwardness of individuals, not also operative in the totality of our political, cultural, and economic history. To think otherwise seems to jeopardize the transcendence of both God and humans, God's transcendence because it would deny the distinction between the "political" and the "religious" as well as the causal primacy of salvation over liberation, transcendence of the person because it is only within the inwardness of intellect, will, and heart that the person transcends and relates to God.

It is in order to preserve God's transcendence and the possibility of human transcendence in freedom and sin that the Vatican insists on the primacy and autonomy of individual inwardness and freedom vis-a-vis society and history. To introduce the sociohistorical elements into the interior of personal existence—not just as its subsequent, external effects—seems to deny the possibility of freedom and sin. To exalt the dignity of the person is not only to affirm the ultimate finality of personal existence as a value and end rooted in one's relation to God and transcendent of anything empirical, but also to assert the causal transcendence and autonomy of the person with respect to everything historical. To assert the transcendent value of the person in the moral order of final causality is possible only because the person—precisely in his or her individual inwardness—is capable of transcending the external pressures of the social and historical in free self-determination, in the metaphysical order of efficient causality.

By way of an overall evaluation, let me begin with the Vatican's tendency to reduce the social to the personal. In its legitimate reaction against certain collectivist tendencies to 'reify' society as an entity in its own right apart from and independent of individuals, the Vatican goes to the other extreme of reducing the social to the individual, in exactly the same way—although for different reasons and purposes—in which bourgeois individualist capitalism has been accused of so doing. For John Paul, humans are "substantial subjects each by himself and separately; the society in itself is exclusively a complex of relations, and therefore an accidental being," "accidental to each and all."[25] The recognition of the sociality of personal existence amounts to no more than the recognition of something purely factual. It means "simply the multiplicity of human activity and existence," that there are "many people as subjects existing and acting,"[26] that "in fact man acts 'together with others'," that "usually—if not always—he in one way or another acts 'together with others'."[27] Social sins are no more than "the result of the accumulation and concentration of many personal sins" (RP, 16).

There is nothing constitutive or irreducible about the social as such. Individuals, already constituted in their proper reality and free in their atomistic isolation, somehow enter into relations with others and produce structures, situations, and systems, good and bad. They may suffer the consequences of their individual actions by creating unjust structures, just as they may benefit from creating just ones. But these evils and benefits of structures are only a posteriori, factual, and external to the constitution of persons in their individuality and freedom, not a priori, constitutive, and intrinsic as well. It is hard to imagine, therefore, why individuals, already constituted free in their isolation, would *want* to enter into all the manifold social relations, create social institutions which more often than not seem to harm and oppress their freedom, and then try to liberate themselves from such institutions and structures. The Vatican is concerned with the social only in two senses, as the "necessary" effect of personal acts and as the factual, extrinsic condition for the exercise of such acts, just as it looks on the personal subject solely from above and from within, as subject of religious transcendence and moral inwardness. It ignores the a priori, intrinsic, constitutive dependence of persons on the social for their very existence and for the very consciousness, content, and development of their freedom and individuality.

Despite all the talk about how "irreplaceable," "necessary," "vital," and "radical" social relations and institutions are to the exercise of freedom, the Vatican construes such relations and institutions as "conditions" in a non-dialectical sense, as something accidental to freedom. Such conditions "can *only* create *better* conditions for the *effective* exercise of freedom" (LC, 31; my emphases). They are, after all, not necessary or irreplaceable; they are helpful only as aids, and thus ultimately dispensable. Being only extrinsic conditions, which have to do with the "effectiveness" or facilitation of the exercise of freedom already constituted as freedom even apart from such conditions, they are not intrinsic to either the very exercise or the very origin and genesis of freedom as such. Liberation "in itself" does not produce human freedom, for "even when freedom is subject to forms of conditioning it is not thereby completely destroyed"; in fact, "people who undergo terrible constraints succeed in manifesting their freedom and taking steps to secure their own liberation" (ibid.).

One may wonder, however, whether it is really possible to consider structures and structural change "in themselves" at all as the Vatican frequently does. Such a conception would be possible, of course, if we were to reify social structures

into autonomous entities wholly independent of those individuals who in varying ways contribute to their creation, something neither John Paul nor Ratzinger
would like to do. Such *conceptual* separation of structures from the humans involved in them seems possible, then, only because one sees, as they do, the *ontological* relation between structures and humans as at best extrinsic and accidental. Such a relation abstracts from all the collective suffering, outrage, excite-
ment, enthusiasm, hope, and actions of interdependent individuals—persons who
create a new structure against the challenges and pressures of an already existing
system, or those who suffer from the system and who are necessarily affected
in their personal inwardness by their involvement in such experiences. A structure or system taken *concretely*, not in abstraction from the experiences and struggles of those involved which are essential to the genesis and maintenance of such
a system, is already, in itself, either good or bad—in varying degrees, of course—
for those who are inseparably involved in it, depending on whether it is liberating
or oppressive. A structure is never so extrinsic to the humans subject to that
structure that we can consider it merely neutral, neither good nor bad in itself,
like a harmless tool (e.g., an axe), which would be extrinsic to an end and could
be used for a good end and abused for a bad.

It is more than curious to note that, while the Vatican thus reminds us that
in itself, structural change does not produce individual freedom and may even
become a tool of oppression, it *never* says that individual freedom in itself, in
isolation from society, is neither possible nor actual. This peculiar blindness
is perhaps not unrelated to the sociological fact that many in already established
democracies or in positions of power in non-democracies tend to take their
freedom for granted, as well as to the historical fact that problems continue to
occur even when one's freedom is guaranteed either by the political system or
by one's social position. Hence one is inclined to dismiss such structural
guarantees as unimportant because they do not, as indeed they could not, in
themselves ensure either personally meaningful freedom or the solution of all
social problems. One fails to appreciate not only the immense sense of liberation originally experienced when the old oppressive structures were toppled but
also the fact that the very indifference to structural protections of freedom, the
continuing search for more meaningful freedom, and the rise and solution of
social problems all presuppose a social, structural context that allows such
indifference and such search in the first place as well as generates both new
problems and the need for their solution.

Is it really true to say that "even when freedom is subject to forms of conditioning it is not thereby completely destroyed"? The answer, I think, is dependent on a number of factors. There are indeed heroic individuals who survive
even torture chambers and concentration camps. It is also praiseworthy to develop
one's inner resources and spirituality so as to be able to survive such pressures
with integrity. Two questions, however, must be asked. First, how many
individuals could be expected to be so heroic? By definition, heroes are rare,

and one wonders how valid it is to base a social doctrine of the church meant for all on the assumption of such heroism. Second, would the heroes still be heroes if they were born, raised, and confined in such concentration camps all their lives? To think they could be would only hide a purely spiritualist or Stoic conception of human existence in all its un-Christian dualism.

Furthermore, depending on the degree of conditioning, these heroes might have died and their freedom been indeed completely destroyed, as witness the millions of people who did die in concentration camps, torture chambers, and drought-ridden areas. If the heroes did survive, it was due not only to their inner strength—their "freedom"—but also because, fortunately, the pain and suffering inflicted on them did not exceed certain objective limits required for survival. Likewise, if "people who undergo terrible constraints succeed in manifesting their freedom and taking steps to secure their own liberation," this would only mean that the "causality" of "conditions" is not mechanical (more on this later), although beyond certain limits, as just mentioned, such causality does operate. After all, both Maximilian Kolbe and Dietrich Bonhoeffer did die. It could not mean that social conditions are not essential to freedom. If not, why would they *want* to take steps to secure their own liberation? Likewise, is it not precisely the challenges and threats posed by the conditions which, along with the inner integrity of the individuals involved, make the heroes heroes and which are therefore intrinsic to heroism *as* heroism?

Social Conditions of Freedom

In exalting the freedom of the individual, the Vatican empties social sin of its distinctive analytic meaning by either reducing it to a cumulative sum of individual sins or dismissing it as sin only in an analogical sense. Social ethics is merely an extension of individual ethics. Just as social structures and conditions are no more than the sum of the results of individual actions, so "they always depend on the responsibility of man, who can alter them, and not upon an alleged determinism of history" (LC, 74). Society or history as such does not "act"; only individuals do. These raise three questions about the relation between the individual and society. (1) In what sense do individuals create or produce their society through their actions? (2) Is it really true to say that institutions and structures never "act" except through the individuals who either represent them as officials and/or promote or exploit them? (3) How is it possible to transform social structures?

First, in what sense do individuals produce or create society through their actions? Certainly not in the sense in which God creates the world according to classical metaphysics, i.e., out of nothing. The creative actions of individuals presuppose many things, which are therefore intrinsic to and constitutive of such actions. Just as individuals do not give birth to themselves, so their actions presuppose a set of preexisting economic, political, and cultural conditions. It is against the challenges and pressures of this already existing structure, as well as by the use of the means already explicitly or implicitly available in it, that individuals contribute their share of actions to the transformation of society; even then, they do not do so equally but in infinitely varying degrees. Even so, it would be difficult to attest that the resulting form of society and its structure correspond exactly to the varied intentions of millions of individual agents. To suppose this would be to presuppose a miraculous degree of homogeneity and consensus among individuals widely separated from one another in time, space, occupation, origin, and class; one would also have to ignore both the conflicts among sexes, classes, races, and nations that have historically burdened human relations and the short-sightedness of individuals whose subjective interests do not always coincide with their objective interests.

Social structures are the results of human action insofar as such structures do not drop down from heaven but are in some infinitely complex way dependent on the actions and passions, commissions and omissions, of numerous individuals who support or exploit the structure for conflicting purposes. They are not results of human design in the sense that such results correspond to the conscious knowledge and will—i.e., freedom—of all individuals taken either separately or collectively. At best, they are results of the design—and thus freedom—of groups, not isolated individuals. These groups, precisely through their common position in the existing social order, have developed common interests and organized themselves into a power sufficient to impose their collective interests on the rest of society in an ongoing struggle for power with other groups and classes; however, the Vatican does not want to recognize this struggle as a fact of history. Even then, we must wonder to what extent the result of the collective action of the winning group or class corresponds to the intention and freedom of that group. Certainly, there remains a gap, a contradiction between its intention and the result of its collective action, as witness the frustrations of capitalists, socialists, and communists alike. Even the collective action of a group is subject to the preexisting conditions of society, its ongoing dialectic, and the basic ontological contingency which pervades all human actions. What Kierkegaard said about the irreducibility of (personal) "existence" to "thought" is equally true of our social existence, which remains irreducible even to collective thought. To think otherwise would indeed be idealistic.

To say, then, that society and its structures are the result of free individual actions, or that social sin in the sense of unjust structures is merely the cumulative result of individual sins, is at best misleading and at worst simply false. It is misleading to say, as does the Vatican, that unjust structures "always depend on the responsibility of man, who can alter them and not upon an alleged determinism of history" (LC, 74) or that sinful structures are reducible to the sum of the unjust acts of individuals. The statements are too vague and general ("man") and fail to specify the groups and classes to which concrete individuals always belong or to note the struggle for power in which some groups are more powerful than others, as though all individuals *as* individuals somehow possessed the freedom and responsibility to "alter" such structures. The statements are false in attributing an almighty power for social change to isolated individuals and in ignoring the reified weight of structures already existing prior to the initiation of change.

Such a view, also characteristic of modern social contract theorists and thinkers such as Jeremy Bentham and Milton Friedman, is ultimately based on an arithmetical conception of human beings in which the whole is not greater than the sum of its parts and where the parts—dead numbers—are devoid of all dialectic with others in their isolated self-sufficiency. Even the so-called 'world-historical' individuals, such as Julius Caesar, Napoleon, Gandhi, and Martin Luther King, became world-historical not only because of their individual daring, wisdom, and insight, which I do not want to minimize, but also because of the social conditions which demanded such leadership and the cooperation of classes and groups whose objective situation made them open and responsive to it. Likewise, those "leaders" who, according to John Paul, "are in a position to avoid, eliminate or at least limit certain social evils" or to "work diligently and wisely for the improvement and transformation of society" (RP, 16) are in that "position" precisely because such a position is supported and needed by the power structure of a society already there prior to their respective individual wills. Ronald Reagan did not create the presidency of the United States any more than John Paul created the papacy. Their individual freedom in their positions, therefore, is derived from the existing power structure of their society and limited by the interests of that structure. They are, of course, free to follow their personal convictions even against the dominant interests and ideologies of that structure, at least in the sense that the structure does not mechanically control their actions; by the same token, of course, they also pay for such convictions.

This is not to deny the importance of individual leadership or to close off the possibility of structural change, but only to show the falsity of the atomistic individualist approach to social phenomena and the inherent conditioning of all attempts at structural change by the reified facticity of the preexisting situation (the given), its ongoing dialectic, and the basic ontological contingency which rules the totality of our existence, both individual and social.

It is important at this point to raise the second question, namely, whether it is true to say that structures as such do not 'act,' that only individuals do. If by 'action' we understand the efficient causality of conscious, deliberate acts—*actus humanus,* not *actus hominis*—as does the Vatican, it is clear that only individuals act. It is on the basis of this conception of causality and action that the claim has been made that society and social sins are "results" and "effects" of individual actions and personal sins, not also "causes" and "sources" of the latter. It is both narrow and superficial, however, to consider the meaning of human action only at the level of conscious, deliberate acts of the individual and to forget the depth dimensions of such acts, namely, the very social and historical conditions of which individuals, usually confined to the immediacy of their actions, are not always conscious but without which such actions would simply be impossible. Human action as concretely exercised, not merely thought about, is always situated in a particular social, historical context, which indeed acts both *on* and *in* the lives of individuals—challenging them to act; providing the material means of such acts, as well as the guiding intellectual and cultural horizon of what is important and desirable and what is not; and in certain limit cases (extreme physical and psychological torture, lack of basic material needs, and so forth) literally causing the subjects of such acts to die.

The kind of "action" proper to structures as "conditions" of individual action is often anonymous and unconscious, but no less important. In a real sense they are more important than individual acts both because their influence on the latter is far more enduring and extensive than the influence of one individual upon another, and because, through that influence, they affect precisely the freedom and dignity of persons that the Vatican so cherishes. As conditions of individual acts they are intrinsic to such acts, not merely "not exterior" (LC, 32) or "external" (RP, 16). Without such conditions individual actions are deprived of all motivations and material means, which provide the psychological origin, concrete specificity, and a determinate range of possibilities to such actions. The socio-historical conditions are intrinsic to actions precisely in the sense that both the very possibility and the concrete particularity, both the existence and essence of an act—whether there can *be* an act at all and what *kind* of an act it will be— depend on such conditions. These conditions are both a priori, in the sense that such conditions provide the general necessity of action, the guiding horizon of values and ideas, and the broad limits of what is possible and what is not, and a posteriori, in the sense that they co-constitute the concrete particularity of an act along with the creative element of personal subjectivity of which they remain the a priori condition.

These conditions do not act in the same way that mechanical causes act. In the case of mechanical causality, the relation between cause and effect is extrinsic. The cause literally determines its effect in a unilateral way; the effect does not react on the cause or enter into the specificity of the result except in the sense that even the unilateral causality of the agent must respect the givenness of the nature of the object. The conditions, on the other hand, do not unilaterally determine individual actions except in limit cases mentioned earlier. Individuals do and can respond and react to such conditions—not, of course, from a position outside such conditions, but as agents already internally subject to and shaped under their challenges, ideologies, and material limitations. Attempts at structural change presupppose the facticity and demands of the existing structure, are subject to the ambiguities of its ongoing dialectic, and remain constrained and limited by the possibilities implicit or explicit in it. Structural change never means starting all over with a clean slate, *de novo*. By the same token, structures do not cause individuals to act in this or that way. Within the general, objective, and basic limits imposed by the structure, individual actions also depend on the perceptions, interpretations, courage, and initiative of the agents themselves.

In this sense of mutually intrinsic and mutually mediating relationship between the 'conditioning' and the 'conditioned,' the concept of 'condition' is essentially a dialectical concept, as opposed to the mechanical concept of unilateral causality and the Vatican's use of condition as something extrinsic to the essence of freedom. Contrary to the claims of John Paul and Ratzinger, the structures and institutions of society are not only "results" or "effects" of human action in the sense of the collective action of the winning groups and classes in the struggle for power—not in the sense of the conscious, deliberate action of all individuals taken separately or collectively—but also themselves condition such collective and individual actions, influencing them to a profounder degree than could any causality of individual action, by promoting or inhibiting the very possibility of such action and in any event setting its limits. To focus on the causality of conscious individual freedom, at the expense of the dialectical conditions which make such causality possible and actual, would be to take a very narrow and partial view of the concrete totality which is human existence, indeed a pre-critical view in the sense in which pre-Kantian metaphysics was pre-critical for Kant.

Conditions of Structural Change

This leads to the third question: How is it possible to transform (unjust) social structures? Who can be the agents of such transformation? The preceding discussion of the dialectic between individuals and social conditions does not mean to rule out the possibility of structural change. History does constrain and limit: we cannot make history arbitrarily, *de novo,* or in a vacuum. By the same token, history is neither closed nor fixed: it also contains openings and possibilities, which it is the task of the agents of liberation to discern and develop. It is the existing conditions which generate the need for change in their ongoing dialectic and make available, at least potentially, the material means for actualizing such change even while setting broad limits for its scope. What are the signs of the times demanding such change; what change would be liberating or oppressive; what means are actually available, and what limits there are to the projected changes—these cannot be decided a priori or purely from outside. Hence the constant need for social analysis with a high sensitivity to the shifting dialectic of history. Besides, the contingencies of history, which overrule both collective and individual intentions and projections, often contain unpredictable surprises, which are knowable only after the fact. Who, under Pius XII, could have predicted the revolution of Vatican II, or foreseen the departure of Ferdinand Marcos from power immediately after the fraudulent Filipino election of February 1986? Hence also the need for courageous action testing the limits of the possible even against the apparent immobility of reified structures, and the hope which, for all its realistic humility, never ceases to hope against the impossible. The 'utopian' principle of hope remains indispensable both in discovering the openings and cracks in the seemingly closed and fixed systems and straining the possibilities of change to their very limit.

Who, then, are the agents of such transformation? The need for change always arises amid social conditions which both generate such need *and* threaten to block its fulfillment. Some oppressed groups demand liberation; others regard such demands as a challenge to their privilege. Likewise, some groups are more power-ful than others in imposing their interests on the rest of society. It is under these conditions of opposing interests and differentiated power that social changes are proposed, attempted, and/or achieved. Individuals *as* individuals, then, as men-tioned earlier, can not be agents of social change. As such, they do not possess the power to impose their purely individual will on the rest of society, nor can there be an agreement among such individuals—a natural harmony—with regard to the goal of such change, which is always *particular* in its content (e.g., the Equal Rights Amendment, socialized medicine, transfer of power from military to civilian rule) and thus will not appeal to all individuals or groups. Only a community—i.e., individuals organized with a sense of interdependence for the realization of a shared purpose and mobilized to acquire sufficient power to over-ride the powers of opposing interests and impose their will on the rest of society—is capable of accomplishing such structural change.

Moreover, the structural change at issue is not just any change; we are con-cerned with only such changes that would be liberating under the given condi-tions of a particular society and history. The urgent practical question is how to locate, organize, educate, and mobilize a collective agent of liberating transfor-mation. It must be a group within which the individuals share a consciousness of their common dignity, their common plight of oppression, their common need for collective action—in short, a sense of common destiny. Such a group is not found ready-made but must be located, educated ("conscientized"), organized, and mobilized. It is here that the basic ecclesial communities assume their historical significance.

John Paul and Ratzinger frequently speak of the need for "solidarity," but such solidarity is understood only as something factual or as a moral virtue yet to be realized in the furture,[28] not as a permanent "existential" (cf. Heidegger) of human existence which is already present as an a priori characteristic of that existence and is capable of becoming self-conscious, purified, and liberated in the integral enrichment of that existence. They speak of a social structure which embodies such solidarity as at best a means to individual dignity and often as something separable ("in itself") from such dignity. They do not recognize solidarity in the very constitution of dignity, experience of oppression, and the activity of liberation. They tend to think of human dignity as primarily the dignity of the individual as individual, not as a dignity intrinsically shared by individuals in their interdependence or solidarity, constituted as such by mutual recogni-tion and support. Such dignity, of course, has and must have a transcendent basis in our relation to God; however, as something proper to humans as historical beings, as an attribute of a concrete totality, it is also intrinsically mediated by solidarity. Human transcendence towards God is possible only as transcendence *in* solidarity, not as transcendence *of* solidarity by the isolated individual or as the sum of such isolated transcendences. Liberating structural change presupposes a consciousness of human dignity, not as something each individual possesses for himself or herself but as something which can be truly possessed only in the solidarity of mutual recognition and support—i.e., a concept of human dignity as a truly *common* good, which is both more and other than the sum of individually pursued goods.

Liberating change also requires a common consciousness of solidarity in oppression and the task of liberation. The agents must become aware that their oppression is due to a *common* cause, *structural* injustice, to which they are subject *together,* not as isolated individuals, and from which, therefore, there is only one way of liberating themselves—namely, collective action or action in solidarity for a just structure. What is necessary for liberation, then, is not the inner conversion of an individual, or even of individuals as individuals, but conversion of individuals *with* and *to* a sense of common destiny in history. It is precisely this sense of common destiny—theological in its transcendent basis, metaphysical–anthropological as an existential of human life, and political in its historical actualization—which the personalism of John Paul and Ratzinger finds it so difficult to accommodate because of its dualism and metaphysical individualism. Personalism might be helpful in illuminating the dynamics of 'dialogical' or 'interpersonal' relations in abstraction from the dialectic of the larger society. It does not have the theoretical resources for understanding the dialectic of history, still less for illuminating the basis of a theology of structural liberation or motivating liberating praxis, however the Vatican might call its own theology a theology of "integral," "definitive," and "authentic" liberation.

Beyond Abstract Personalism

Human existence, I have argued many times thus far, is a concrete totality of all the essential relations, broadly the relation to transcendence and the relation to history and nature. As moments within a totality, these relations are indeed distinct, but as moments of concrete totality they are also mutually mediated and mediating in a constitutive relationship; each can neither exist nor develop apart from the mediation by the other. The human relation to nature and history is human, not animal, because it is intrinsically mediated by our relation to transcendence; similarly our relation to transcendence is human, not angelic, because it is mediated by our relation to history and nature. And just as human existence as such a totality cannot be reduced to pure nature, nor can it be reduced to pure transcendence. Our relationship to God as a human relationship is intrinsically conditioned by the mediation of the natural and the historical, our dependence on nature, our social interdependence, and the objectification of our natural and social dependences in economics, politics, and culture.

The Vatican never ceases to emphasize the finitude of human existence as created by God, and in this they are only joining the long line of classical theologians, spiritual writers, and contemporary existentialists. Sin manifests itself in the revolt of the finite creature against the creator and the denial of one's own nature as a finite creature. It is important to note, however, that this finitude has consistently been understood only metaphysically, as contingency or lack of ontological self-sufficiency, and only in our vertical relation to God. It is as though human finitude—I don't know about the finitude of angels—consisted only in the ontological dependence on God, as if humans were self-sufficient in relation to others in society and history. What has not been adverted to is the fact that our natural and social dependences in concrete history are simply the other side of the same coin, the humanly finite expression and mediation of our ontological dependence on God. We are intrinsically dependent not only on God but also on nature and our fellows. As intrinsically finite beings we do not cease to be finite in our sociohistorical relations. Our double dependences on God and on finite creatures in nature and history are the two sides—mutually mediated and mediating—of one and the same ontological fact: the contingency of our existence *(esse)*.

John Paul and Ratzinger abstract totally from this sociohistorical dimension in their account of sin and freedom, which as a result ultimately renders sin and freedom incomprehensible as realities of concrete human existence. They construe sin as a transaction in the inwardness of the individual before God, and freedom as the act of a person without essential social mediation. The subject of sin and freedom is not the person as a concrete totality, already immersed in history where one must act and thus discover and develop one's consciousness of self, freedom, the need for God and salvation, and the sense of sin through the experience of the manifold historical forms of ontological contingency. Instead, the subject of sin is identified with the "inner" person directly confronted with God and God alone. As LC put it earlier;

> Culpable ignorance of God unleashes the passions, which are causes of imbalance and conflicts in the human heart. From this there inevitably come disorders which affect the sphere of the family and society: sexual license, injustice and murder (39).

The causal sequence is always from the transcendent to the historical, from the person to society, from the inner to the outer.

Consider, however, the a priori conditions for the very possibility of such a sequence and whether the fundamentally asocial subject—the "worldless subject" (Heidegger)—of John Paul and Ratzinger could fulfill such conditions. How is it possible to be even culpably ignorant of God? This presupposes, of course, our need for God and our capacity for knowledge of God. After all, minerals, plants, and animals do not have such a need and capacity. This, however, is not sufficient. If it is true that we do not have an innate idea of God, that we cannot even develop an intuitive knowledge of God in her essence in this life, as Aquinas insists, then we must derive our knowledge of God from the analogy with creatures; this necessity presupposes our exposure to society. It is also in the midst of our social existence in history that we develop the need for God and salvation, through the experience of sickness, frustrations, oppressions, the beauty and fragility of love, the possibility of death, alienation and reconciliation, the grandeur and misery of nature, and the tragedies of war, poverty, and starvation. To say that we acquire a knowledge of God through our social existence and its culture is also to acknowledge that our knowledge of God is exposed to the relativities of the dominant ideologies and values of a particular society, which often distort our knowledge of God. In other words, both our need for and our knowledge of God as a human need and human knowledge presuppose, as their a priori condition, our involvement in society and history. John Paul's and Ratzinger's abstract subject, unsituated and withdrawn from the necessities of social life, could not even get an idea of God, contingency, and sin, still less be culpably ignorant.

Consider also the a priori conditions for the possibility of passions, imbalances, and conflicts in the human heart. These presuppose something like what the Thomists call the powers of the soul—intellect, will, irrational appetites, or passions—as the essential potentialities of the person. In their human concreteness, however, they also presuppose more. As the phenomenologists have been telling us, intellect, will, passions, imbalances and conflicts in the heart are always 'intentional': they are directed to specific objects, through which they also become actual and concrete. A passion which is not a passion for or against something is no passion, as conflicts which are not about anything in particular can not be real conflicts. These objects come to us produced, interpreted, and evaluated by the culture and society in which we live. It is in society that we develop the power to discriminate among different objects, and it is through society that objects become available to fulfill or frustrate the passions of the heart. The dominant values of society, as John Paul never ceases to point out in his encyclicals and addresses, also pressure us in favor of certain values, such as material comfort, easy sex, indifference to the value of life, worship of money and profit, and so forth, and thus reinforce our passions, imbalances, and disorders in these areas. The powers and passions of human interiority need the mediation of society for both their specificity and actuality.

Consider, finally, the a priori conditions for the possibility of the sins singled out by LC: sexual license, injustice, and murder. These presuppose not only certain characteristics on the part of the person—such as sexual desire, the need and power to assert oneself against another, and the physical and psychological power to kill—but also the existence of sexual objects and other persons who are themselves always found only in a culture with a particular system of values and laws regarding the relation of human beings to one another. Sexual license, injustice, and murder do not exist as abstractions; they are always particular according to object, situation, and the society in which they occur. Murder for private revenge, murder for political reasons, murder on the battlefield, murder out of economic pressure, even murder for the sake of God: these are not all the same but require different explanations, evaluations, and responses, which are conditioned by the existing political, legal, economic, and cultural conditions of a particular society. Again, how and why the abstract, unsituated subject of the Vatican would want to commit sexual license, injustice, and murder remains incomprehensible. There is, of course, a certain arbitrariness about sin, but such arbitrariness or wilfulness is always *about* something within a certain situation. The Vatican's anthropology concentrates on the arbitrariness of self-assertion in sin without providing anything to be arbitrary *about* and a situation to be arbitrary *in*.

This is ironic. The intention of John Paul and Ratzinger is to defend the reality of sin and the dignity of humans by exalting freedom, but by ignoring the historical condition and content of sin, freedom, and dignity, they end up by rendering these concepts so superhuman and angelic as to make them simply incomprehensible, indeed impossible, as *human* realities. They insist that "in the process of liberation, one cannot abstract from the historical situation of the nation or attack the cultural identity of the people" (LC, 75). It is curious why, in the treatment of sin from which we are meant to be liberated, LC does "abstract from the historical situation" of the sinner and thus reifies sin.

Freedom, sin, conversion, and human dignity: these are activities and attributes of a subject with a nature which is finite, not in the angelic but in the concretely human sense. They are comprehensible only as experiences of human existence as a concrete, dialectical totality of transcendence and history, a totality which transcends only *in* history, not *over* history except as an ideal limit. It is in history, the totality of economic, political, and cultural conditions, and against the challenges, opportunities, and limitations posed by these conditions, that individuals both acquire and grow in their consciousness of their identity, their freedom to sin or not sin, their need for God and conversion, and their transcendent dignity—and through history that they develop and actualize identity, freedom, and moral and religious transcendence. Both the transcendent dignity of humans in the order of ends and the power of freedom to transcend in the order of efficient causality are themselves discovered, realized, and in any case always in the process of becoming, in a dialectic of co-constitution of the individual and the manifold social relations to which he or she is subject as a concrete totality. It is true that "man becomes free to the extent that he comes to a knowledge of truth, and to the extent that this truth—not only other forces—guides his will" (LC, 26), but this knowledge of truth is not independent of or simply prior to our praxis in society and history. It is precisely *in* and *through* such praxis that we acquire and grow in the knowledge of truth.

Contrary to John Paul and Ratzinger, then, it is not possible to either appreciate or defend the reality of freedom, sin, and human dignity by maximizing the capacity of the individual for self-determination and minimizing the conditioning power of situations and structures over that capacity; such a view only denatures these experiences and attributes of humanly finite natures, either by exalting them to the angelic level or by emptying them of their humanly necessary historical content and historical dialectic. This historically dialectical conception rejects both mechanistic reductionism, which denies the possibility of human freedom altogether, and the exaltation of human freedom to the unsituated, ahistorical freedom of angels, which denies the humanly finite character of that freedom. It preserves both the possibility and humanity of human freedom. It is precisely because of the challenge and resistance of social reality that heroes can become heroes, that people can suffer oppression and demand liberation. Human dignity is precious not because humans can determine themselves for themselves in any arbitrary way, in a historical vacuum, or over all historical situations, but precisely because it is primarily rooted in God's loving transcendence of her transcendence towards us in history, to which we only respond in a transcendence appropriate to our human, historical mode, not in an ahistorical transcendence towards God, and because it always remains fragile, demanding constant reaffirmation and structural protection against the negativities of history.

The abstract personalism of John Paul and Ratzinger, which lacks this sense of historical mediation of human existence as a concrete totality, not only denatures the human reality of sin, freedom, and dignity but also tends to distort the nature of the poor, the salvific significance of the death and resurrection of Jesus Christ, and the meaning of the Magnificat. It does so by consistently emptying them of their concrete, often painful historical content and thus 'spiritualizing' them. Let me confine myself to the interpretation of the poor in LC.

For LC, it is "one of the principal errors" since the Enlightenment and "a misunderstanding of the depths of freedom and its needs" to think that improvements in the material conditions of life "should serve as a basis for achieving freedom" (21). Why? Because "the little ones and the poor," who lack such conditions, experience "the liberating joy" which comes from their faith–knowledge that "they are the object of God's infinite love," which gives them "the dignity which none of the powerful can take away from them" (ibid.). In an assertion of the "hermeneutic privilege" of the poor in the context of the popular devotion to the Cross, LC goes on to state:

> Here we have a fact of fundamental theological and pastoral significance:
> it is the poor, the object of God's special love, who understand best and
> as it were instinctively that the most radical liberation, which is liberation

from sin and death, is the liberation accomplished by the Death and Resurrection of Christ. (22)

The "poor of Yahweh" know that communion with him is the most precious treasure and the one in which man finds his true freedom. For them, the most tragic misfortune is the loss of this communion. Hence their fight against injustice finds its deepest meaning and its effectiveness in their desire to be freed from the slavery of sin. (47)

Why did Christ identify himself with the poor? Because such misery is "the obvious sign of the natural condition of weakness in which man finds himself since original sin and the sign of his need for salvation" (68).

Just as LC consistently separates sin in its essence from its sociohistorical conditions and content and thus reifies and spiritualizes it, so does it do the same with the poor. Material conditions are not even *a* basis of freedom. The poor of LC are indifferent to the experience of a lack of basic necessities, in all its concrete pain, anxiety, and helplessness, although this experience, one would think, is precisely what makes them poor. They "understand best" that "true freedom" lies in "liberation from sin and death" in their communion with God, not also in the overcoming of their material poverty. The reason why Jesus had compassion on them was that poverty was a sign of our need for salvation—not also because poverty was poverty, i.e., the painful lack of elementary physical needs without which they would literally die. That is, the poor of LC are not really poor. They do not care about poverty; they already enjoy true freedom in a direct communion with God. They are only concerned about sin against God and God's salvation from that sin. LC suppresses all that is specific about the experience of poverty *as* poverty, even while talking about the poor *as* poor.

One only wonders, then, how it is possible at all for the poor to engage in the "fight against injustice" with concern for "its effectiveness" (47). Why do the poor, who are poor but do not suffer the consequences of poverty, fight, and try to fight effectively, against the injustice that makes them poor? What exactly is it from which "they live in hope of deliverance" (ibid.), if not their poverty? Why do they have such hope and "place their trust in Yahweh" (ibid.) at all unless they suffer the pain, helplessness, and despair as a result of poverty? How is it possible to experience injustice *as* injustice except in its concrete social forms, such as denial of basic needs, forced seizure of land, low wages, systematic discrimination in employment, excessive taxation, robbery, and slavery—all of which do hurt the poor as poor in the most materially painful ways? How could injustice to the poor be a "grave sin" which destroys communion with God" (46) when it does not really touch them *as* poor? How is it possible for the poor to "understand" that the "liberation from sin and death" is "the liberation accomplished by the Death and Resurrection of Christ" (22) except through the experience of their own poverty, which constitutes their existential and historical situation, unless, of course, one supposes an unmediated, direct, almost angelic intuition on the part of the poor? If the poor experience the "liberating joy," what exactly is it a liberation *from,* if not from the degradation and helplessness of poverty as well? Why are the poor "the object of God's special love," if they are not really helpless, dependent, and not really different from other groups of people? How is poverty a sign of our "need" for salvation when it is poverty only in name?

By systematically abstracting from the concrete material and social experiences of poverty which make the poor poor, LC spiritualizes poverty and ends up by denying the concretely *human* reality of the poor and making its own assertions incomprehensible. Again, it refuses to acknowledge the concrete sociohistorical mediation as the essential human condition for the very possibility of the spiritual experience of injustice, sin, liberation from sin, and the knowledge of radical liberation through Christ which it attributes to the poor. For LC, as for TL, the poor possess both theological and epistemological privilege over other groups, but whereas TL attributes such privilege to the poor precisely in their material, historical reality, LC does so by consistently ignoring such human reality and emphasizing instead a spirituality unmediated by the experience of poverty in its most ordinary sense. In order to affirm the transcendent meaning of poverty, it transcendentalizes poverty itself and denies poverty *as* poverty.

Both John Paul and LC use the language of totality, such as 'unity,' 'whole' person, and 'all' dimensions of human life.[29] Their use, however, is formal and abstract: 'unity' means no more than the sum of all the dimensions in their formal distinction, without a sense of a totality mediating and mediated by the dimensions or of the dimensions mediating and mediated by one another. It is at best an extrinsic unity and thus an abstract, not concrete, totality. History does not intrinsically mediate our transcendence to God in freedom and sin. On the contrary, freedom and sin unilaterally 'cause' our history as their 'effect,' while also preserving their transcendence *over* history and their distinctness *from* history. The *whole* person, therefore, is reduced either to transcendent subjectivity without an essential relation to history, as in the account of sin, freedom, and poverty, or to an incomprehensible juxtaposition of transcendence and history, accomplished by the addition of the word "and" in its argument for liberation ("first of all as a member of the City of God, *and* then as a member of the earthly city") (LC, 63; my emphasis).

Given the Vatican's abstract personalism, then, which wavers between a spiritualist monism and a not-so-covert dualism, it is no wonder that its commitment to liberation often appears ambiguous and half-hearted. One cannot avoid the impression of a dilemma: on the one hand its deeper conviction seems to lean in the monist direction, but on the other it seems to find it impossible to ignore the weight and challenge of unjust structures and the demand for liberation. Even when LC insists that the Church's speaking about the promotion of social justice "is not going beyond her mission," it does not forget to warn that "this mission should not be absorbed by preoccupations concerning the temporal order or reduced to such preoccupations" (64). Even while asserting that the "temporal" task of serving one's neighbor and society is "urgently demanded", it also tempers this urgency by warning against "an unrealistic and ruinous search for a perfect world, 'for the form of this world is passing away'"(62), just as LN combines the strongest appeal yet for the social commitment of the entire church with a simultaneous warning and reservation about "temporal messianism" and "historicist immanentism" (xi, ix, and x). If indeed historical and social forms of love of neighbor are "indissolubly" linked to the work of salvation as part of God's "singular" plan, it is curious why the Vatican is forever so anxious to issue such a reservation. It certainly does not worry about "preoccupations" with the love of God, sacramental piety, and individual conversion, even though the possibility of deviation or excess in these areas, if history is any evidence, is certainly not less.

To conclude, the Vatican's own version of theology of liberation suffers from a pervasive dualism in its view of transcendence and history, which renders its soteriological, Christological, and anthropological doctrines incomprehensible and irrelevant to our human reality in its concrete historical existence. There seems no doubt that the Vatican feels the need for a theological development in the direction of some sort of a theology of liberation. It even insists that such a development "remains constantly open to the new questions which continually arise" (72). It also insists, however, as we saw earlier in this chapter, that it must be in "strict connection" with and "fully adherent" to the tradition of the magisterium, to the "principles that are always valid" even in the midst of "the changing circumstances of history" (ibid.). Unless this tradition and its principles are somehow disengaged from the underlying anthropological assumptions—whether neo-Platonist, Augustinian, Thomist, or personalist—and unless we are allowed to rethink the tradition on new anthropological bases, the range of possibility of development, I submit, remains severely restricted. Certainly, a theology of liberation developed on traditional anthropological foundations, as I have been arguing all along, would be at best a half-hearted attempt, always in the grip of a dualistic schizophrenia.

CHAPTER VI

Signs of the Times and the Future of Theology: Concluding Reflections

Thus far I have covered some of the major issues having to do with the central themes of TL. Beginning with a survey of the issues and an outline of the book in the first chapter, I presented the Marxian and Hegelian sources of TL (Chapter 2) and discussed the relation between theology and praxis (Chapter 3), the dialectic of salvation and liberation (Chapter 4), and the Vatican's own version of a theology of freedom and its social doctrine of liberation (Chapter 5). In each case, I tried to take the criticisms very seriously and to respond to them as fully as possible from the perspective of TL. From the very beginning, my intention, I think, has been clear: it was to save TL from many of its distortions and defend it against some of its critics. Whether I have succeeded in doing so is not for me to judge. Doubtless, some issues demand further elaboration and discussion, while a host of others have not even been broached.

In this concluding chapter, I would like to reflect on the larger significance of the confrontation between TL and the Vatican, its official critic. Over and beyond the particular issues that have been discussed, the confrontation raises two fundamental questions: How does Christianity respond to the contemporary "signs of the times"? and How adequate is a theology to such a task? Both are questions of Christian praxis in the contemporary world: the first is a question about the challenges facing that praxis, the second about the task of Christian theory in responding to such challenges.

SIGNS OF THE TIMES

A cloud has been hanging over humanity for some time. Sometimes it seems to be gathering, at other times to be dispersing. Sometimes it turns into a storm of unimaginable disaster, often into merely uncomfortable rain and snow; always it casts long shadows of gloom over the planet Earth and always threatens to become a tornado ready to hit us all in our moments of uneasy complacency and feigned peace. What Matthew Arnold said of the nineteenth century seems truer of the twentieth. The world

> Hath really neither joy, nor love, nor light,
> Nor certitude, nor peace, nor help for pain;
> And we are here as on a darkling plain
> Swept with confused alarms of struggle and flight,
> Where ignorant armies clash by night.
> (From "Dover Beach")

Not all of us, of course, are so "confused" or so "ignorant." Many, especially those with power and privilege, seem to know exactly what they are doing when they struggle to maintain and extend their power over the rest of society and the world. The result of such struggles for power and domination has indeed been "a darkling plain," which "has really neither joy, nor love, nor light, nor certitude, nor peace, nor help for pain."

This is how the contemporary world might appear to a sensitive and compassionate observer from the First World. The world is gloomy and unpleasant indeed. The threats of tornados and storms and earthquakes always seem to be there. Still, the world is tolerable. After all, the threats of political repressions, military conflicts, and economic disasters seem to remain only threats. If they flare up, they do so only in regions so far away that they do not seem to touch us with the immediacy of the concrete, only in countries whose cultures seem so strange to our own. We do not suffer the disasters ourselves. Nor are we really responsible for them. The problems are, after all, so it seems, *theirs,* not ours. The picture of the world is depressing, the turn of events disheartening, but overall, life remains quite tolerable, occasionally even enjoyable.

To the absolute majority of humanity today, however, many of them in the First and Second Worlds but mostly in the Third, the disasters are not threats but bloody realities of the everyday world. From the Palestinians in refugee camps to the women and children slaughtered by the Nicaraguan contras; from those caught in the brutal struggle between Hindus and Buddhists in Sri Lanka and between Hindus and Sikhs in India to the victims of the conflict between Catholics and Protestants in Northern Ireland; from the victims of the war between Iran and Iraq to the oppressed black majority in South Africa; from the displaced refugees and victims of death squads in Central America to the uprooted Cambodians in Thai camps; from the starving campesinos in Latin America to the victims of drought in Africa; from the slum dwellers of Manila to the exploited workers of Seoul; from the political criminals silently languishing and 'disappearing' in the jails of right-wing regimes to the silenced majorities of left-wing regimes; from the blacks, Hispanics, whites, and the elderly living under the poverty line in the United States to the "guest workers" in Germany; from the women and racial and religious minorities in all the regions of the world whose sufferings are compounded by sexism, racism, and discrimination to the more than one billion humans in absolute poverty and on the verge of starvation—and the list could go on endlessly—suffering and oppression are not abstract threats of the future but concrete realities of the immediate present. They are victims of economic exploitation and political repression, of the colossal indifference of those with power and privilege, of the structural inequities of an increasingly interdependent world, of economic, political and military imperialism and its local cronies. Some of the victims muster enough courage and hope to scream to the television sets of the First World, while the majority, it seems, feel powerless and languish in quiet despair.[1]

How should Christians respond to these horrors of massive poverty and brutal repression throughout the world? How should they heed these signs of the times? Many Christians, individually and collectively, have been responding at great personal and institutional cost. Many courageous leaders and groups have arisen to speak and act prophetically for the silent, suffering majority of humanity. In recent years the vigorous statements and activities of such bodies as the World Council of Churches, the National Council of Churches in the United States, the Methodist and Roman Catholic bishops, the Presbyterian national assemblies, the Friends Service Committee, and a host of others have been most encouraging. It is clear, however, that these efforts, laudable as they indeed are, are scarcely adequate to the screaming needs of the world's poor and oppressed. It is equally clear that Christians committed to the praxis of prophetic responsibility are all too few and powerless even in their own denominations. The conversion of the churches *as* institutions still awaits its realization,.

The challenge of theology of liberation is not primarily a challenge of *theology* of liberation or even some of its outspoken theologians. It is primarily the challenge of *liberation,* the screaming demand of these billions of 'non-persons' for liberation from the conditions which literally kill them. In this respect the confrontation between TL and the Vatican is not a matter of church discipline between some rebellious theologians and their highest authority, nor is it even a matter of academic dissent and freedom, which might be relevant only to academic theologians. Neither is it a mere product of media sensationalism: it was not created by the media, and it is not likely to go away because the media lose interest in it. Individual liberation theologians may come and go, but the problem of liberation will remain as long as the conditions of oppression persist, and so long will it remain a challenge to the Christian conscience and church leadership. In the final analysis, the confrontation between TL and the Vatican is a confrontation of a Christian church with its own evangelical identity. Is the church going to treat the problem of global poverty simply as one of the corporal works of mercy, something which may make us better Christians but without which we could still be Christian, something which is therefore ultimately peripheral to the Gospel? Or is the church going to take the problem of liberation seriously and take it as a challenge to reexamine its own theological identity and radicalize its evangelical praxis? Is liberation a matter of the social doctrine that applies and follows from a theology centered on personal sin and salvation, or is it an integral part of the very theology of sin and salvation? In other words, do we have only a social doctrine or a theology of liberation?

The Catholic Church in the modern world has faced a number of crises, from the Reformation through the Enlightenment to the "apostasy" of the working class. Through internal self-discipline and external expansion by missionary activity, the church weathered the storm of the Reformation. After an unqualified rejection of the spirit of the Enlightenment and the ideals of the French Revolution in the Syllabus of Errors and the condemnation of Modernism, it has, some one hundred and fifty years later, finally come to terms with the challenge of modernity, political liberty, and critical reason. In its personalist moral theology it tried to meet Kant's demand for the autonomy of the person as an end in itself, and in the transcendental Thomism of Marechal, Rahner, and Lonergan it also tried to accept his demand for a "critical" approach in dogma. In the Pastoral Constitution on the Church in the Modern World and the Declaration on Religious Liberty of Vatican II and in the political theology of John Courtney Murray, the church also placed itself on the side of political modernity, with the acceptance of basic human rights. In each instance the adjustment has not been without cost. The response to the Reformation was accompanied by internal rigidity and siege mentality. The long-delayed response to the challenge of the Enlightenment was preceded by the triumphalism and absolutism of Vatican I, not to speak of the loss of intellectual credibility of Catholicism and the massive alienation of European intellectuals from the church.

As for the challenge of the working class in the nineteenth and twentieth centuries, it seems clear that this challenge was simply not met. With a feudal, aristocratic mentality, the Church could not appreciate the historical significance of the industrial revolution, and when it did try to respond—*Rerum Novarum, Quadragesimo Anno,* the worker priests, the Young Christian Worker's movement, and so on—it was too little, too late. There can be little wonder, therefore, that the largest communist party in the West has sprung up in Italy, right in the heart of Catholicism, or that the magnificent cathedrals of Europe have been turning into museums. If the church somehow muddled through the first phase of the Enlightenment and its demand for political autonomy and critical rationality, a demand confined to the bourgeoisie and the intellectuals, its response to the second phase of the Enlightenment and its demand for critical social praxis, as represented by Marx and the socialist movements, was nothing short of disastrous.

The present challenge of liberation is far more serious than that of the European working class in the nineteenth century. The problem of the poor and oppressed has since then become global, no longer confined to one continent.

The challenge, therefore, is the challenge of otherness in two forms, the otherness of poverty and that of non-Western cultures. The challenge of liberation is a challenge to enter into the strangeness of the other in its most painful form. Whether the church leadership could meet the present global challenge any more effectively than it did the older European one would depend on whether they appreciate the full gravity and magnitude of the crisis, in which regard there does not seem to be much ground for optimism. Neither in their theory nor in their political practice do Pope John Paul II and Joseph Cardinal Ratzinger seem to show a convincing evidence that they appreciate the gravity of the signs of the times. Their intellectual horizon is still largely medieval with a dash of modern personalism, their political preference for evolutionary reformism too clearly on the side of the political and economic status quo, despite the occasional radicalism of their rhetoric.

As the discussion in the preceding chapter should have made clear, their thinking remains essentialist in the classical tradition, in contrast to the dialectical thinking of TL in the tradition of Hegel and Marx. They stress the essential specificity and distinctions among the different dimensions of reality while TL stresses the inner relation and dynamic interaction among them. Where TL sees mediation in process within a concrete totality, they find only irreducible differences within a unity that is at best extrinsic and accidental. Theologically, this leads to their primary concern for the transcendence of the Kingdom over the historical, of personal freedom and dignity over the social. In contrast, TL's basic conern is the actualization of salvation through and for the historical praxis of humans here below, just as Hegel stressed the active (*wirklich*) immanence of the Absolute in history against agnostics and transcendentalists, and as Marx stressed the actual (*wirklich*) liberation that would make human freedom concrete and effective in history and society as opposed to the merely ideal. The Vatican's main fear is reductionism and immanentism, that of TL idealism and spiritualism. Whereas TL tries to see a dialectical, historical, inner mediation between transcendence and history, between the personal and the social, the Vatican locates the very essence—the specific distinction—of Christian faith in their irreducible difference. Hidden in the personalism of the Vatican is a profound contempt of the social and the historical, which equips it to appreciate the gravity of the sociohistorical undercurrents about as well as does Kierkegaardian existentialism.

In their approach to the problem of political involvement, therefore, John Paul and Ratzinger are either frankly dualistic or always on the verge of dualism. John Paul does preach a strong commitment to social justice and structural change but immediately goes on to warn about the danger of reducing faith to political liberation; he does not see an inner mediation between the two. He recognizes "labor" as a "fundamental" dimension of human existence,[2] but does not use it consistently as a totalizing principle of his theology. He too talks of praxis and action, but he means them in the Kierkegaardian sense of personal moral commitment to which social commitment is at best extrinsic and accidental. Rat-zinger habitually opposes personal freedom and historical determinism, ethics and history, as though they were exhaustive alternatives and there were no media-tion between personal freedom and historical conditions. Both John Paul and Ratzinger reduce the social to the personal, the global structural crisis to that of personal sins.[3] They recognize structural injustice but see it only as a byproduct of personal sins, not also as their cause. They virtually admit the existence of an ongoing class struggle by calling attention to the "shocking inequality between the rich and the poor" (LN, I, 6) and the realities of neo-colonialism and neo-imperialism, but they are not willing to accept the moral ambiguities of the struggle and insist on moral purity at all costs. We are even urged to struggle "for" justice but never "against" others.[4] The difference between the Vatican and TL, then, is clearly not a matter of differences of opinion on particular issues but one of the very horizon and basic mode of thinking underlying such opinions, not a matter of "contingent" but "structural" misunderstanding between two radically opposed theologies.[5]

On the more practical level of politics, both ecclesiastical and secular, John Paul has been launching a forceful conservative offensive marked by emphasis on narrowly conceived orthodoxy of doctrine, a return to traditional sacramen-tal and personal piety, and centralization of authority. Both the crackdown on dissenting clerics and theologians in recent years (Archbishop Hunthausen of Seattle, Schilleebeckx, Küng, Boff, Gutierrez, Curran, and others) and the pro-ject of theological purification of seminaries have been well publicized in the press. What is perhaps not as well known but far more significant is the use of the papal power of episcopal appointment, the greatest potential threat to the future of theology of liberation in Latin America, through which John Paul, hav-ing already appointed fully one-third of all active bishops (about 1,200 of them), has been reshaping the Catholic Church throughout the world in his own con-servative image.[6] Efforts also seem under way to undermine episcopal collegiality and the authority of national episcopal conferences,[7] stifling the constructive inter-action between the universal and the local churches as well as the creativity and flexibility of the regional churches in responding to their regional crises. The Church of John Paul is a church increasingly turned inward, to the past, and directed from the center.

No wonder, therefore, that some see the papacy of John Paul as a move-ment toward a 'church of Neo-Christendom.' While always warning clerics against political involvements, the Vatican has been quite active in supporting the ultraconservative political agenda of such organizations as Opus Dei, Commun-ion and Liberation, and the Order of Malta; all of these groups are marked by a strong anti-communist ideology, and some are suspected to have connections with the CIA and the conservative and neo-conservative establishments in the United States. In this regard one could not overlook the political significance of the convergence of interests between the Vatican and the conservative political forces in the United States, especially the ideology of anti-communism, attack on theology of liberation and clerical involvement in 'radical' politics, support (often disguised) of the Nicaraguan contras, and the emphases on personal and family morality and "justice with freedom."[8]

All of these seem to argue for a certain pessimism with regard to the capacity of the Catholic Church to respond adequately and swiftly to the gathering crisis of global liberation. As long as the See of Peter is occupied by persons of the essentially medieval, authoritarian, and traditionalist mentality of John Paul and Ratzinger, one might be tempted to give up all hope. It is clear, however, that the challenge of the present crisis to Catholicism is not a matter of the contingent mentality of those who happen to govern the Church at the present time. It is, more basically, a matter of the very structure of authority in the Church, so centralized in the person of the pope, without any procedure of accountability, and so affirmed even by Vatican II, which—not accidentally but structurally—makes the fulfillment of the evangelical mission of the church, to serve the poor and oppressed of this world, contingent on who happens to sit in the chair of Peter. Should the mission of the whole church remain so dependent on the accidents of papal personalities? The present crisis presses with an urgency greater than ever before an issue endemic to Catholicism, a reexamination of its ecclesiology in light of its evangelical identity.

TOWARDS A FOUNDATIONAL THEOLOGY OF CONCRETE TOTALITY

How should a Christian theology respond to the screams and cries of 'the wretched of the earth'? What changes are required in its theoretical structure so as to respond to such screams adequately? I have already indicated, throughout the book, the importance of the anthropological presuppositions of a theology and my preference for an anthropology of concrete totality. In this final section, let me outline—and no more than outline—the significance and content of an anthropology of concrete totality as a foundation of theology or a foundational theology of concrete totality.

At every critical juncture of history a new theology has arisen in response to the emerging signs of the times. Such a new theology has always begun with a critique of what it considers to be the fundamental defect of its predecessors and ended with a systematic reconstruction of the content of faith on a new foundation. Where one locates this central defect and the new foundation, therefore, and whether such an alleged foundation is indeed foundational, have been crucial tests of every new theology. For Barthian neo-orthodoxy, the vitiating defect of both Thomistic and liberal theology was the subordination of the sovereignty of the self-revealing God to the demand of 'natural theology,' and the new foundation was the restoration of the sovereignty of grace. For Bultmann, Tillich, and Rahner the main culprit was extrinsicism and dualism, and the new foundation a hermeneutic of faith in correlation with the structural necessities of human existence. Process theologians have found the culprit in the metaphysics of 'substance' underlying classical theologies and the new foundation in White-headian process. In recent years both political theology and the many varieties of theology of liberation—black, feminist, and Latin American—have been finding traditional, transcendental, and existentialist theologies guilty of intellectualism, individualism, ethnocentrism, sexism, and ideological indifference to the crying problems of historical liberation.

As I have argued all along in this book, I consider the anthropological assumptions of a theology as among the foundations of a Christian theology, along with biblical and other traditions and contemporary experience. If an old theology proves fundamentally inadequate, the source of that inadequacy must be looked for, perhaps above all, in the inadequacy of its anthropology, as a new theology should build its new synthesis only on a foundation that is anthropologically adequate. In this regard I consider it a permanent contribution of modern liberal theology, *pace* Barth, to have revealed the essential correlativity of faith and existence. Without denying the importance of the reciprocal dialectic among the sources of Christian theology—tradition, contemporary experience, and contributions of contemporary philosophy and other sciences—I stress the importance of adequate anthropology for a number of reasons.

As the history of biblical exegesis clearly shows, how one interprets and appropriates Scripture into theology is itself a function of one's anthropological assumptions. Aristotelian theology (Aquinas) interprets Scripture in Aristotelian anthropoligical 'categories,' as existentialist theology interprets it in terms of anthropological 'existentials.' The same text of Scripture, which has been there for two thousand years and longer, has been interpreted monistically and dualistically, as demanding both the salvation of the soul and that of the whole person, as justifying both triumphalistic theocracy and the separation of religion and politics, all in function of the anthropological assumptions of the interpreter. In this regard it should not be too difficult to expose the anthropological assumptions underlying the variety of approaches in contemporary biblical interpretation, such as literary, form, tradition, redaction, structural, and, most recently, sociohistorical or materialist criticisms.

What is true of biblical hermeneutics, of course, has been true all along of systematic or dogmatic theologies. How the anthropological categories of prevailing philosophies have shaped the theologies of the Trinity, Christology, sin and grace, faith and justification, divine providence, the sacraments, spiritual life, the Church, and the responsibility of Christians in and for the world is clear enough from the prevalence of such categories as 'person,' 'nature,' 'soul,' 'body,' 'intellect,' 'will,' 'spirit,' and 'matter' in the theologies of the Fathers and the Medieval Scholastics, as it is from the prevalence in modern and contemporary theologies of such categories as 'feeling,' 'moral will,' 'transcendence,' 'existence,' 'intersubjectivity,' 'person,' 'sinner,' 'commitment,' 'hope,' 'praxis,' 'narrative,' and others. How one interprets the signs of the times and the nature of the challenge they pose to Christian faith and theology is likewise conditioned by one's anthropological assumptions. The moral personalism of John Paul and Ratzinger reduces the challenge to one of individual moral conversion, just as the existentialism of Bultmann reduces it to one of existential "authenticity" and as Rahner's transcendental theology sees it largely in terms of rendering Christian faith *intelligible* and credible by reinterpreting it as transcendent fulfillment of the transcendental structures of human existence.

And there is nothing surprising or in principle untheological about this. As the classical epistemological principle states, whatever is known is known according to the mode of the knower. The knowledge of God—whether through reason or through revelation—is still human knowledge, and is necessarily reflective—even by way of analogy—of the structure of human existence as a condition of both its possibility as human knowledge and its relevance as salvific knowledge. Theology presupposes our 'obediential potency' and salvific need to know or hear God, and thus an essential relation to the structure of human existence as a cognitive subject who is at the same time in need of salvation. This does not deny, as no Christian theology should, that the initiative must come from God, or that such a potency and need is itself something posited by God, but it does deny that we can theologize from a purely divine point of view, from outside history altogether.

In some sense the anthropological assumptions are even more important than the metaphysical–cosmological ones, although an adequate anthropology must, no doubt, be based on an adequate metaphysics. The general conception of being as being and its universal structure is largely dependent on one's conception of human being; even the demand for transcendence of anthropocentrism, as in process theology, implies a relation—at least a negative one—to human being as one understands it, unless, of course, one takes refuge in Heideggerian *Gelassenheit* and seeks to transcend even the attempt to transcend anthropocentrism.

The decisive question, therefore, is not whether a theology can do without an anthropology but whether that anthropology is adequate to both the normative tradition of Christian faith and the task of theology to interpret that tradition in view of the central crisis of the time. In this regard, without going into the question of whether the various anthropologies of modern and contemporary theology have been adequate to the normative tradition of faith, it is safe to say, as I have tried to show in preceding chapters, that many of them have been inadequate as hermeneutic tools for interpreting and responding to the crises of contemporary history. Typically they are asocial and ahistorical; when they do not deny the sociality and historicity of human existence, they do not take them seriously enough as constitutive dimensions of that existence. They are basically anthropologies of individual inwardness and individual transcendence.

Metz recently pointed out that there are three basic challenges facing Christian theology today. The challenge of Marxism means the end of theology's historical and social innocence. The challenge of the Jewish Holocaust means the end of unsituated and subjectless systematics. The challenge of the Third World means the end of theology's cultural monocentrism. In response, Metz argued for a "post-idealistic" paradigm of theology beyond neo-Scholastic, existentialist, and transcendental paradigms, for which we would need a critical and productive confrontation with Marxism. In this regard the attempt of TL has a significance for the whole church.[9]

I have used the term *concrete totality* throughout the book to indicate precisely the 'post-idealistic' anthropology that underlies TL without always being explicitly formulated by liberation theologicans. By keeping all the essential relationships—transcendence and history—in mutual dialectic, it keeps us from the one-dimensional view of human existence—what Hegel called "understanding"—as well as from a preoccupation with 'specific differences' which forgets their intrinsic unity and mutual mediation. By taking the dialectic in all its concrete historicity, it also keeps us from taking human existence as an abstract universal and alerts us to the historical relativity—not relativism—of our individual and collective perspectives. It views a human being as one who has to make a living, live with one's fellows, create a world of values and ideals, and who must, *through* such experiences—not just 'also,'—become aware of her or his need for God's salvation, all in a particular society with a particular structure and a particular set of social conflicts at a particular point in time. It is as a concrete historical totality of these essential dimensions and relationships that humans relate to God, just as their relationship to God also mediates their existence as a concrete totality.

And the bearer or locus of this dialectic of concrete totality is praxis or action. For a human being, to be is to act. To act is always to act in a definite constellation of sociohistorical conditons, economic, political, and cultural, given from the past yet also in process towards the future. To act is to affirm these conditions as internally constitutive of my subjectivity, not accidental to it. To act is also to judge and protest against them as they are and to affirm the possibility of transcending them towards what they should be. To act is to co-act or co-labor with other subjects on whose action I depend for the very possibility of my own, and thus to affirm community or interdependence as constitutive of my subjectivity. To act is to actualize myself in community with others within these conditions and against their pressures and challenges, by objectifying my inwardness, my intellect and will, and my motives and intentions, and thereby also to affirm my subjectivity as self-determining and thus transcendent over the given. I not only affirm my transcendence but also co-affirm the absolute future as the horizon of that transcendence. If the problem of human existence is essentially a problem of action, the problem of action is essentially a problem of cooperative action in society and history: i.e., collective action of individuals as a self-conscious community of interdependence for the sake of creating the sociohistorical conditions of human existence under the horizon—itself historically conditioned—of what transcends history, the problems of finitude, mortality, and final salvation.

In this sense the problem of liberation is not something superimposed on the problem of action from outside but an intrinsic necessity of the latter. The demand for liberation arises out of oppressive social relations and structures which obstruct the actualization of humane existence and which could be perceived as oppressive only by subjects of action in society, and implicitly affirms the common value and dignity of human beings as attributes which transcend the instrumental values of oppressive structures for those who profit from them. Liberation can become actual only through political action which equalizes the social power of one individual or group over another by an equitable distribution of the material embodiments of power, freeing the sphere of culture for its own intrinsic ends from the alien encroachments of both economic and political power. Liberation thus presupposes a community of action with a sense of collective agency, responsibility, and destiny. It also presupposes sensitivity to the dialectic of shifting power arrangements in concrete history, in which it must locate the source of oppression and in which it must discern the real possibilities of social transformation. To liberate is to protest against a given historical status quo and to transform it within its real, although concealed or not perceived, possiblities, not to transcend all history.

The concept of action—in the Hegelian sense of *Begriff,* the intelligible structure of action as *actus exercitus,* not merely as a bare 'idea,' something merely thought about—thus brings together all the essential dimensions of human existence in their historical concreteness and dialectical tensions. It keeps together transcendence and history; thought and reality; interiority and exteriority; intentions and consequences; subjectivity and objectivity; personal and social existence; the facticity of the past and the demands of the future; materiality and spirituality; oppression and liberation; the existential problems of finitude, mortality, and sin; and the social problems of poverty, opression, and liberation in history. It does so intrinsically and simultaneously, not extrinsically or purely factually, and thus avoids the traditional dualisms and fragmentations of existence, not by denying the importance of the dimensions emphasized in the tradition but by integrating them into the context of lived praxis in which they originate, in which they become concrete, and for the sake of which they fulfill their properly human function. Apart from this concrete totality of lived praxis, subjectivity, inwardness, transcendence, and reason become angelic, no longer human, attributes; they slide into subjectivism, interiorism, transcendentalism, and rationalism, so many routes of escape from the burdens and responsibilities of lived human existence; and 'history' and 'society' become unintelligible as *human* history and society. From the perspective of the concrete totality of praxis, the cardinal sin of anthropology would be "reification"—i.e., considering a particular dimension in isolation from its place in and its inner, dialectical relation to the totality, absolutizing it as sufficient unto itself, and thus denaturing it as human reality and dehumanizing the human subject of the totality both in thought and ultimately in practice.

It is this anthropology of concrete totality, formulated here all too briefly, which I argue must be the anthropological foundation or correlative of all theological hermeneutics if theology is to remain truly human and humane, not a subtlely disguised angelic and dehumanizing theology. Elaborated more systematically and with its implications for theology spelled out, without its actual integration into the elaboration of particular theological topics, such a theology would also be what I earlier meant by 'foundational theology.' By foundational theology I certainly do not mean 'foundationalism' in the epistemological sense, the basically Cartesian search for an indubitable, presuppositionless, absolutely prior epistemological basis and starting point from which all else could logically be derived, which would not be humanly possible if humans are concrete totalities with a built-in hermeneutic circle. Nor do I mean 'fundamental theology' in the traditional sense, a philosophical discipline that deals with the *preambula fidei*, the rational demonstration of God's existence and the immortality of the human soul, the credibility of revelation, and the extrinsic, human basis of faith, which remains both preliminary and external to dogmatic theology proper. I use 'foundational' in the sense of Bernard Lonergan and Francis Fiorenza, for whom "foundations present, not doctrines, but the horizon within which the meaning of doctrines can be apprehended."[10]

That is, foundational theology is foundational in the sense that it elaborates the basic horizon that governs the interpretation of particular dogmas and raises further questions about existing interpretations. It is both intrinsic to and constitutive of the very content of dogmatic theology and is transcendent and regulative of its ongoing elaboration. The initial hermeneutic option is not something that occurs at the beginning of theological construction and then is simply left behind, as is traditional fundamental theology, as that construction progresses. It continues, implicitly or explicitly, to exercise both a "constitutive" and a "regulative" (Kant) function for the subsequent phases of theological reflection and thus infects the whole of theology, both its content and its direction. In this sense the choice of a basic horizon is a matter of decisive importance for all theologies. To put my argument thus far in another way, then, much traditional and contemporary theologizing is inadequate, among other reasons, precisely because its anthropological horizon is inadequate. An adequate dogmatic or systematic theology must be based on a foundational theology whose basic horizon includes an anthropology of concrete totality.

A dogmatic theology proceeding against the horizon of concrete totality would always ask about the conditions of possibility, meaning, and demands of a particular dogma (God, Trinity, Christ, sin, salvation, grace, church, sacraments, and so on) in and for the human subject to whom the dogma is addressed and who is to be taken as a concrete totality. What does 'God'—or sin, salvation, grace—mean for and demand of a human being who has to make a living, live with her or his fellows, and search for meaning and value under concrete historical conditions, suffering their contradictions in the most concrete way and screaming for liberation from such contradictions? From the very beginning, this sort of dogmatic theology of concrete totality would enjoy a built-in antidote against the dualisms and reifying fragmentation of human existence often perpetuated in the name of Christian faith. Theology of liberation, as elaborated and interpreted in this book, already demonstrates the potential of a dogmatic theology of concrete totality. I have tried to show how an anthropology of concrete totality guides its reconstruction of the very method of theology, the conceptions of God, faith, sin, and salvation, as well as its biblical hermeneutics.

Notes

CHAPTER ONE

1. On the theological problem of pluralism, see David Tracy, *The Analogical Imagination: Christian Theology and the Culture of Pluralism* (New York: Crossroad, 1981) and *Plurality and Ambiguity: Hermeneutics, Religion, Hope* (San Francisco: Harper & Row, 1987); also Claude Geffre et al. (eds.), *Concilium* 171 (January 1984) ("Different Theologies, Common Responsibility: Babel or Pentecost?").

2. On the dialectic of essence and history, the universal and the particular, I find Ernst Troeltsch's essay still one of the most succinct and profound statements; see his essay, "What Does the 'Essence of Christianity' Mean?" in Ernst Troeltsch, *Writings on Theology and Religion,* translated and edited by Robert Morgan and Michael Pye (Atlanta: John Knox Press, 1977), pp. 124–79. For a recent discussion of the theological implications of modern historical consciousness, see Trutz Rendtorff, "The Modern Age as a Chapter in the History of Christianity; or, The Legacy of Historical Consciousness in Present Theology," *Journal of Religion* 65:4 (October 1985), 478–99.

3. For a discussion of the criteria for Christian theology, see Schubert Ogden, *Faith and Freedom: Towards a Theology of Liberation* (Nashville: Abingdon Press, 1979), pp. 26–7, 46–7, 122–3, and his essay, "The Concept of a Theology of Liberation: Must a Christian Theology Today Be So Conceived?" in Brian Mahan and L. Dale Richesin (eds.), *The Challenge of Liberation Theology* (Maryknoll, NY: Orbis Books, 1981), pp. 132–3.

4. Joseph Cardinal Ratzinger, with Vittorio Messori, *The Ratzinger Report,* tr. Salvator Attanasio and Graham Harrison (San Francisco, CA: Ignatius Press, 1985), p. 175.

5. *Ibid.,* pp. 176–7.

6. For an overview of conservative critiques of liberation theology, see Ronald Nash (ed.), *Liberation Theology* (Milford, MI: Mott Media, 1984), which contains articles by, among others, Michael Novak, James V. Schall, Edward Norman, Carl F. H. Henry, and Richard John Neuhaus. For a sympathetic but critical account of theology of liberation from the Latin American evangelical perspective, see Emilio A. Nunez, *Liberation Theology,* translated by Paul E. Sywulka (Chicago, IL: Moody Press, 1985). For a conservative Protestant critique, see Gerard Berghoef and Lester DeKoster, *Liberation Theology: The Church's Future Shock* (Grand Rapids, MI: Christian's Library Press, 1984);

for a critique by a conservative Catholic ecclesiastic, see Bonaventure Kloppenburg, *The People's Church: A Defense of My Church* (Chicago, IL: Franciscan Herald Press, 1978). For a critique from the European perspective, see Johann Baptist Metz (ed.), *Die Theologie der Befreiung: Hoffnung oder Gefahr für die Kirche?* (Düsseldorf: Patmos Verlag, 1986), especially the articles by Peter Ehlen and Walter Kasper. For an excellent introduction and survey of theology of liberation, see Phillip Berryman, *Liberation Theology* (Oak Park, IL: Meyer Stone Books, 1987); also Robert McAfee Brown, *Theology in a New Key* (Philadelphia, PA: Westminster Press, 1978), and Rebecca S. Chopp, *The Praxis of Suffering: An Interpretation of Liberation and Political Theologies* (Maryknoll, NY: Orbis Books, 1986).

7. See Schubert Ogden, *Faith and Freedom* (cited earlier) and *The Point of Christology* (San Francisco: Harper & Row, 1982).

8. See the Congregation for the Doctrine of the Faith, "Instruction on Certain Aspects of the 'Theology of Liberation'," *Origins* 14:13 (September 13, 1984), 194–204; all references in parentheses in this chapter are to this document by section and paragraph.

9. Juan Luis Segundo, *Theology and the Church,* translated by John W. Dierckmeier (New York: Winston Press, 1985), p. 13.

10. Ibid., p. 14.

11. Ibid., p. 66.

12. Ibid., pp. 68–85.

13. On the difference between theology of liberation and political theology, see Francis Fiorenza, "Liberation Theology and Political Theology," in Thomas McFadden (ed.), *Liberation, Revolution and Freedom: Theological Perspectives* (New York: Seabury, 1975), pp. 3–29, and Chopp, *The Praxis of Suffering.*

14. For example, on the nature and method of theology in Aquinas, see Yves Congar, *History of Theology,* translated by Hunter Guthrie (Garden City, NJ: Doubleday, 1968), pp. 91–114; Marie Dominique Chenu, *Is Theology a Science?,* translated by A. H. N. Green-Armytage (New York: Hawthorn Books, 1959), pp. 48–96; Per Erik Persson, *Sacra Doctrina: Reason and Revelation in Aquinas,* translated by Ross Mackenzie (Philadelphia, PA: Fortress Press, 1970).

15. On the controversy of whether Catholic social doctrine is dead—occasioned by M. D. Chenu's critique of social doctrine as ideology—and on John Paul II's attempt to revive it, see Peter Hebblethwaite, "The Popes and Politics: Shifting Patterns in 'Catholic Social Doctrine'," *Daedalus* 111:1 (Winter 1982): 85–99.

CHAPTER TWO

---

1. For a review of the relation between Christianity and Marxism, see Fernando Castillo, "Die Christen und der Marxismus: Ein Problem mit Geschichte," in Peter Rottländer (ed.), *Theologie der Befreiung und der Marxismus* (Münster: Edition Liberacion, 1986), pp. 23–36. All translations from this book are mine.

2. For a recent discussion of this issue, see the special issue of *Journal of Ecumenical Studies,* 22:3 (Summer 1985), which is devoted to the question of whether atheism is essential to Marxism. See also Arthur F. McGovern, *Marxism: An American Christian Perspective* (Maryknoll: Orbis Books, 1980), pp. 245–77, and René Coste, *Marxist Analysis and Christian Faith* (Maryknoll, NY: Orbis Books, 1985), pp. 27–63. For a most recent study of the Marxian view of religion, see David McLellan, *Marxism and Religion* (New York: Harper & Row, 1987).

3. For a history of the attitudes of recent Popes towards Marxism, see Christine E. Gudorf, *Catholic Social Teaching on Liberation Themes* (Washington, DC: University Press of America, 1981), pp. 167–248; McGovern, *Marxism,* pp. 90–131.

4. All references in parentheses in this chapter are references, by section and paragraph, to the Congregation for the Doctrine of the Faith, "Instruction on Certain Aspects of the 'Theology of Liberation'," dated August 6, 1984 and published in *Origins* 14:13 (September 13, 1984): 194–204.

5. See Quentin L. Quade (ed.), *The Pope and Revolution* (Washington, DC: Ethics and Public Policy Center, 1982), pp. 78–9.

6. See Anselm Min, "John Paul II's Anthropology of Concrete Totality," in the *Proceedings of the American Catholic Philosophical Association* 58 (1984): 120–29.

7. The National Conference of Catholic Bishops, *Pastoral Letter on Marxist Communism* (Washington, DC: U. S. Catholic Conference, 1980), p. 9.

8. On the use of Marxism in John Paul II's *Laborem Exercens,* see Gregory Baum, *The Priority of Labor* (New York: Paulist Press, 1982); Yves Ledure, "L'encyclique de Jean-Paul II sur le travail humain," *Nouvelle Revue Theologique* 105:2 (March–April 1983); 226–27; John F. Kavanaugh, "The Moral Dialectic of *Laborem Exercens,*" *Proceedings of the Forty-Sixth Annual Convention of the Jesuit Philosophical Association* (April 1984): 17–27; Clodovis Boff, "Die ambivalente Haltung der 'Instruktion zur Theologie der Befreiung' gegenüber dem Marxismus," in Rottländer, *Theologie,* p. 115.

9. Quoted in Jose Porfirio Miranda, *Marx and the Bible* (Maryknoll, NY: Orbis Books, 1971), xiii.

10. See Enrique Dussel, *History and the Theology of Liberation* (Maryknoll, NY: Orbis Books, 1976), pp. 135–37.

11. On the relation between theology and philosophy, see Karl Rahner, *Theological Investigations,* VI (Baltimore, MD: Helicon Press, 1969), 71–81, and IX (New York: Seabury Press, 1972), 28–63.

12. Quoted in Boff, p. 112.

13. See Clodovis and Leonardo Boff, *The National Catholic Reporter* (August 28, 1987), pp. 14 and 23–25, where the Boffs criticize the U.S. bishops for lacking a sense of "class" conflict, the "structural" defect of capitalism, and the need for "political" action.

14. Giulio Girardi, "Die Gegenwärtigen Auseinandersetzungen um Marxismus, Theologie der Befreiung und 'Kirche des Volkes'," in Rottländer, *Theologie,* p. 128.

15. Ibid., pp. 127–29.

16. For a critique of the Vatican's monolithic conception of Marxism, see ibid., pp. 131–37.

17. For right-wing criticisms of the "Marxism" of liberation theology, see Dale Vree, "'Christian Marxists': A Critique," in Quade, *The Pope and Revolution*, pp. 37–46; Gerard Berghoef and Lester DeKoster, *Liberation Theology: The Church's Future Shock* (Grand Rapids, MI: Christian's Library Press, 1984), pp. 29–70; Bonaventure Kloppenburg, *The People's Church: A Defense of My Church* (Chicago, IL: Franciscan Herald Press, 1978), p. 95.

18. Girardi, *op. cit.*, p. 130.

19. Ignacio Ellacuria, "Theologie der Befreiung und Marxismus: Grundlegende Reflexionen," in Rottländer, p. 97.

20. Gustavo Gutierrez, *The Power of the Poor in History* (Maryknoll, NY: Orbis Books, 1983), pp. 62 and 147 respectively.

21. Hugo Assmann, *Theology for a Nomad Church* (Maryknoll, NY: Orbis Books, 1976), p. 55.

22. See Gutierrez, p. 69; his *A Theology of Liberation* (Maryknoll, NY: Orbis Books, 1973), p. 238; and Dussel, p. 143.

23. Gutierrez, *Theology*, p. 177.

24. See Juan Luis Segundo, *Faith and Ideologies* (Maryknoll, NY: Orbis Books, 1984), pp. 140–42.

25. This is based on Jose Miguez Bonino, *Christians and Marxists* (Grand Rapids, MI: Eerdmans, 1976), pp. 91–94, and Clodovis Boff, "Zum Gebrauch des 'Marxismus' in der Theologie der Befreiung: Einige Thesen," in Rottländer, *Theologie*, pp. 37–40.

26. For a contemporary account of the concept of "concrete totality," see Karel Kosik, *Dialectics of the Concrete* (Dordrecht: D. Reidel, 1976); my review, "Karel Kosik, *The Dialectics of the Concrete*," *The New Scholasticism* 55:2 (Spring 1981): 247–54; Martin Jay, *Marxism and Totality* (Berkeley, CA: University of California Press, 1984).

27. On the relation between the economic base and the ideological superstructure, see Michael Harrington, *The Twilight of Capitalism* (New York: Simon and Schuster, 1976), pp. 60–82; John McMurtry, *The Structure of Marx's World-View* (Princeton, NJ: Princeton University Press, 1978), pp. 157–239.

28. Miguez Bonino, p. 92.

29. Ibid.

30. Ibid., p. 93.

31. See Gutierrez, *Theology*, p. 10.

32. My presentation here is based on Ellacuria, pp. 88–94. This article contains a proposition-by-proposition response to the Vatican's 1984 Instruction.

33. See Clodovis Boff in Rottländer, pp. 39–44; see also ibid., p. 34 (Castillo), pp. 50–59 (Gutierrez), pp. 94–96 (Ellacuria), and pp. 129–30 (Girardi); also Gudorf, p. 172.

34. See Gutierrez, "Theologie und Sozialwissenschaften: Eine Ortsbestimmung," in Rottländer, p. 52; see also ibid., pp. 127–29 (Girardi) and p. 96 (Ellacuria).

35. On my interpretation of Hegel with responses to the usual objections to Hegel (atheism, pantheism, rationalism, and so on), see my articles, as follows: "Hegel on the Foundation of Religion," *International Philosophical Quarterly* 14:1 (March 1974): 79–99; "Hegel's Absolute: Transcendent or Immanent?" *Journal of Religion* 56:1 (January 1976): 61–87; "Hegel's Retention of Mystery as a Theological Category," *CLIO* 12:4 (Summer 1983): 333–53; "The Trinity and the Incarnation: Hegel and Classical Approaches," *Journal of Religion* 66:2 (April 1986); 173–93.

36. For an exposition of Hegel's dialectic, see the preface in his *Phenomenology of Spirit* and the last chapter ("The Absolute Idea") of his *Science of Logic*. Since this is not a book on Hegel, I do not want to cite the numerous commentaries on the Hegelian dialectic.

37. For a recent discussion of the theological meaning of politics in Hegel, see Ludger Oeing-Hanhoff, "Das Christentum als 'Religion der Freiheit,'" *Theologischer Quartalschrift* 164:1 (1984): 16–34, and Paul Lakeland, *The Politics of Salvation: The Hegelian Idea of the State* (Albany, NY: SUNY Press, 1984).

CHAPTER THREE

1. For a history of the concepts of theory and praxis, see Nicholas Lobkowicz, *Theory and Practice: History of a Concept from Aristotle to Marx* (Notre Dame: University of Notre Dame Press, 1967); Richard J. Bernstein, *Praxis and Action: Contemporary Philosophies of Human Activity* (Philadelphia, PA: University of Pennsylvania Press, 1971); and Jürgen Habermas, *Theory and Practice* (Boston, MA: Beacon Press, 1973). On the significance of praxis for contemporary theology, see Dermot A. Lane, *Foundations for a Social Theology: Praxis, Process and Salvation* (New York: Paulist Press, 1984). For a typology of the relation between theory and praxis in contemporary Christian theology, see Matthew Lamb, "The Theory-Praxis Relationship in Contemporary Christian Theologies," *Proceedings of the Catholic Theological Society of America* 31 (1976): pp.149–78.

2. Gustavo Gutierrez, *A Theology of Liberation* (Maryknoll, NY: Orbis Books, 1973), p. 13.

3. Ibid.; my emphasis.

4. See the Congregation for the Doctrine of the Faith, "Instruction on Certain Aspects of the 'Theology of Liberation'," *Origins* 14:13 (September 13, 1984): 194–204. All references in the body of this chapter are to this document by section and paragraph.

5. This fear of "classism" in theology of liberation is also shared by James M. Gustafson, *Ethics From a Theocentric Perspective,* I (Chicago, IL: University of Chicago Press, 1981), p. 74.

6. For an evaluation of Ogden's "more adequate" alternative to theology of liberation, see my article, "How Not to Do a Theology of Liberation: A Critique of Schubert Ogden," *The Journal of the American Academy of Religion* (forthcoming).

7. Schubert Ogden, *Faith and Freedom: Toward a Theology of Liberation* (Nashville: Abingdon Press, 1979), p. 33.

8. Ibid., p. 34.

9. Ibid., p. 33.

10. Ibid., p. 116.

11. Ibid., p, 117.

12. Ibid., p. 118.

13. Ibid., p. 120.

14. Ibid., pp. 119–21.

15. See ibid., p. 123.

16. Ibid.

17. Ibid.

18. Ogden, "The Concept of a Theology of Liberation: Must a Christian Theology Today Be so Conceived?" in Brian Mahan and L. Dale Richesin (eds.), *The Challenge of Liberation Theology* (Maryknoll, NY: Orbis Books, 1981), p. 131.

19. Ibid., pp. 131–32.

20. Ibid., p. 134.

21. Ogden, *Faith,* p. 123.

22. See Ogden, in Mahan and Richesin, p. 134.

23. On the distinction between "explicit" and "implicit" witness of Christian witness, see Ogden, *Faith,* p. 60.

24. Ibid., p. 124.

25. Dennis P. McCann and Charles R. Strain, *Polity and Praxis: A Program for American Practical Theology* (Minneapolis, MN: Winston Press, 1985; A Seabury Book), p. 54.

26. See ibid., pp. 3, 5, 9, 16, 40, 43.

27. Ibid., p. 4.

28. Ibid., p. 9.

29. For a discussion and evaluation of Habermas from the perspective of practical theology, see Charles Davis, *Theology and Political Society* (Cambridge: Cambridge University Press, 1980), pp. 79–103.

30. McCann and Strain, *Polity,* p. 36.

31. Ibid., p. 25.

32. Ibid., p. 14.

33. See *ibid.*

34. Gustavo Gutierrez, *The Power of the Poor in History* (Maryknoll, NY: Orbis Books, 1983), p. 42. The quotation is from Johann B. Metz, *Theology of the World* (New York: Herder & Herder, 1969), p. 112.

35. Gutierrez, *Power,* p. 60; my emphasis.

36. Clodovis Boff, *Theology and Praxis* (Maryknoll, NY: Orbis Books, 1987), p. 38.

37. Ibid.

38. For a critique of the intellectualist conception of salvation, faith, and revelation, see ibid., pp. 105–107 and 116.

39. Ibid., p. 38.

40. Ibid.

41. Ibid.

42. Jon Sobrino, *The True Church and the Poor* (Maryknoll, NY: Orbis Books, 1984), p. 74; also, pp. 73 and 282–83.

43. Clodovis Boff, *Theology,* p. 203.

44. Gutierrez, *Power,* p. 60.

45. Ibid., p. 17.

46. Boff, *Theology,* p. 37.

47. Ibid., p. 39. On the problem of the absolute and relative, the universal and particular in faith and the necessity of concretization of faith, see Juan Luis Segundo, *The Liberation of Theology* (Maryknoll, NY: Orbis Books, 1976), pp. 97–124 ("Ideologies and Faith") and 154–82 ("Ideologies and Relativity").

48. On the autonomy of theology and its critical mediation of faith, see further Clodovis Boff, *Theology,* pp. 109–14; Gutierrez, *Theology,* p. 12.

49. Boff, *Theology,* p. 40. On the transcendent dimension of theology, see further pp. 38–41.

50. Boff's *Theology and Praxis* was originally the author's doctoral dissertation, presented at Louvain in 1976, and was translated into English only in 1987. I regret the ten-year delay between the dissertation and the translation. If it had been translated in the 1970s, I think it would have gone a long way towards preventing many of the misunderstandings of TL in the English-speaking world. This extremely fine work, rich with relevant distinctions and sophisticated analyses, would have silenced many of the charges of methodological innocence and conceptual confusion often hurled at TL. As should be clear from the notes in this chapter, I am heavily indebted to Boff for much of the discussion.

51. Ibid., p. 159.

52. Ibid., pp. 160–61.

53. See ibid., pp. 159–62.

54. Ibid., p. 166.

55. See ibid., pp. 162–64.

56. Ibid., p. 165.

57. Ibid., p. 167.

58. See ibid.

59. Ibid., p. 176.

60. See further ibid., pp. 176–77.

61. See ibid., p. 182. Boff here makes an important distinction between "relevance" and "pertinency." The first is a category of the relationship of theory with praxis, of knowledge with power, of a theory with a given historical problematic. The second is a category of the intratheoretical relation of a question with a given theoretical problematic.

62. See ibid., pp. 182–84.

63. Ibid., p. 187.

64. Ibid., p. 190.

65. Ibid.

66. Ibid., p. 191.

67. Gutierrez, *Power*, p. 91.

68. Ibid., p. 213.

69. See G. W. F. Hegel, *Hegel's Philosophy of Right,* translated by T. M. Knox (Oxford: Oxford University Press, 1967), p. 11.

70. See Gutierrez, *Power*, p. 93.

71. Ibid., p. 66.

72. Hegel, *Philosophy*, p. 11.

73. See Gutierrez, *Theology*, pp. 12, 14, and *Power*, pp. 16, 61, 65; also Leonardo Boff, *Liberating Grace* (Maryknoll, NY: Orbis Books, 1979), p. 80.

74. Gutierrez, *Theology*, p. 32.

75. See Gutierrez, *Theology*, p. 11; see further Charles Davis, "Theology and Praxis," *Cross Currents* 23:2 (Summer 1973): 154–68; and Jon Sobrino's illuminating comparative discussion of the theoretical orientation of traditional European theology and the practical orientation of Latin American theology in his *The True Church and the Poor* (Maryknoll, NY: Orbis Books, 1984), pp. 7–38, and "Theologisches Erkennen in der europäischen und der lateinamerikanischen Theologie," in Karl Rahner (ed.), *Befreiende Theologie* (Mainz: Kohlhammer, 1977), pp. 123–43.

76. See Jon Sobrino, *Christology at the Crossroads* (Maryknoll, NY: Orbis Books, 1978), xxi and p. 13; Roger Haight, *An Alternative Vision: An Interpretation of Liberation Theology* (New York: Paulist Press, 1985), pp. 53–56.

77. Gutierrez, *Power*, p. 266.

78. See Sobrino, *Christology*, p. 22; Hugo Assmann, *Theology for a Nomad Church* (Maryknoll, NY: Orbis Books, 1976), p. 121; Clodovis Boff, *Theology*, p. 40.

79. Clodovis Boff, *Theology*, p. 40.

80. For a brief account of the historical reality of Latin America, see Rebecca S. Chopp, *The Praxis of Suffering* (Maryknoll, NY: Orbis Books, 1986), pp. 8–14; Enrique Dussel, *History and the Theology of Liberation* (Maryknoll, NY: Orbis Books, 1976), pp. 75–109.

81. Gutierrez, *Power*, p. 197.

82. Ibid., p. 58.

83. Ibid., p. 44.

84. Ibid.; on the change of perspective brought about by the experience of poverty, see further Sobrino, *True Church*, pp. 125–59 ("The Experience of God in the Church of the Poor").

85. See Sören Kierkegaard, *Concluding Unscientific Postscript*, translated by David F. Swenson and Walter Lowrie (Princeton, NJ: Princeton University Press, 1941), p. 296.

86. See Gutierrez, *Power*, p. 103, and *Theology*, p. 14.

87. Clodovis Boff, *Theology*, p. 169.

88. Ibid.

89. See ibid., pp. 170–71.

90. Ibid., p. 171.

91. Ibid.

92. Ibid., p. 173.

93. My presentation here is based on Juan Carlos Scannone, "Das Theorie-Praxis Verhältnis in der Theologie der Befreiung," in Rahner (ed.), pp. 77-96. A similar but simpler account of the three levels of liberation theology, professional, pastoral, and popular, is given in Leonardo Boff and Clodovis Boff, *Introducing Liberation Theology* (Maryknoll, NY: Orbis Books, 1987), pp. 11-21.

94. See further Dussel, p. 148.

95. See Boff, *Theology*, pp. 20-24.

96. Ibid., pp. 24-5.

97. See ibid., pp. 26-7.

98. See ibid., pp. 27-9.

99. Ibid., p. 29.

100. Ibid., p. 30.

101. Ibid., p. 25.

102. Ibid., p. 30.

103. Ibid., p. 31.

104. Ibid.

105. For a similar view, see Gutierrez, "Theologie und Sozialwissenschaft: eine Ortsbestimmung," in Peter Rottländer (ed.), *Theologie der Befreiung und der Marxismus* (Munster: Edition Liberacion, 1986), pp. 55-58.

106. See Boff, *Theology*, pp. 51-55.

107. See ibid., pp. 57-60.

108. See ibid., pp. 60-61.

109. Gutierrez, *Theology*, p. 13.

110. On the Biblical foundation of theology of liberation and liberationist hermeneutics, see Norman K. Gottwald (ed.), *The Bible and Liberation: Political and Social Hermeneutics* (Maryknoll, NY: Orbis Books, 1983); also his *The Tribes of Yahweh* (Maryknoll, NY: Orbis Books, 1979); Walter Brueggemann, *Hope Within History* (Atlanta, GA: John Knox Press, 1987); Fernando Belo, *A Materialist Reading of the Gospel of Mark* (Maryknoll, NY: Orbis Books, 1981); Michel Clevenot, *Materialist Approaches to the Bible* (Maryknoll, NY: Orbis Books, 1985); Walter E. Pilgrim, *Good News to the Poor* (Minneapolis, MN: Augsburg Publishing House, 1981); Juan Luis Segundo, *The Historical Jesus of the Synoptics* (Maryknoll, NY: Orbis Books, 1985) and *The Humanist Christology of Paul* (Maryknoll, NY: Orbis Books, 1986); Jose Porfirio Miranda, *Marx and the Bible*

(Maryknoll, NY: Orbis Books, 1971); John R. Donahue, "Biblical Perspectives on Justice," in John C. Haughey (ed.), *The Faith That Does Justice* (New York: Paulist Press, 1977), pp. 68–112; John C. Haughey, "Jesus as Justice of God," ibid., pp. 264–90; Rudolf Schnackenburg, "Befreiung in der Blickweise Jesu und der Urkirche," in Johannes B. Metz (ed.), *Die Theologie der Befreiung: Hoffnung oder Gafahr für die Kirche?* (Düsseldorf: Patmos Verlag, 1986), pp. 11–28; Horst Goldstein, "Skizze einer biblischen Begründung der Theologie der Befreiung," in Rahner (ed.), *Theologie,* pp. 62–76; Christine E. Gudorf, "Liberation Theology's Use of Scripture: A Response to First World Critics," *Interpretation* 41:1 (January 1987): 5–18; J. Severino Croatto, *Biblical Hermeneutics: Toward a Theory of Reading as the Production of Meaning* (Maryknoll, NY: Orbis Books, 1987).

111. C. Boff, *Theology,* p. 136.

112. Ibid., p. 137.

113. Ibid.

114. Ibid.

115. Ibid., p. 138.

116. Ibid.

117. Ibid.

118. Ibid., p. 141.

119. Ibid., p. 140.

120. Ibid.

121. Ibid.

122. Ibid.

123. Ibid., pp. 141–42.

124. The following discussion of the three models of the hermeneutic mediation of political praxis in TL is based on Clodovis Boff, *Theology,* pp. 142–50.

125. Impressions to the contrary notwithstanding, it should be pointed out that this 'correspondence of terms' model is generally rejected by liberation theologians. See Segundo, *Liberation* p. 117; Gutierrez, *Theology,* p. 226, and *Power* p. 4; Rosemary Radford Ruether, *To Change the World: Christology and Cultural Criticism* (New York: Crossroad, 1985), pp. 7–18; Sobrino, *True Church,* pp. 217–27.

126. C. Boff, *Theology,* p. 149.

127. *Ibid.*

128. *Ibid., p. 150.*

129. Gutierrez, *Power,* p. 15.

130. Segundo, *Liberation*, p. 8.

131. *Ibid.*, p. 9.

132. This is in response to Gregory Baum's sympathetic critique of Segundo's hermeneutic circle; see Gregory Baum, "The Theological Method of Segundo's *The Liberation of Theology," Proceedings of the Catholic Theological Society of America* 32 (1977): 120–24. See also Segundo's more recent elaboration of the hermeneutic circle in his *Historical Jesus*, pp. 32–39.

133. See Dorothee Sölle's critique of Bultmann in her *Political Theology* (Philadelphia, PA: Fortress Press, 1974) and Johann Metz's critique of Karl Rahner in his *Faith in History and Society: Toward a Practical Fundamental Theology* (New York: Seabury Press, 1980), pp., 62–64, 157–66.

134. I elaborate on this criticism in my article, "How Not to Do a Theology of Liberation: A Critique of Schubert Ogden," *Journal of the American Academy of Religion* (forthcoming).

135. See Karl Mannheim, *Ideology and Utopia: An Introduction to the Sociology of Knowledge,* translated by Louis Wirth and Edward Shils (New York: Harcourt, Brace & World, 1936; a Harvest Book), pp. 147–63.

136. This is no place to discuss the relative weight of class, race, and gender as factors of oppression, but it seems clear, without reducing the racial and sexual differences to purely economic terms, that both racism and sexism increase their historical weight and social significance as modes of oppression precisely because of their economic origin and expression, with all its dialectical consequences at the political and cultural levels. Should all the races and sexes enjoy real, not merely formal, economic equality, and acquire real, not merely legal, equality of opportunity for political and cultural self-expression, both racism and sexism would certainly lose much of their significance as social issues. Economic oppression is a kind of "infrastructural" expression of all other forms of oppression. Furthermore, as the Boff brothers point out, in a class-divided society the struggle between economic classes remains the "main" form of struggle because it embodies an "antagonistic" contradiction that could be resolved only if each would cease to be what it is in the relationship, i.e., only if the exploiter would cease to exploit and the exploited cease to be exploited, i.e., only if the wealthy would cease to be wealthy and the poor cease to be poor, whereas sexism and racism are "nonantagonistic" contradictions that could be resolved without women ceasing to be women and without blacks ceasing to be black. See Leonardo Boff and Clodovis Boff, *Introducing*, pp. 28-30.

137. On the Biblical and explicitly Marxian basis of the hermeneutical privilege of the oppressed, see Lee Cormie, "The Hermeneutical Privilege of the Oppressed: Liberation Theologies, Biblical Faith, and Marxist Sociology of Knowledge," *Proceedings of the Catholic Theological Society of America* 33 (1978): 155–81.

138. In an illuminating discussion Karl Mannheim distinguishes "relationism" from "relativism," and tries to show how sociology of knowledge is the logical extension of the classical bipolar conception of human knowledge to the anthropology of human existence conceived as a historical totality. See his *Ideology and Utopia*, pp. 78–79, 84–87.

139. See further Clodovis Boff, *Theology,* pp. 206–20.

140. McCann and Strain, *Polity,* pp. 49–50.

141. For a trenchant critique of Habermas on this point, see Rudiger Bubner, "Habermas's Concept of Critical Theory," in John B. Thompson et al. (eds.), *Habermas: Critical Debates* (Cambridge, MA: The MIT Press, 1982), pp. 42–56.

142. For a further critique of "pluralism" in a divided church and a divided world, see Sobrino, *True Church,* pp. 194–227.

CHAPTER FOUR

1. Leonardo Boff and Clodovis Boff, *Liberation Theology: From Confrontation to Dialogue,* translated by Robert R. Barr (San Francisco, CA: Harper & Row, 1986), pp. 13–14.

2. See Ibid., pp. 24–25.

3. See "Instruction on Certain Aspects of the 'Theology of Liberation'," issued by the Congregation for the Doctrine of the Faith and dated August 6, 1984. I follow the English version published in *Origins* 14:13 (September 13, 1984): 194–204. All references in parentheses in this chapter are to this text according to section and paragraph.

4. See Joseph Ratzinger, *Politik und Erlösung* (Opladen, Westdeutscher Verlag, 1986), pp. 7–36.

5. Ibid., p. 16 (my translation).

6. See ibid., pp. 16–17.

7. See ibid., pp. 18–20.

8. See ibid., pp. 20–21.

9. Stanley Hauerwas, "Some Theological Reflections on Gutierrez's Use of 'Liberation' as a Theological Concept," *Modern Theology* 3:1 (October 1986): 69.

10. Ibid., p. 76.

11. John B. Cobb, Jr., *Process Theology as Political Theology* (Philadelphia, PA: Westminster Press, 1982), p. 126.

12. Ibid., p. 132.

13. Ibid., p. 117. Basically the same charge of "anthropocentrism" or "homocentrism" resulting in the instrumentalizing exploitation of nature is shared by Schubert M. Ogden, *Faith and Freedom: Toward a Theology of Liberation* (Nashville, IN: Abingdon, 1979), pp. 97–124. Ogden directs the charge explicitly against the theologies of liberation.

14. Leonardo Boff and Clodovis Boff, *Liberation Theology,* p. 20.

15. Ibid., p. 21.

16. Ibid.

17. Ibid.

18. Gustavo Gutierrez, *The Power of the Poor in History* (Maryknoll, NY: Orbis Books, 1983), p. 69.

19. Gutierrez, *A Theology of Liberation* (Maryknoll, NY: Orbis Books, 1973), p. 238.

20. Enrique Dussel, *History and the Theology of Liberation* (Maryknoll, NY: Orbis Books, 1976), p. 143.

21. Ignacio Ellacuria, *Freedom Made Flesh: The Mission of Christ and His Church* Maryknoll, NY: Orbis Books, 1976),p. 108.

22. Gutierrez, *Theology,* p. 35.

23. Ibid., pp. 175–6.

24. Ibid., p. 263.

25. Ibid., p. 176.

26. Ibid., p. 177.

27. The relationship between salvation and liberation is a contemporary variant on the classical issue of the relation between nature and grace, an issue I cannot go into here. On the history of this issue, see Henri de Lubac, *The Mystery of the Supernatural,* translated by Rosemary Sheed (New York: Herder and Herder, 1967); Karl Rahner, *Theological Investigations,* IV, translated by Kevin Smyth (Baltimore, MD: Helicon Press, 1966), pp. 165–188 ("Nature and Grace"); Gutierrez, *Theology,* pp. 45–72; Juan Luis Segundo, *Grace and the Human Condition,* translated by John Drury (Maryknoll, NY: Orbis Books, 1973), pp. 62–74; Leonardo Boff, *Liberating Grace,* translated by John Drury (Maryknoll: Orbis Books, 1979), pp. 39–46; Edward Yarnold, *The Second Gift: A Study of Grace* (Slough, England: St. Paul Publications, 1974).

28. In a doctrine not widely recognized, the later Barth also holds the basically Hegelian theory that the "true" infinity and freedom of God requires not only that God is *not* finite but also that God has the power to transcend his own transcendence and "over-reach" the finite in creation, redemption, and providence. See Karl Barth, *Church Dogmatics,* 1/2, translated by G. T. Thompson and H. Knight (Edinburgh: T & T Clark, 1956), pp. 31–32; 2/1, translated by Parker, Johnston, Knight, and Haire (Edinburgh: T & T Clark, 1957), pp. 298–305, 465–468; *The Humanity of God* (Atlanta, GA: John Knox Press, 1960), pp. 48–52.

29. On Rahner's ontologically oriented theology of the symbol, see his *Theological Investigations,* 4, translated by Kevin Smyth (Baltimore, MD: Helicon Press, 1966), pp. 221–252 ("The Theology of the Symbol"). I am not, of course, arguing here that Hegel's theology as a whole is compatible with the normative tradition of Christian faith, which is a separate issue. I am fully aware of the traditional objections to Hegel on the part of the existentialist and Thomist theologians, although I am not convinced that their

objections are based on an accurate understanding of Hegel. I am concerned here only with the Hegelian *Denkform* which I think underlies that of TL. On my interpretation of Hegel, see Chapter 2, n. 35.

30. Gutierrez, *The Power of the Poor in History* (Maryknoll, NY: Orbis Books, 1983), p. 4; emphasis added.

31. Jon Sobrino, *Christology at the Crossroads* ((Maryknoll, NY: Orbis Books, 1978), p. 391; emphasis added.

32. Gutierrez, *Power* p. 7.

33. Ibid.; emphasis added.

34. Ibid., p. 13; emphasis added.

35. Gutierrez, *Theology,* p. 168.

36. Ellacuria, p. 27.

37. Sobrino, *Christology,* p. 352; also p. 352; also p. 275. On the importance of the "historical Jesus" in Latin American Christology, see further Sobrino, *Jesus in Latin America* ((Maryknoll, NY: Orbis Books, 1987), p. 55–77.

38. Gutierrez, *Theology,* p. 151; emphasis added.

39. Ibid., p. 168; emphases added.

40. Gutierrez, *Power,* p. 32.

41. Gutierrez, *Theology,* p. 177; emphasis added.

42. Leonardo Boff, "Salvation in Jesus Christ and the Process of Liberation," *Concilium* 96 (1974): 89 (emphasis added).

43. Ibid., p. 88.

44. Juan Luis Segundo, *Faith and Ideologies* ((Maryknoll, NY: Orbis Books, 1984), p. 129.

45. Gutierrez, *Power* p. 69.

46. Gutierrez, *Theology, p. 177.*

47. *Ibid., p. 237.*

48. *Segundo, Grace,* pp. 95–96.

49. Sobrino, *The True Church and the Poor* (Maryknoll, NY: Orbis Books, 1984), pp. 73, 74, and 283.

50. See Juan Carlos Scannone, "Das Theorie-Praxis Verhältnis in der Theologie der Befreiung, " in Karl Rahner (ed.), *Befreiende Theologie* (Mainz: Kohlhammer, 1977), p. 82.

51. Leonardo and Clodovis Boff, *Liberation Theology*, pp. 24–25.

52. Gutierrrez, *Theology*, p. 153; also *Power*, p. 31; emphasis added.

53. Gutierrez, *Theology*, p. 177.

54. Ibid.

55. See Gutierrez, *Theology*, pp. 36–37; Leonardo Boff, *Liberating Grace*, pp. 79–80; Scannone, p. 79.

56. On the significance of the Enlightenment in TL, see Gutierrez, *Theology*, pp. 28–32; Sobrino, *Christology*, p. 19; and *True Church*, pp. 10–15. On the difference between liberation and development and a critique of the ideology of development, see Gutierrez, *Theology*, pp. 26–27, 36–37 and 82–84.

57. Gutierrez, *Theology*, p. 146.

58. See ibid.

59. See ibid. p. 33.

60. See ibid. pp. 36, 146, 235–36; Boff, *Liberating Grace*, pp. 79–80.

61. Gutierrez, *Theology*, p. 32.

62. Ibid. p. 231.

63. Ibid., p. 35.

64. Boff, *Liberating Grace*, p. 155.

65. Gutierrez, *Theology*, p. 176.

66. See Sobrino, *Jesus*, pp. 19–29; Gutierrez, *Power*, pp. 95–96.

67. Gutierrez, *Theology*, p. 234.

68. This dichotomy, opposing personal freedom and mechanistic necessity, ethics and history, seems characteristic of Ratzinger's thought as a whole. See his "Freedom and Liberation: the Anthropological Vision of the Instruction "Libertatis Conscientia'," *Communio* 14 (Spring 1987): 56–57, 70.

69. Gutierrez, *Theology*, p. 153; emphasis added.

70. Ibid., pp. 15, 213–14, 233, 237.

71. Ibid., pp. 234 and 217.

72. See Karl Rahner, *Hörer des Wortes: Zur Grundlegung einer Religionsphilosophie*, edited by Johann Baptist Metz (Munich: Kösel Verlag, 1963).

73. See Gutierrez, *Theology*, pp. 236–38; Leonardo Boff, *Liberating Grace*, pp. 79–80, 153; and Scannone, p. 83.

74. Gutierrez, *Theology*, pp. 221 and 236; also see Scannone, "Das Theorie-Praxis Verhältnis," pp. 79–80.

75. Gutierrez, *Theology*, p. 237.

76. Ibid., p. 177.

77. Gutierrez, *Power* p. 63.

78. Gutierrez, *Theology*, p. 145.

79. Ibid., p. 231–32.

80. Ibid., p. 35.

81. Ibid., p. 36.

82. Ibid., p. 176.

83. Ibid., p. 177.

84. Ibid., p. 160.

85. Ibid., p. 238.

86. Segundo Galilea, "Liberation as an Encounter with Politics and Contemplation," *Concilium* 96 (1974): 22.

87. Gutierrez, *Theology*, p. 238.

88. Ibid.

89. Ibid., p. 165.

90. Ibid., p. 237.

91. Ibid., pp. 238–239.

92. See Scannone, pp. 82–83.

93. Gutierrez, "Liberation, Theology and Proclamation," *Concilium*, 96 (1974), p. 73.

94. See further Scannone, p. 85.

95. On the importance of effective means and method ("ideology") for faith itself, see Segundo, *Faith*, pp. 120–30.

96. Gutierrez, *Theology*, p. 157.

97. Ibid.

98. Gutierrez, *Power*, pp. 9–10; emphasis added.

99. Segundo, *Grace*, p. 128; emphasis added. For different approaches to the interpretation of the Exodus, see the special issue of *Concilium*, 189 (February 1987), entitled "Exodus—A Lasting Paradigm," and Michael Walzer, *Exodus and Revolution* (New York: Basic Books, 1985).

100. See Gutierrez, *Theology,* p. 37.

101. See Leonardo Boff, *Liberating Grace,* pp. 80–82.

102. See Scannone, pp. 81–83.

103. See Segundo, *Grace* p. 38.

104. Ibid.

105. For a further discussion of this basic "sociality" of human existence and its application to the theology of sin and grace, see ibid., pp. 37–39; Boff, *Liberating Grace,* pp. 8–25, 28, 84–86, 124–127, 141–143.

106. See Paul Tillich, *The Courage To Be* (New Haven: Yale University Press, 1952), pp. 40–63.

107. Gutierrez, *Theology,* p. 172.

108. Gutierrez, *Power,* p. 62.

109. Ibid., p. 147.

110. Leonardo Boff, "Salvation in Jesus Christ and the Process of Liberation," *Concilium* 96 (1974): 88.

111. Gutierrez, *Theology,* p. 35.

112. Gutierrez, *Power,* p. 47.

113. Segundo, *Grace,* p, 39.

114. Boff, *Liberating Grace,* p. 153; see also Ellacuria, p. 106.

115. See Jose Miguez Bonino, *Christians and Marxists* (Grand Rapids, MI: Eerdmans, 1976), p. 93.

116. Gutierrez, *Power* p. 47.

117. Ibid.; see further Segundo, *The Historical Jesus of the Synoptics* (Maryknoll, NY: Orbis Books, 1985), pp. 80–85, 178–88.

118. Sobrino, *Christology,* pp. 391–92; emphasis added.

119. For an interpretation of the meaning of ministry and authority within a political ecclesiology of concrete totality, see Leonardo Boff, *Ecclesiogenesis: The Base Communities Reinvent the Church* (Maryknoll, NY: Orbis Books, 1986), pp. 61–98.

120. For a critique of existentialism on this point, see Georg Lukacs, *Marxism and Human Liberation* (New York: Dell, 1973), pp. 243–266; and Theodor W. Adorno, *The Jargon of Authenticity* (Evanston, IL: Northwestern University Press, 1973).

121. Joseph Ratzinger, "Freedom and Liberation," p. 61.

122. Cobb, p. 128.

123. See Karl Marx, *The Economic & Philosophic Manuscripts of 1844,* edited by Dirk J. Struik (New York: International Publishers, 1964), p. 139.

124. Cobb, p. 128.

125. Boff, *Liberation Theology,* p. 22.

126. See Gutierrez, *Theology,* p. 173; Joseph Comblin, "Freedom and Liberation as Theological Concepts," *Concilium* 96 (1974): 96.

127. Gutierrez, *Power,* p. 63.

128. This and the preceding quotation is from Segundo, "Capitalism–Socialism: A Theological Crux," *Concillium* 96 (1974): 123.

129. Ellacuria, p. 106.

130. Gutierrez, *Power,* p. 98.

131. Alvaro Barreiro, *Basic Ecclesial Communities* (Maryknoll, NY: Orbis Books, 1982), p. 32.

132. Ellacuria, pp. 104 and 105.

133. See Dussel, p. 170, and Sobrino, *True Church,* pp. 185–92.

CHAPTER FIVE

---

1. For an account of Leonardo Boff's relationship with the Vatican, see his "Summons to Rome: A Personal Testimony" in Leonardo Boff and Clodovis Boff, *Liberation Theology* (San Francisco: Harper & Row, 1986), pp. 75–91. For a fascinating recent account of the controversy between Boff and Joseph Cardinal Ratzinger and an evaluation of the controversy from an ecclesiological perspective, see Harvey Cox, *The Silencing of Leonardo Boff: The Vatican and the Future of World Christianity* (Oak Park, IL: Meyer Stone Books, 1988).

2. See respectively the Sacred Congregation for the Doctrine of the Faith, "Instruction on Certain Aspects of the 'Theology of Liberation'," *Origins* 14:13 (September 13, 1984), and "Instruction on Christian Freedom and Liberation" (Vatican City: Vatican Polyglot Press, 1986). In this chapter I use the abbreviations LN and LC from their respective Latin titles, *Libertatis Nuntius* and *Libertatis Conscientia.* All references in the body of this chapter are to these two instructions by section and paragraph (LN) or by paragraph (LC).

3. I have already discussed the reactions to LN in chapter 1, section two ("Issues in Theology of Liberation"). For reactions to LC, see *The National Catholic Reporter* (April 18, 1986), pp. 1, 10, 15–16; *Commoweal* (April 25, 1986), pp. 227–28; *America* (May 24, 1986), pp. 425–28.

4. The excerpts of this letter are found in *The National Catholic Reporter* (May 9, 1986), p. 14.

5. Peter Hebblethwaite, *The National Catholic Reporter* (May 9, 1986), p. 6.

6. Ibid., p. 14.

7. Ibid.; emphasis added.

8. Ibid.

9. Ibid. The same stringent qualifications for acceptable theology of liberation were stated by Pope John Paul II in his March 13, 1986 address to a meeting of Brazilian bishops at the Vatican; see *Origins* 15:42 (April 3, 1986), 684–685. As recently as his May 1988 visit to Peru, he also warned of the errors of some theologies of liberation and told a closed-door meeting of Peru's fifty-three bishops to adhere closely to the two Vatican Instructions; see *National Catholic Reporter* (June 3, 1988), p. 20.

10. Joseph Cardinal Ratzinger, "Freedom and Liberation: The Anthropological Vision of the Instruction 'Libertatis Conscientia'," *Communio* 14 (Spring 1987): 64. This is the text of a paper presented in Lima, Peru on July 19, 1986.

11. Ibid., p. 58. Pope John Paul II also reaffirms the criticism of TL contained in the Instruction of 1984 in his latest encyclical, *Sollicitudo Rei Socialis* (Vatican City: Libreria Editrice Vaticana, 1988), para. 46.

12. *The National Catholic Reporter* (May 9, 1986), p. 6.

13. See Ratzinger, "Freedom and Liberation," p. 55.

14. See Pope John Paul II, "Apostolic Exhortation on Reconciliation and Penance" (*Reconciliatio et Paenitentia*), issued on December 2, 1984, in response to the controversy on "social sin," and found in the special supplement to the January 17, 1985 issue of *The Wanderer*, pp. 3–16. This will be referred to in the body of this chapter by RP, followed by paragraph number.

15. See Karol Wojtyla, *The Acting Person* (Boston: Reidel, 1979).

16. John Dewey makes this necessary distinction between private and public in his *The Public and Its Problems* (New York: Henry Holt, 1927; reprints by Ohio University Press, 1980, 1981, and 1985), pp. 12–36.

17. The language of 'social sin' was also used by the Roman Catholic Bishops of the United States in their *Economic Justice For All: Pastoral Letter on Catholic Social Teaching and the U. S. Economy* (Washington, DC: U.S. Catholic Conference, 1986), p. 49 (para. 77). The personalist understanding of 'social sin' is reaffirmed in the most recent encyclical of Pope John Paul II, *Sollicitudo Rei Socialis*, para. 36.

18. See Joseph Ratzinger, *Politik und Erlösung* (Opladen: Westdeutscher Verlag, 1986), p. 21.

19. See ibid., p. 22.

20. Ibid., p. 23; my translation and emphasis.

21. See ibid., p. 23.

22. See ibid., p. 24. On the importance of education as "the core of every praxis of liberation," see Ratzinger, "Freedom and Liberation," p. 62.

23. Synod of Bishops, "Justice in the World" (1971) (Introduction), found in David J. O'Brien and Thomas A. Shannon (eds.), *Renewing the Earth: Catholic Documents on Peace, Justice and Liberation* (Garden City, NJ: Doubleday, 1977), p. 391.

24. This, of course, is the main thesis of Karl Rahner's classic work on philosophy of religion, *Horer des Wortes: Zur Grundlegung einer Religionsphilosophie,* edited by Johann B. Metz (Munich: Kosel Verlag, 1963); translated by Michael Richards as *Hearers of the Word* (New York: Herder & Herder, 1969).

25. Karol Wojtyla, "The Person: Subject and Community," *Review of Metaphysics* 33:2 (December 1979: 289.

26. Wojtyla, "Participation or Alienation?" *Analecta Husserliana* 6 (1977): 70.

27. Wojtyla, *The Acting Person,* p. 315.

28. On the purely factual or moral (but not ontological) use of "solidarity" in the Vatican documents, see LC, 89–91; John Paul II, *On Human Work* (Washington, DC: U.S. Catholic Conference, 1981), para. 8; *The Acting Person,* pp. 284–287; *Sollicitudo Rei Socialis,* paras. 38–40.

29. For a detailed discussion of John Paul II's use of the term 'totality,' see Anselm K. Min, "John Paul II's Anthropology of Concrete Totality," *Proceedings of the American Catholic Philosophical Association* 58 (1984): 120–29. I must note here that in this article I did not go into the kind of ciritical evaluation that I am making in this chapter.

CHAPTER SIX

1.For a brief but essential description of the dimensions of the global and U.S. domestic economic crises, see the National Conference of Catholic Bishops, *Economic Justice For All: Pastoral Letter on Catholic Social Teaching and the U.S. Economy* (Washington, DC: U.S. Catholic Conference, 1986), paras. 2–21.

2. See Pope John Paul II, *On Human Work* (Washington, DC: U.S. Catholic Conference, 1981), para. 1.

3. Much more "communal," concrete, and biblical than the two Vatican Instructions on liberation is the U.S. Catholic bishops' Pastoral Letter; see *Economic Justice For All,* especially paras. 5, 25, 28, and 64–67, on the communal understanding of human existence.

4. See Pope John Paul II, *On Human Work,* para. 20.

5. See further Giulio Girardi, "Die gegenwartigen Auseinandersetzungen um Marxismus, Theologie der Befreiung und 'Kirche des Volkes' (iglesia popular)," in *Theologie der Befreiung und Marxismus,* edited by Peter Rottlander (Munster: Edicion Liberacion, 1986), pp. 137–42.

6. See Peter Rottländer, "Zur Einfuhrung," in his edited volume, *Theologie der Befreiung und Marxismus,* pp. 8–17, where he discusses the Vatican's double strategy regarding theology of liberation, the strategy of confrontation exemplified by the Instruction of 1984 *(Libertatis Nuntius),* and the campaign of conservative Latin American and West German bishops and professors of 'social doctrine,' the strategy of integration exemplified in the Instruction of 1986 *(Libertatis Conscientia)* which tries to integrate theology of liberation into the church's social doctrine. On the reshaping of the Catholic Church through the appointment of conservative bishops, see John Thavis, "The Bishops: Shaping the Hierarchy," *North Carolina Catholic* (January 31, 1988), pp. 2 and 12.

7. See Arthur Jones, "Vatican Document Targets Collegiality," *National Catholic Reporter* (February 19, 1988), pp. 1 and 5.

8. For a documentation of these trends, see Ana Maria Ezcurra, *The Vatican and the Reagan Administration* (New York: Circus Publications, 1986), pp. 91–136.

9. See Rottländer, pp. 175–79 ("Politische Theologie und die Herausforderung des Marxismus: Ein Gespräch des Herausgebers mit Johann Baptist Metz").

10. Bernard J. F. Lonergan, *Method in Theology* (New York: Herder & Herder, 1972), p. 131; and Francis S. Fiorenza, "Political Theology as Foundational Theology," *Proceedings of the Catholic Theological Society of America* 32 (1977): 142–43. For a critique of foundationalism and the historical background of the concept and discipline of fundamental theology, see Francis S. Fiorenza, *Foundational Theology: Jesus and the Church* (New York: Crossroad, 1984), pp. 5–55 and 247–321. I am not here ready to comment on the difference between Fiorenza's conception of foundational theology as "reconstructive hermeneutics" and my conception of the same as an anthropology of concrete totality. I share the same formal conception of a foundational theology—i.e., that of its function in relation to the whole of dogmatic theology—but differ with him in the content of such a theology.

References

Adorno, Theodor. *The Jargon of Authenticity*. Evanston, IL: Northwestern University Press, 1973.

Assmann, Hugo. *Theology for a Nomad Church*. Maryknoll, NY: Orbis Books, 1976.

Barreiro, Alvaro. *Basic Ecclesial Communities*. Maryknoll, NY: Orbis Books, 1982.

Barth, Karl. *Church Dogmatics*. Vol. 1, Part 2. Translated by G. T. Thompson and H. Knight. Edinburgh: T & T Clark, 1956.

———. *Church Dogmatics*. Vol. 2, Part 1. Translated by Parker, Johnston, and Haire. Edinburgh: T & T Clark, 1957.

———. *The Humanity of God*. Atlanta, GA: John Knox Press, 1960.

Baum, Gregory. "The Theological Method of Segundo's *The Liberation of Theology*." *Proceedings of the Catholic Theological Society of America* 32 (1977): 120–24.

———. *The Priority of Labor*. New York: Paulist Press, 1982.

Belo, Fernando. *A Materialist Reading of the Gospel of Mark*. Maryknoll, NY: Orbis Books, 1981.

Berghoef, Gerard, and Lester DeKoster. *Liberation Theology: The Church's Future Shock*. Grand Rapids, MI: Christian's Library Press, 1984.

Bernstein, Richard J. *Praxis and Action: Contemporary Philosophies of Human Activity*. Philadelphia, PA: University of Pennsylvania Press, 1971.

Berryman, Philip. *Liberation Theology*. Oak Park, IL: Meyer Stone Books, 1987.

Boff, Clodovis. *Theology and Praxis: Epistemological Foundations*. Translated by Robert R. Barr. Maryknoll, NY: Orbis Books, 1987.

———. "Die ambivalente Haltung der 'Instruktion zur Theologie der Befreiung' gegenüber dem Marxismus." In *Theologie der Befreiung und Marxismus*, edited by Peter Rottländer, 109–116.

———. "Zum Gebrauch des 'Marxismus' in der Theologie der Befreiung. Einige Thesen." In *Theologie der Befreiung und Marxismus*, edited by Peter Rottländer, 37–44.

———, and Leonardo Boff. *Liberation Theology: From Confrontation to Dialogue*. San Francisco: Harper & Row, 1986.

————, and Leonardo Boff. *Introducing Liberation Theology.* Maryknoll, NY: Orbis Books, 1987.

Boff, Leonardo. "Salvation in Jesus Christ and the Process of Liberation." *Concilium* 96 (1974): 78–91.

————. *Liberating Grace.* Maryknoll, NY: Orbis Books, 1979.

Bonino, Jose Miguez. *Christians and Marxists.* Grand Rapids, MI: Eerdmans, 1976.

Brown, Robert McAfee. *Theology in a New Key.* Philadelphia, PA: Westminster Press, 1978.

Brueggeman, Walter. *Hope Within History.* Atlanta, GA: John Knox Press, 1987.

Bubner, Rudiger. "Habermas's Concept of Critical Theory." In *Habermas: Critical Debates,* edited by John B. Thompson and David Held, 42–56. Cambridge, MA: MIT Press, 1982.

Castillo, Fernando. "Die Christen und der Marxismus: ein Problem mit Geschichte." In *Theologie der Befreiung und der Marxismus,* edited by Peter Rottländer, 23–36. Munster: Edicion Liberacion, 1986.

Chenu, Marie Dominique. *Is Theology a Science?* Translated by A.H. N. Green-Armytage. New York: Hawthorn Books, 1959.

Chopp, Rebecca S. *The Praxis of Suffering: An Interpretation of Liberation and Political Theologies.* Maryknoll, NY: Orbis Books, 1986.

Clevenot, Michel. *Materialist Approaches to the Bible.* Maryknoll, NY: Orbis Books, 1985.

Cobb, John B., Jr. *Process Theology as Political Theology.* Philadelphia, PA: Westminster Press, 1982.

Comblin, Joseph. "Freedom and Liberation as Theological Concepts." *Concilium* 96 (1974): 92–104.

Congar, Yves. *History of Theology.* Translated by Hunter Guthrie. Garden City, NJ: Doubleday, 1968.

Congregation for the Doctrine of the Faith. "Instruction on Certain Aspects of the 'Theology of Liberation'." *Origins* 14:13 (13 September 1984): 194–204.

————. *Instruction on Christian Freedom and Liberation.* Vatican City: Vatican Polyglot Press, 1986.

Cormie, Lee. "The Hermeneutical Privilege of the Oppressed: Liberation Theologies, Biblical Faith, and Marxist Sociology of Knowledge." *Proceedings of the Catholic Theological Society of America* 33 (1978): 155–81.

Coste, René. *Marxist Analysis and Christian Faith.* Maryknoll, NY: Orbis Books, 1985.

Cox, Harvey. *The Silencing of Leonardo Boff.* Oak Park, IL: Meyer Stone Books, 1988.

Croatto, Severino. *Biblical Hermeneutics: Toward a Theory of Reading as the Production of Meaning.* Maryknoll, NY: Orbis Books, 1987.

Davis, Charles. "Theology and Praxis." *Cross Currents* 23: 2 (Summer 1973): 154-68.

———. *Theology and Political Society.* Cambridge, MA: Cambridge University Press, 1980.

De Lubac, Henri. *The Mystery of the Supernatural.* New York: Herder & Herder, 1967.

Dewey, John. *The Public and Its Problems.* New York: Henry Holt, 1927.

Donahue, John R. "Biblical Perspectives on Justice." In *The Faith That Does Justice,* edited by John C. Haughey, 68-112. New York: Paulist Press, 1977.

Dussel, Enrique. *History and the Theology of Liberation.* Maryknoll, NY: Orbis Books, 1976.

Ellacuria, Ignacio. *Freedom Made Flesh: The Mission of Christ and the Church.* Maryknoll, NY: Orbis Books, 1976.

———. "Theologie der Befreiung und Marxismus: Grundlegende Reflexionen." In *Theologie der Befreiung und Marxismus,* edited by Peter Rottländer, 77-108.

Ezcurra, Ana Maria. *The Vatican and the Reagan Administration.* New York: Circus Publications, 1986.

Fiorenza, Francis S. "Liberation Theology and Political Theology." In *Liberation, Revolution and Freedom: Theological Perspectives,* edited by Thomas McFadden, 3-29. New York: Seabury Press, 1975.

———. "Political Theology as Foundational Theology." *Proceedings of the Catholic Theological Society of America* 32 (1977): 142-77.

———. *Foundational Theology: Jesus and the Church.* New York: Crossroad, 1984.

Galilea, Segundo. "Liberation as an Encounter With Politics and Contemplation." *Concilium* 96 (1974): 19-33.

Girardi, Giulio, "Die gegenwärtigen Auseinandersetzungen um Marxismus, Theologie der Befreiung und 'Kirche des Volkes'." In *Theologie der Befreiung und Marxismus,* edited by Peter Rottländer, 117-154.

Goldstein, Horst. "Skizze einer biblischen Bergründung der Theologie der Befreiung." In *Befreiende Theologie,* edited by Karl Rahner, 62-76. Mainz: Kohlhammer, 1977.

Gottwald, Norman K. *The Tribes of Yahweh.* Maryknoll, NY: Orbis Books, 1979.

———, ed. *The Bible and Liberation: Political and Social Hermeneutics.* Maryknoll, NY: Orbis Books, 1983.

Gudorf, Christine E. *Catholic Social Teaching on Liberation Themes.* Washington, DC: University Press of America, 1981.

——. "Liberation Theology's Use of Scripture: A Response to First World Critics." *Interpretation* 41:1 (January 1987): 5–18.

Gutierrez, Gustavo. *A Theology of Liberation.* Maryknoll, NY: Orbis Books, 1973.

——. "Liberation, Theology and Proclamation." *Concilium* 96 (1974): 57–77.

——. *The Power of the Poor in History.* Maryknoll, NY: Orbis Books, 1983.

——. "Theologie und Sozialwissenschaften: eine Ortsbestimmung." In *Theologie der Befreiung und Marxismus,* edited by Peter Rottländer, 45–76.

Habermas, Jürgen. *Theory and Practice.* Boston, MA: Beacon Press, 1973.

Haight, Roger. *An Alternative Vision: An Interpretation of Liberation Theology.* New York: Paulist Press, 1985.

Harrington, Michael. *The Twilight of Capitalism.* New York: Simon and Schuster, 1976.

Hauerwas, Stanley. "Some Theological Reflections on Gutierrez's Use of 'Liberation' as a Theological Concept." *Modern Theology* 3:1 (October 1986): 67–76.

Haughey, John C., ed. *The Faith That Does Justice.* New York: Paulist Press, 1977.

Hebblethwaite, Peter. "The Popes and Politics: Shifting Patterns in 'Catholic Social Doctrine'." *Daedalus* 111:1 (Winter 1982): 85–99.

Jay, Martin. *Marxism and Totality.* Berkeley, CA: University of California Press, 1984.

John Paul II, Pope. *On Human Work.* Washington, DC: U.S. Catholic Conference, 1981.

——. "Apostolic Exhortation on Reconciliation and Penance." *The Wanderer* (January 17, 1985), 3–16.

——. *Sollicitudo Rei Socialis.* Vatican City: Libreria Editrice Vaticana, 1987.

Journal of Ecumenical Studies 22:3 (Summer 1985).

Kavanaugh, John F. "The Moral Dialectic of *Laborem Exercens.*" *Proceedings of the Forty-Sixth Annual Convention of the Jesuit Philosophical Association* (April 1984): 13–40.

Kloppenburg, Bonaventure. *The People's Church: A Defense of My Church.* Chicago, IL: Franciscan Herald Press, 1978.

Kosik, Karel. *Dialectics of the Concrete.* Dordrecht: D. Reidel, 1976.

Lakeland, Paul. *The Politics of Salvation: The Hegelian Idea of the State.* Albany, NY: The State University of New York Press, 1984.

Lamb, Matthew. "The Theory-Praxis Relationship in Contemporary Christian Theologies." *Proceedings of the Catholic Theological Society of America* 31 (1976): 149–78.

Lane, Dermot A. *Foundations for a Social Theology: Praxis, Process and Salvation.* New York: Paulist Press, 1984.

Ledure, Yves. "L'encyclique de Jean-Paul II sur le travail humain." *Nouvelle Revue Theologique* 105:2 (March–April 1983): 218–27.

Lobkowicz, Nicholas. *Theory and Practice: History of a Concept from Aristotle to Marx.* Notre Dame: University of Notre Dame Press, 1967.

Lonergan, Bernard J. F. *Method in Theology.* New York: Herder & Herder, 1972.

Lukács, Georg. *Marxism and Human Liberation.* New York: Dell, 1973.

Mannheim, Karl. *Ideology and Utopia: An Introduction to the Sociology of Knowledge.* Translated by Louis Wirth and Edward Shils. New York: Harcourt, Brace & World, 1936.

Marx, Karl. *The Economic and Philosophic Manuscripts of 1844,* edited by Dirk J. Struik. New York: International Publishers, 1964.

McCann, Dennis P., and Charles R. Strain. *Polity and Praxis: A Program for American Practical Theology.* Minneapolis, MN: Winston Press, 1985.

McGovern, Arthur F. *Marxism: An American Christian Perspective.* Maryknoll, NY: Orbis Books, 1980.

McLellan, David. *Marxism and Religion.* New York: Harper & Row, 1987.

McMurtry, John. *The Structure of Marx's World-View.* Princeton, NJ: Princeton University Press, 1978.

Metz, Johann Baptist. *Theology of the World.* New York: Herder & Herder, 1969.

———. *Faith in History and Society: Toward a Practical Fundamental Theology.* New York: Seabury Press, 1980.

———. ed. *Die Theologie der Befreiung: Hoffnung oder Gafahr für die Kirche?* Düsseldorf: Patmos Verlag, 1986.

Min, Anselm Kyongsuk. "Hegel on the Foundation of Religion." *International Philosophical Quarterly* 14:1 (March 1974): 79–99.

———. "Hegel's Absolute: Transcendent or Immanent?" *Journal of Religion* 56:1 (January 1976): 61–87.

———. "Karel Kosik, *The Dialectics of the Concrete.*" *The New Scholasticism* 55:2 (Spring 1981): 247–54.

———. "Hegel's Retention of Mystery as a Theological Category." *CLIO* 12:4 (Summer 1983): 333–53.

———. "John Paul II's Anthropology of Concrete Totality." *Proceedings of the American Catholic Philosophical Association* 58 (1984): 120–29.

———. "The Vatican, Marxism, and Liberation Theology." *Cross Currents* 34:4 (Winter 1984–85): 439–55.

———. "The Trinity and the Incarnation: Hegel and Classical Approaches." *Journal of Religion* 66:2 (April 1986): 173–93.

———. "Praxis and Theology in Recent Debates." *Scottish Journal of Theology* 39:4 (November 1986): 529–49.

———. "How Not To Do a Theology of Liberation: A Critique of Schubert Ogden." *Journal of the American Academy of Religion* (forthcoming).

Miranda, Jose Porfirio. *Marx and the Bible.* Maryknoll, NY: Orbis Books, 1971.

Nash, Ronald, ed. *Liberation Theology.* Milford, MI: Mott Media, 1984.

National Conference of Catholic Bishops (USA). *Pastoral Letter on Marxist Communism.* Washington, DC: U.S. Catholic Conference, 1980.

———. *Economic Justice For All: Pastoral Letter on Catholic Social Teaching and the U.S. Economy.* Washington, DC: U.S. Catholic Conference, 1986.

Nunez, Emilio A. *Liberation Theology.* Translated by Paul E. Sywulka. Chicago, IL: Moody Press, 1985.

Ogden, Schubert M. *Faith and Freedom: Towards a Theology of Liberation.* Nashville, TN: Abingdon Press, 1979.

———. "The Concept of a Theology of Liberation: Must a Christian Theology Be So Conceived?" In *The Challenge of Liberation Theology,* edited by Brian Mahan and L. Dale Richesin, 127–140. Maryknoll, NY: Orbis Books, 1981.

———. *The Point of Christology.* San Francisco, CA: Harper & Row, 1982.

Oeing-Hanhoff, Ludger. "Das Christentum als 'Religion der Freiheit'." *Theologischer Quartalschrift* 164:1 (1984): 16–34.

Persson, Per Erik. *Sacra Doctrina: Reason and Revelation in Aquinas.* Translated by Ross Mackenzie. Philadelphia, PA: Fortress Press, 1970.

Quade, Quentin L., ed. *The Pope and Revolution.* Washington, DC: Ethics and Public Policy Center, 1982.

Rahner, Karl. *Hörer des Wortes,* edited by Johann Baptist Metz. Munich: Kösel Verlag, 1963.

———. *Theological Investigations.* Vol. 4. Baltimore: Helicon Press, 1966.

———. *Theological Investigations.* Vol. 6. Baltimore: Helicon Press, 1969.

———. *Theological Investigations.* Vol. 9. New York: Seabury Press, 1972.

———, ed. *Befreiende Theologie.* Mainz: Kohlhammer, 1977.

Ratzinger, Joseph Cardinal. With Vittorio Messori. *The Ratzinger Report.* Translated by Salvator Attanasio and Graham Harrison. San Francisco, CA: Ignatius Press, 1985.

————. *Politik und Erlösung.* Opladen: Westdeutscher Verlag, 1986.

————. "Freedom and Liberation: The Anthropological Vision of the Instruction 'Libertatis Conscientia'." *Communio* 14 (Spring 1987): 55–72.

Reuther, Rosemary Radford. *To Change the World: Christology and Cultural Criticism.* New York: Crossroad, 1985.

Rendtorff, Trutz. "The Modern Age as a Chapter in the History of Christianity; or, The Legacy of Historical Consciousness in Present Theology." *Journal of Religion* 65:4 (October 1985): 478–99.

Rottländer, Peter, ed. *Theologie der Befreiung und der Marxismus.* Münster: Edicion Liberacion, 1986.

Scannone, Juan Carlos. "Das Theorie-Praxis Verhältnis in der Theologie der Befreiung." In *Befreiende Theologie,* edited by Karl Rahner, 77–96. Mainz: Kohlhammer, 1977.

Schnackenburg, Rudolf. "Befreiung in der Blickweise Jesu und der Urkirche." In *Die Theologie der Befreiung: Hoffnung oder Gefahr für die Kirche?* edited by Johann B. Metz, 11–28. Düsseldorf: Patmos Verlag, 1986.

Segundo, Juan Luis, *Grace and the Human Condition.* Maryknoll, NY: Orbis Books, 1973.

————. "Capitalism–Socialism: A Theological Crux." *Concilium* 96 (1974).

————. *The Liberation of Theology.* Maryknoll, NY: Orbis Books, 1976.

————. *Faith and Ideologies.* Maryknoll, NY: Orbis Books, 1984.

————. *Theology and the Church.* Translated by John W. Dierckmeier. New York: Winston Press, 1985.

————. *The Historical Jesus of the Synoptics.* Maryknoll, NY: Orbis Books, 1985.

————. *The Humanist Christology of Paul.* Maryknoll, NY: Orbis Books, 1986.

Shannon, Thomas, ed. *Renewing the Earth: Catholic Documents on Peace, Justice, and Liberation.* Garden City, NJ: Doubleday, 1977.

Sobrino, Jon. "Theologisches Erkennen in der europäischen und der lateinamerikanischen Theologie." In *Befreiende Theologie,* edited by Karl Rahner, 123–43. Mainz: Kohlhammer, 1977.

————. *Christology at the Crossroads.* Maryknoll, NY: Orbis Books, 1978.

————. *The True Church and the Poor.* Maryknoll, NY: Orbis Books, 1984.

————. *Jesus in Latin America.* Maryknoll, NY: Orbis Books, 1987.

Sölle, Dorothee. *Political Theology.* Philadelphia, PA: Fortress Press. 1974.

Tillich, Paul. *The Courage To Be.* New Haven, CT: Yale University Press, 1952.

Tracy, David. *The Analogical Imagination: Christian Theology and the Culture of Pluralism*. New York: Crossroad, 1981.

———. *Plurality and Ambiguity: Hermeneutics, Religion, Hope*. San Francisco, CA: Harper & Row, 1987.

Troeltsch, Ernst. *Writings on Theology and Religion*. Translated by Robert Morgan and Michael Pye. Atlanta, GA: John Knox Press, 1977.

Wojtyla, Karol (Pope John Paul II). *The Acting Person*. Boston: D. Reidel, 1979.

———. "The Person: Subject and Community." *Review of Metaphysics* 33:2 (December 1979): 273–308.

———. "Participation or Alienation?" *Analecta Husserliana* 6 (1977): 61–73.

SUBJECT INDEX

AUTHOR INDEX

Adorno, Theodor, 188n
Althusser, Louis, 9
Aquinas, Thomas, 1, 18, 73, 132, 164, 172n
Arnold, Matthew, 158
Aristotle, 17, 27, 38, 73, 132, 164
Arrupe, Pedro, 20
Assman, Hugo, 174n
Augustine, 1, 124, 126, 132, 155

Barreiro, Alvaro, 189n
Barth, Karl, 1, 4, 9, 163, 164, 184n
Baum, Gregory, 173n, 182n
Belo, Fernando, 180n
Bentham, Jeremy, 144
Berghoef, Gerard, 171n, 174n
Bernstein, Richard J., 175n
Berryman, Philip, 172n
Bloch, Ernst, 96, 98, 132
Blondel, Maurice, 9
Boethius, 18
Boff, Clodovis, 7, 21, 30, 45–51, 54–56,
    58–60, 62–67, 79, 85–86, 94, 114, 173n,
    174n, 175n, 177n, 178n, 179n, 180n, 181n,
    182n, 183n, 186n, 189n
Boff, Leonardo, 7, 21, 117, 162, 173n, 179n,
    180n, 182n, 183n, 184n, 185n, 186n, 188n,
    189n
Bonhoeffer, Dietrich, 9, 142
Brown, Robert McAfee, 172n
Brueggemann, Walter, 180n
Buber, Martin, 9
Bubner, Rudiger, 183n
Bultmann, Rudolf, 1, 4, 104, 164, 165

Castillo, Fernando, 172n, 175n
Chenu, Marie-Dominique, 172n
Chopp, Rebecca S., 172n, 179n
Clevenot, Michel, 180n
Cobb, John B. Jr., 80, 84, 112–113, 183n,
    189n
Congar, Yves, 172n
Coreth, Emerich, 9
Cormee, Lee, 182n
Coste, Rene, 173n
Cox, Harvey, 189n
Croatto, J. Severino, 181n
Curran, Charles, 162

Davis, Charles, 177n, 179n
DeKoster, Lester, 171n, 174n
Descartes, Rene, 72
Dewey, John, 12, 73, 105, 190n
Donahue, John R., 181n
Dussel, Enrique, 19, 86, 173n, 179n, 184n,
    189n

Ehlen, Peter, 172n
Ellacuria, Ignacio, 28, 86, 174n, 184n, 185n
Engels, Friedrich, 98
Eusebius of Caesarea, 132
Ezcurra, Ana Maria, 192n

Feuerbach, Ludwig, 9, 12, 27
Fiorenza, Francis Schussler, 168, 172n, 192n
Freud, Sigmund, 12
Friedman, Milton, 144

205

DATE DUE

MAR 0 3 1994			

HIGHSMITH # 45220